T0305262

International Business in Korea

International Business in Korea

The Evolution of the Market in the Globalization Era

by

O. Yul Kwon

Korea Foundation Chair in Korean Studies
Director, Australian Centre for Korean Studies
Griffith University, Australia

Edward Elgar
Cheltenham, UK • Northampton, MA, USA

Published by
Edward Elgar Publishing Limited
The Lypiatts
15 Lansdown Road
Cheltenham
Glos GL50 2JA
UK

Edward Elgar Publishing, Inc.
William Pratt House
9 Dewey Court
Northampton
Massachusetts 01060
USA

A catalogue record for this book
is available from the British Library

Library of Congress Cataloguing in Publication Data: 2007941686

ISBN 978 1 84720 570 4

Printed on FSC approved paper
Printed and bound in Great Britain by Marston Book Services Ltd, Oxfordshire

Contents

Tables

Preface

This book investigates the knowledge on the environmental dynamics and operational nature of international business in South Korea (Korea hereafter). From the early 1960s, the Korean economy continued to surge through to the financial crisis that suddenly struck a number of East Asian economies in mid-1997. The decisive recovery from the financial crisis, which saw this national economy resurge unlike any of the other crisis-afflicted economies, helped establish Korea as the world's eleventh-largest economy by 2005. Government measures for structural reform moved well beyond the recovery program imposed by the International Monetary Fund to push the state-led industrial economy to a market-oriented, knowledge- and information-based economy. Korean society has transformed its social stratification and value system. Also, the Korean political system has transformed from a series of authoritarian regimes to a fully fledged democracy. In parallel with the Korean economy, society and politics, the international business environment and business practices have undertaken a remarkable evolution in the recent past. This evolution, which has drawn little attention in the literature, is the subject of this book.

The book has a number of distinctive features. First, it adopts an institutional perspective in exploring the evolution of the Korean market under the emerging globalization and information era. The institutional approach, drawing upon various disciplines of political science, sociology and economics, enables careful analysis of the institutional transition that has been at the core of the transformation of the business environment and operational practices under examination here. Viewing through an institutional lens produces the assessment that the Korean market and business practices will maintain some *sui generis* characteristics because the nation's idiosyncratic culture and institutions are inevitably entrenched in the business environment and practices, even while globalization serves to help homogenize business behavior and market practices worldwide.

Second, the comprehensive approach of this study covers both macro-international business environments and micro-business operations. At the macro level, analysis reaches across business opportunities and cultural influences to country risk and configuration of the import market, which have drawn little attention in the literature. Micro-level analysis includes examination of the overlooked areas of business negotiation style, business ethics and management of international joint ventures. In this way the book provides valuable information for those seeking to understand the Korean example of international business, whether for scholarly purposes or for the more immediately practical purposes of considering entrance into the Korean market or improving performance of foreign firms already operating in this market.

Third, this book draws extensively not only from sources in the English and Korean languages, including electronic as well as published materials, but also from the author's experiences as both a scholar and business person. In preparing this study, the author has been informed by broad experience in Korean business. He has many years of experience involving visits to Korea for academic purposes and as consultant on projects concerned with the Korean market. His experiences as a business person engaging with Korean companies, as an interpreter, and as a director on the board of a Korean bank have provided rich opportunities to develop first-hand knowledge of Korean business and insights into the transformation of international business in Korea during the post-crisis transition to a market-led economy. The author has also conducted surveys and interviews with foreign business people in Korea and these contribute to the empirical work informing the study for this book.

The need for this book became clearer to the author while teaching a course entitled 'International Business in Korea', at Griffith University in Australia, since 1996. There was no comprehensive treatment of this subject in a single book and the sources of pertinent information were scattered and inadequate for presenting a fully informative picture. The transition in the Korean economy, as indeed in Korean political, social and cultural life, since the abandonment of a state-led system has seen considerable development in international business. This development is crucial for understanding the evolution of international business in Korea but has eluded the careful examination that it deserves in view of the economic strength of the nation in a strategically dynamic region of Northeast Asia. Some chapters have been rewritten a number of times as the speed of institutional reforms and their consequences overtook production of this book. A number of former students commented on some chapters of the book over the several years of its creation.

Many people have made valuable contributions to the production of this book. Its preparation has been part of a research project funded by the Korea Foundation in Seoul, to which the author expresses sincere thanks. He thanks Larry Crump, Peter Ross and David Schak, colleagues at Griffith University, who commented on draft chapters. Daniel Halvorson deserves special mention for his excellent research assistance and for meticulous editing of this book. Thanks are also due to Robyn White for her careful attention to detail and her efficiency in preparing the manuscript to meet the exacting specifications of the publisher. Perhaps most importantly, the author expresses deep thanks to his wife, Joanne Kwon, who stayed home alone without much demur or complaint, while the author was buried in researching and writing this book in his office over what seemed like day and night for several years. He therefore dedicates this book to her with thanks and affection. He of course remains solely responsible for any errors and shortcomings in the content of this book.

Introduction

This book seeks to analyze the transition in South Korean business environments and business practices from the roughly three decades of unprecedented economic growth (1963–96) to the recovery period after the 1997 financial crisis. It also critically assesses the prospects of international business in South Korea (hereafter Korea) under globalization. Korean business environments and practices since the national economy began to take off in the wake of the Korean War have not been analyzed critically in the context of recent developments in international business. Nor have the implications of post-war economic developments for future international business in Korea been considered carefully. This book is intended to help fill the void in the literature by providing academic analysis as well as practical information on international business as an ever more important dimension of the Korean economy.

Prior to the financial crisis in 1997, many observers saw Korea as one of the most difficult places in the world for foreigners to do business. These difficulties drew international attention to the distinctive features of the Korean market, business culture and management system as foreign businesses sought to understand the international business environment in Korea to capitalize on emerging business opportunities. However remedial measures in response to the 1997 crisis have transformed Korea's international business environment and business practices by removing many of the obstacles that deterred foreign business. The domestic market has been opened widely to the global business community, and business systems and practices have been shifted toward those of Western counterparts. Yet for all the change in the decade since the crisis, an idiosyncratic culture deeply ingrained in Korean society together with a singular way of institutional development in the recent past ensures that the Korean market and business practices remain *sui generis*.

The success of the Korean economy from the 1960s is well documented and attests to how a country can leap from being one of the poorest in the world to one of the richest in just one generation. The national economy recorded an annual growth of 8.8 per cent between 1963 and 1996, while per capita income increased a hundredfold from US$100 to US$10 548 (Kwon 1997). In 1996 Korea joined the OECD as its 29th member, and as a textbook example of successful economic development it stimulated broad international discussion.

Suddenly and unexpectedly, however, the Korean economy was drawn into the financial crisis that struck various Asian economies in mid-1997. Here Korea experienced its worst economic setback since the early 1960s, recording negative growth of 6.9 per cent in 1998. The Korean government quickly accepted an IMF rescue package with conditionality attached and accordingly began a program of sweeping reform to liberalize the national economy through privatization, labor-market adjustments and other measures. Signs of early recovery from the crisis emerged in the national economic data from early 1999, with annual average growth of 5.6 per cent over the 1999–2005 period (Bank of Korea 2006). Korea's GDP increased to US$791 billion and per capita GDP to US$16 438 in 2005, a performance that made the Korean economy the eleventh-largest in the world by that time. Such a performance has once again stimulated broad international discussion of the distinctive features of the Korean economy, this time relating to the features that enabled, or were changed to achieve, such a rapid and strong recovery.

Clearly, the national response to the 1997 financial crisis produced a metamorphosis in Korean business environments and practices. The conditions attached to the IMF recovery package required the Korean government to implement specific reforms to internationalize and liberalize the economy, particularly through institutions that shape business operations (Kwon 1998). Internationalizing required opening the economy to foreign competition, while liberalizing required inducing the transition from a state-led to a market-oriented economy.

These major systemic reforms, conducted through the nation's economic, political and social institutions, have been the main driver of the transition in Korean business and management over the decade since the crisis. They have increased transparency and accountability in business operations through improvements in corporate governance, decreased transaction and agency costs, and yielded a more competitive and efficient Korean market. The Korean political system has been transformed from a series of authoritarian regimes to a vibrant and fully fledged democracy. Korean society and culture have inevitably changed in tandem with the economic and political transformation. In the wake of these fundamental shifts that have transformed the Korean business environment and management system, Korea presents a fascinating case for enquiry into the evolution of a national market – from remarkably successful in the short term while heavily controlled and protected, to liberalized, internationalized and again highly successful under conditions of economic globalization.

This national economic drama, unfolding since the 1997 crisis, begs critical interpretation and re-evaluation of the literature on the Korean international business environment and business systems, since earlier studies were largely without access to the information and insights now available a decade after the crisis struck. Reappraisal is needed to shed light on the profound transition in international business in Korea and its future prospects. Because of the sudden, unexpected and revolutionary nature of this development, new knowledge on Korea's business transition and the nature of its international business is still in the early stages of development. Kwon (2001, 2004, 2005, 2006), Lee (2004), Rowley (2002) and Rowley and Bae (2003, 2004) have attempted to explore aspects of this rich terrain. However there is clearly the need for a comprehensive study that draws together detailed information, analysis and assessment of future prospects to capture the 'big picture' of the international business environment and management in Korea today. The present book pursues this task.

Another important aspect to which the existing literature has paid little attention is foreign perspectives on the recent developments of Korean business. How foreign firms view the evolution of Korea's international business environment and practices would be critically important not only for those foreign firms that are already in Korea or planning to enter, but also for Korea if the nation truly seeks to attract foreign businesses. This important issue has remained beyond the scholarly radar, and this book attempts to address the task.

As this book makes clear, international business in Korea differs from that in other countries mainly because of differences in the dynamics of the business environment and operations. Foreign firms that are inexperienced and unfamiliar with this environment in Korea therefore have much to learn if their business venture is to succeed. Business environments cover numerous spheres including business opportunities, country risk, culture, the configuration of the market and the regulations related to foreign direct investment (FDI) as well as its profitability. When making a decision on entry to the Korean market, foreign businesses have to weigh up the balance of business opportunities and political and country risk. They also need to understand the norms of business practices in Korea. Knowledge of particular aspects of Korean business and their underpinnings in Korean culture, ranging from negotiation processes and business ethics to general business management, and human resource management, is just as vital as more specific knowledge about conducting international joint ventures in Korea. The comprehensive nature of topics addressed in this book is a direct response to these information needs.

Redding (2005) argues that the weakness of the traditional approach to explaining international business lies in poor treatment of context, including the influences of history, culture and institutions. This book acknowledges Redding's position and adopts an institutional perspective, guided by the argument of Whitley (1999) that business systems are institutionally structured and institutional differences result in different kinds of business. As Hodgson (1998) points out, the institutional approach enables one to delineate the transition of social, political and economic institutions and to focus on the impacts of institutional transformation on the behavior of firms and business environments. This book uses the concept of institutions proposed by North (1990), which sees institutions as the 'rule of the game' in society and includes unwritten informal rules or culture as well as formal written rules.

The institutional approach is openly interdisciplinary, recognizing the insights of political science, sociology and anthropology as well as economics. It is also evolutionary rather than attempting to generate all-embracing general theories. The present study therefore examines the Korean institutional context through the multiple lenses of history, society, culture and politics, and analyzes various aspects of the Korean market and business systems in this light. It should be noted that the logical loop of the influences of business operations on institutions is not ignored. Rather, in order to keep the task manageable, the focus will be placed on the causality flow from institutional changes to changes in business environment and operations in Korea.

A set of eight propositions has been drawn from the extensive survey of English- and Korean-language literature on this subject. These propositions summarize the relevance of institutional changes for business environments and operations in Korea. They are:

1. A metamorphosis of formal institutions in the wake of the 1997 financial crisis has been the main force for determining the transition path of Korean business and management.
2. In response to the emergence of the globalization and information era, Korea's economic policy paradigm has shifted from developing a state-led industrial economy with extensive state intervention to promoting a market-oriented and knowledge-based economy. This paradigm shift has important implications for business opportunities and market configuration in Korea.
3. The shock of the financial crisis and the ensuing institutional reforms, alongside globalization, have led to changes in Korean society and culture. Koreans have come to value foreign business and culture, and their extreme patriotism of earlier times has faded significantly. Another

manifestation of cultural change is the lower importance of personal relationships and higher importance of impersonal operations in conducting and managing business.

4. Fully fledged political democratization coincident with institutional reforms in Korea will help to increase transparency and accountability in the political process and decrease political risk for international business.

5. Internationalization resulting from institutional reforms has enhanced the attractiveness of Korea's international business environment to foreign businesses. This has facilitated not only trade in goods and services but also inflows of FDI to Korea.

6. Moves to liberalize the market have reduced state paternalism – state intervention, protection and subsidies – towards domestic firms and in particular towards chaebol business conglomerates. This provides a more level playing field for foreign competitors in the Korean market.

7. Improvement in corporate governance through greater transparency, accountability and protection of minority shareholders has decreased both financial and operational risk and transaction and agency costs for international business. This has made the market in Korea more efficient and competitive.

8. Labor market reforms and demographic changes in Korean society in the recent past have changed the dominant mode and ethos of human resource management.

These propositions recur across the following ten chapters where they are explored carefully. A broad variety of topics of particular relevance to the Korean case is explored in these chapters, taking the analytical reach of this book beyond that of most conventional analyses of international business. This book considers not only business negotiation and business ethics but also takes up issues related to international joint ventures since these have become an important sphere of international business in Korea. Each chapter begins with a description of the international business context relevant to the subject of the chapter, and then explains its evolution and examines recent institutional reforms and their consequences.

Since the book is concerned with two interrelated lines of enquiry – the environmental dynamics and the nature of business operations in Korea – it has two sections. The first five chapters form Part I, which explores the macro-environment of international business in Korea to explain the nature and motivations of Korean and foreign firms and the features of trade and investment. Part II, which comprises the last five chapters, deals with the micro-processes of business operations and business management in Korea.

Chapter 1 opens Part I's discussion of the macro-environment of international business in Korea with examination of the business opportunities in Korea. This is one of the most critical issues in international business, particularly from a foreign perspective. As a way of assessing business opportunities, this chapter reviews Korea's rapid economic development over the last 40 years and the key contributing factors, particularly the important institutional settings. It then critically examines the transition of the Korean economy from this period of successful performance to the 1997 financial crisis and to a very rapid resurgence with the advent of the new millennium. The inability of institutions to adapt efficiently, particularly because of heavy state intervention, is identified as the major reason for the crisis. The drastic institutional reforms pursued in response to the crisis are then critically investigated. This chapter also proposes a set of policy guidelines and assesses the medium-term prospects of the economy under the emerging policy environments.

Chapter 2 turns to country risk which is an increasingly important concern in conducting international business. Korea's international geopolitical relationships, given its location in Northeast Asia, and its relationship with North Korea in particular, make country risk a serious concern for foreign business people contemplating market entry to Korea. This chapter assesses Korea's country risk with respect to these international relationships, paying special attention to inter-Korea economic relations as a way of assessing political and military conflicts between the two Koreas. The chapter recognizes that domestic circumstances are also instrumental in assessing country risk and hence considers political stability, democratic accountability and government–business relations in Korea to provide assessments of the major factors that shape country risk for Korea.

The critical importance of understanding a host country's culture for conducting international business is widely accepted. As Whitley (1999) argues, culture underpins formal institutions that in turn underpin business systems. In the case of Korea, not only does culture underpin formal institutions, but it also influences, directly and indirectly, all spheres of international business in Korea as examined in this book. Chapter 3 examines the nature of Korean culture and its historical development. It explores the salient aspects of traditional culture and the causes and extent of cultural change in the recent past as it influences Korea's international business environment and practices.

Chapter 4 turns to the configuration of the Korean market, with comprehensive assessment of the transition from 1990 to the present as a way of market screening. Attention is given to the information that foreign firms require for their export screening processes, including trends in Korea's import market, relevant institutional changes, the distribution system, socio-cultural forces, demographic changes and trends in e-commerce. The distribution system is examined because Korea's complex and idiosyncratic distribution system has been seen as a major obstacle to market entry by foreign businesses. E-commerce is a rapidly emerging new phenomenon of the Korean market configuration.

Chapter 5 examines recent trends in inward foreign direct investment (FDI) in Korea and investigates the causes for Korea's relatively poor performance in attracting FDI. Since government policy has been the key variable for inward FDI, particular consideration is given to the paradigm shift in FDI policy and the rationales that underpin these policy shifts. Attention is also given to foreign investors' perceptions of the Korean FDI environment given the importance of this factor in determining the flow of FDI into Korea.

Chapter 6 takes us into Part II of this book to consider the micro-processes of business operations and business management in Korea. Chapter 6 examines business negotiation, which is an integral part of international business in Korea. As Graham (1981) noted, the importance and difficulty of successful negotiation in international business can hardly be overemphasized. International business negotiation is intercultural negotiation since negotiation processes and practices are embedded in the culture within which negotiators usually conduct business. This chapter examines Koreans' approach to business negotiation from a cultural perspective and considers their distinctive approach to negotiation ethics, since this is becoming an important issue in international business.

Chapter 7 focuses on Korean business ethics. Ethics has become a much more important concern in Korean business after the string of corporate crashes brought on by the financial crisis and the massive US corporate debacles, which have forced the need for tighter compliance with a code of ethics appropriate for business conduct. Guidelines on business ethics have thus been institutionalized through domestic and intergovernmental organizations, and maintaining an ethical business culture has come to be recognized as a sensible strategy for business success and long-term survival. This chapter explores reasons for the relative underdevelopment of ethical behavior in corporate life in Korea until the crisis, and assesses the actions of government and private corporations to build a more ethical business environment post-crisis.

The institutional framework related to business management has also changed markedly since the financial crisis and has helped to shape profoundly the transition in the Korean management system. Chapter 8 examines the salient characteristics of the Korean management system until the crisis and the transition in this system in the post-crisis period from an institutional perspective. The current status and future prospects of the management system are also assessed, with consideration of the views that foreign business people in Korea have of this management system in its present form.

Chapter 9 examines human resource management (HRM) in Korea. While businesses in Korea face unprecedented competition domestically and internationally, Korean companies must respond to major institutional changes that seek to eliminate inefficiency in the HRM system, while maintaining workers' commitment and loyalty and adjusting to demographic changes. This chapter analyzes how and why Korea's system of HRM has been transformed. It also considers the perceptions that foreign business people in Korea have of this evolving HRM system. Reaching beyond HRM, this chapter also gives some consideration to the labor market and labor standards in Korea since this information is particularly useful for foreigners seeking to understand and/or to enter the Korean market.

Given the recent proliferation of international joint ventures (IJVs), Chapter 10, the final chapter, focuses on the salient characteristics and management of IJVs in Korea. The intensification of globalization and diffusion of new technologies have encouraged Korean companies to pursue aggressively global strategic partnerships inside Korea with leading foreign companies. Despite their advantages and popularity as a form of market entry, IJVs in Korea have a high failure rate that is largely attributable to management problems arising from the incompatibility of partners. This chapter uses a set of established criteria to assess IJVs in Korea in terms of the compatibility of partners.

Overall the analysis in this book weaves together the rich array of pertinent topics considered across the ten chapters to present an informative and comprehensive picture of international business in Korea at this early stage of the twenty-first century. It does so largely by using an institutional analytical framework that examines both informal (cultural) and formal institutions. Thus, although the influence of Korean culture is discussed at length in one chapter, the fuller picture of cultural influence upon business conduct surfaces across all ten chapters. This applies to the treatment of many topics that recur throughout the discussion that follows. The choice of topics most pertinent to this discussion has been guided by the nature and direction of institutional transformation in Korean business life in the wake of the 1997 financial crisis.

This book is shaped by a keen awareness of the nature of globalization and its impact on international business worldwide. Some observers will argue that the globalization process will precipitate further changes in international business in Korea, while drawing all or most nations towards a global standard. However, this book maintains that the distinctive nature of Korean culture and institutional frameworks will continue to shape the Korean market and business practices. These circumstances make knowledge of the Korean business environment and system and their idiosyncrasies, as revealed in this book, particularly valuable for those seeking to understand international business in Korea or indeed to become actively engaged in it.

REFERENCES

Bank of Korea (2006), 'Economic statistics system', http://ecos.bok.or.kr/ EIndex_en.jsp.

Graham, J.L. (1981), 'A hidden cause of America's trade deficit with Japan', *Columbia Journal of World Business*, Fall, 5–15.

Hodgson, Geoffrey M. (1998), 'The approach of institutional economics', *Journal of Economic Literature*, 36 (1), 166–92.

Kwon, O. Yul (1997), 'Korean economic developments and prospects', *Asian-Pacific Economic Literature*, 11 (2), 15–39.

Kwon, O. Yul (1998), 'The Korean financial crisis: diagnosis, remedies and prospects', *Journal of the Asia Pacific Economy*, 3 (3), 331–57.

Kwon, O. Yul (2001), 'Korea's international business environment before and after the financial crisis', in O. Yul Kwon and William Shepherd (eds), *Korea's Economic Prospects: From Financial Crisis to Prosperity*, Cheltenham, UK and Northampton, MA, USA: Edward Elgar, pp. 245–65.

Kwon, O. Yul (2004), 'Causes for sluggish foreign direct investment in Korea: a foreign perspective', *Journal of the Korean Economy*, 5 (1), 69–96.

Kwon, O. Yul (2005), 'A cultural analysis of South Korea's economic prospects', *Global Economic Review*, 34 (2), 213–31.

Kwon, O. Yul (2006), 'Recent changes in Korea's business environment: views of foreign business people in Korea', *Asia Pacific Business Review*, 12 (1), 77–94.

Lee, Y.I. (2004), 'South Korean companies in transition: an evolving strategic management style', *Strategic Change*, 13 (1), 29–35.

North, D.C. (1990), *Institutions, Institutional Change and Economic Performance*, Cambridge: Cambridge University Press.

Redding, Gordon (2005), 'The thick description and comparison of societal systems of capitalism', *Journal of International Business Studies*, 36 (2), 123–55.

Rowley, C. (2002), 'South Korean management in transition', in M. Warner and P. Joynt (eds), *Managing Across Cultures*, London: Thomson, pp. 178–92.

Rowley, C. and J. Bae (2003), 'Culture and management in South Korea', in M. Warner (ed.), *Culture and Management*, London: Curzon, pp. 187–209.

Rowley, C. and J. Bae (2004), 'Human resource management in South Korea after the Asian financial crisis', *International Studies of Management and Organization*, 34 (1), 52–80.

Whitley, Richard (1999), 'Competing logics and units of analysis in the comparative study of economic organizations', *International Studies of Management and Organization*, 29 (2), 113–26.

PART I

The international business environment in
Korea

1. Business opportunities: Korea's economic prospects

1.1 INTRODUCTION

The Korean development model has attracted international attention due to the country's well-documented economic transformation from one of the world's poorest countries to one of the richest between 1963 and 1996. Despite a lack of natural resources, a high population density, severe wartime devastation, heavy defense expenditure and authoritarian military regimes, economic growth averaged 8.7 per cent per annum between 1963 and 1996 (Table 1.1). Per capita GDP, just $87 in 1962, had increased to $10 548 by 1996. Nominal GDP increased from $2.3 billion in 1962 to $480.4 billion in 1996, establishing Korea as the world's eleventh-largest economy. In 1996, Korea became the 29th member of the OECD. Korea's economic miracle ended abruptly in November 1997 during the Asian financial crisis, experiencing a negative growth rate of 6.7 per cent and depreciation of its currency value by 50 per cent in 1998. However, unlike other economies affected by the crisis, Korea recovered quickly with 10.7 per cent growth in 1999, followed by an 8.8 per cent growth rate in 2000. Once again, Korea's economic performance stimulated broad international discussion, this time as a model for overcoming financial crisis, rather than as the developmental model of the past.

As a way of assessing business opportunities, this chapter reviews and critically examines the Korean economy's transition from success to financial crisis, and then to resurgence in the new millennium. The following section analyzes the rapid growth period from 1963 to 1996. Section 1.3 examines the 1997 financial crisis, including its causes, and evaluates the subsequent structural and institutional reforms. Section 1.4 examines the potential and future direction of the Korean economy, and section 1.5 briefly reviews the major findings of the study and provides concluding remarks.

1.2 MIRACULOUS DEVELOPMENT: 1963–96

1.2.1 Extensive State Intervention

Economic development in Korea can be broadly divided into two historical periods: the period of rapid growth from 1963 to 1996, and that of financial crisis in 1997 and post-crisis restructuring. During the rapid growth period, the government intervened extensively in the economy. Until the late 1980s, the government, rather than market forces, controlled the direction and pace of industrialization in Korea. Consecutive five-year plans commencing in 1962 provided clear and consistent signals to both domestic and international economic players.

In the 1960s, maximum growth was sought through export-led industrialization in light, labor-intensive industries. All policy and regulatory instruments were mobilized to support this strategy, including tax, trade, credit, foreign exchange allowances and interest rates. The most powerful of these was the allocation of funds at preferential interest rates for export and investment in specific industries. In the 1970s, the focus of industry policy changed to heavy and chemical industries. All policy tools, particularly credit allocation, were reoriented to the six targeted industries of steel, petrochemicals, metals, shipbuilding, electronics and machinery. In the early 1980s, structural adjustment measures toward economic liberalization were adopted due to the severe economic imbalances caused by overinvestment in heavy industry at the expense of other sectors and pressure from international partners.

In the late 1980s, the Roh Tae-Woo government pursued political democratization in parallel with economic liberalization, ending four decades of authoritarian rule. The transition from state-led economic management to a free market approach imposed considerable adjustment costs in the forms of rampant labor disputes, wage hikes and inflationary pressures. In 1993, the first civilian government in three decades was elected. The Kim Young-Sam government focused on reforms to open Korea to globalization, such as deregulation of the financial sector.

1.2.2 Transformation of the Economy

The Korean economy was profoundly transformed during its rapid growth period. Table 1.1 shows that growth in the manufacturing and service sectors resulted in a drastic decline in agriculture's share of GDP from 43.5 per cent in 1963 to 5.8 per cent in 1996. The manufacturing and service sectors grew from 11.6 to 28.9 per cent, and from 44.9 to 65.3 per cent of GDP respectively. Another striking transformation was the acceleration in trade. Exports increased from $90 million in 1963 to $130 billion in 1996. As a percentage of GDP, exports rose from 3.9 to 30.3 per cent, a direct result of increased manufactured exports. By 1996, manufactured goods comprised 92.9 per cent of total exports. The Korean economy is import-dependent on raw materials, crude oil, agricultural products and intermediate capital goods. Consequently, imports also increased from $500 million in 1963 to $150 billion in 1996. As a percentage of GDP, imports increased from 16.1 to 32.6 per cent. Korea became the world's twelfth-largest trading nation as a result of this rapid import and export growth.

Rapid increases in saving and investment were another striking feature of Korean economic development. The gross investment rate increased from 18.1 per cent in 1963, to 38.1 per cent in 1996. Such a sustained accumulation of capital would not be possible without a significant increase in domestic saving. The gross saving rate increased from 14.4 per cent of GDP in 1963 to 33.8 per cent in 1996. Over the period 1971–96, labor productivity increased by 9.8 per cent per year. Demand for labor also grew, and employment rose from 7.7 million to 20.9 million over the 1963–96 period – a 3.1 per cent annual growth rate. Unemployment declined from 8.2 per cent in 1963 to 2 per cent in 1996.

Another important aspect of post-1962 Korean economic development was the concentration of economic power in large, family-owned and managed industrial conglomerates, or chaebols, characterized by central planning and close ties with government. With the diversification of the economy, chaebols rapidly expanded the scope of their businesses. In 1970, the 30 largest chaebols each had 4.2 subsidiaries on average. By 1989, this figure had increased to 17.1 (K.U. Lee 1994).[1] By 1995, total sales of the 30 largest chaebols were equivalent to 90 per cent of Korea's GDP (DFAT 1996, p. 1). Unlike Japanese keiretsu, centered on banking institutions, chaebols could not hold majority ownership of commercial banks. Ownership control was maintained by means of intercompany cross-ownership, and cross-debt guaranteeing among subsidiaries.

During the initial stage of Korea's rapid growth in the 1960s, little attention was paid to income distribution and social development. However, due to successful land reforms over the 1947–50 period, and the physical destruction of the Korean War, the population had to start from similar levels of poverty. This resulted in an income distribution that ranked among the most equitable in the developing world. In addition, cultural homogeneity and the lack of entrenched regional, religious or class differences in Korean society have provided for a genuine equality of opportunity, particularly in the area of education. Korea's labor-intensive development contributed to the egalitarian income distribution by providing employment for workers with minimal levels of education.

1.2.3 Factors Contributing to Korea's Economic Success

State intervention

Extensive state intervention occurred in all sectors of the Korean economy over the high-growth period. State intervention was easily justifiable in

Table 1.1 Korea's major economic indicators (1963–2005)

	1963	1970	1980	1990	1996	2000	2002	2003	2004	2005
Population (million)	27	32	38	43	46	47	48	48	48	48
Annual population growth (%)	2.82	2.21	1.57	0.99	0.96	0.72	0.55	0.49	0.49	0.44
GDP per capita (US$)	100	250	1 673	6 151	11 422	10 888	11 485	12 707	14 161	16 306
GDP (US$ billion)	2.3	8	64	264	520	512	547	608	681	787
GDP growth rate (%)	9.1	7.5	-1.5	9.2	6.8	8.5	7.0	3.1	4.7	4.0
Gross saving rate (%)	14.4	17.8	24.7	37.5	33.8	33.7	31.3	32.8	34.9	33.0
Gross investment rate (%)	18.1	24.8	31.9	37.4	38.1	31.1	29.1	30.1	30.3	30.2
Share of GDP (%)										
Agriculture	43.5	26.5	14.9	8.5	5.8	4.9	4.1	3.6	3.3	3.3
Manufacturing	11.6	22.7	29.8	29.6	28.9	29.8	27.2	26.9	25.8	28.8
Services	44.9	50.8	55.3	61.9	65.3	65.3	68.7	69.5	70.9	67.9
Employed (million)	7.7	9.6	13.7	18.1	20.9	21.2	22.2	22.1	22.6	22.9
Unemployment rate (%)	8.2	4.4	5.2	2.4	2.0	4.1	3.1	3.4	3.5	3.4
Inflation rate (%)	20.2	12.8	28.7	8.6	4.9	2.2	2.7	3.6	3.6	2.7
Exchange rate (won/US$)	130	317	660	716	844	1 260	1 200	1 198	1 044	1 013
Exports (US$ billion)	0.09	0.8	17.5	65.0	130	173	162	194	254	284
Imports (US$ billion)	0.50	2.0	22.3	69.8	150	160	152	179	224	261
Trade balance	-4.1	-1.2	-4.8	-2.0	-20	+17	+8	+15	+30	+23
Exports/GDP (%)	3.9	13.6	32.1	28.6	30.3	33.7	29.6	31.9	44.1	36.1
Imports/GDP (%)	16.1	23.8	40.0	29.0	32.6	31.3	27.7	29.4	39.7	33.2

Table 1.1 (continued)

	1963–69	1970–79	1980–89	1990–99	1963–96	1963–2004	2000–05
Average annual growth rate (%)	9.8	9.7	8.3	6.2	8.7	8.0	5.2
Annual productivity growth (%)[a]	n.a	8.9[b]	9.6	11.2	9.8[c]	9.4[d]	3.65

Notes:
[a] Labor productivity is measured as the index of constant GDP divided by the index of labor man-hour input.
[b] indicates value for 1971–79.
[c] for 1971–96.
[d] for 1971–2002.

Sources: Korean National Statistical Office (KNSO) (2002), KNSO (2005), KNSO (2006), Bank of Korea (2003), Bank of Korea (2005), Bank of Korea (2007), Korea Labor Institute (2003), and Korea Productivity Centre (2004).

the initial stages of economic development. Markets were small, inefficient and lacked effective institutionalization. Deficiencies in technology and economies of scale also necessitated government intervention and promotion. Not only was intervention justified during the initial stage of Korean economic development, but it also worked well until the latter 1980s because of clear social consensus on policy goals and high organizational capabilities pervaded by strong Korean nationalism, in addition to a cooperative external environment. Important institutions were established during the rapid growth period. In 1962, the powerful Economic Planning Board assumed a central policy-making role, including budgetary authority and administrative control over the banking system. Competent technocrats were secured through competitive civil service examinations, and most ministries established their own research centers. The bureaucracy enjoyed a high degree of independence from political interference because of the societal respect and prestige associated with the economic ministries.

Export-led industrialization
Due to its lack of natural resources and small domestic market, export-led industrialization has been fundamental to Korea's development. The focus of this strategy has changed over time. In the 1960s, Korea's comparative advantage in surplus labor was utilized by the promotion of exports of labor-intensive manufactures. In the 1970s, industrialized countries imposed trade restrictions on labor-intensive products, and upward pressure on wages eroded the comparative advantage of labor-intensive industries. Korea also needed to reduce its imports of capital goods to rectify chronic trade deficits. The composition of exports was thus restructured toward more sophisticated, value-added products in heavy and chemical industries, and trade partnerships were diversified. In the 1980s, Korea's export strategy was again modified, with international pressure to open its economy resulting in further import liberalization and a greater harmonizing of its export drive with domestic and international pressures. In the 1990s, Korea further opened its economy and reduced export subsidies under its WTO obligations. With rapidly rising domestic wages together with intensifying international competition, Korea has transformed its industrial structure toward high value-added, knowledge- and technology-oriented industries, and focused its exports in these areas.

Over the rapid export growth period, numerous policy incentives were used to implement Korea's export strategy, including tax and foreign exchange benefits, and export loans at artificially low interest rates. The government also established a variety of institutions integral to export promotion, including the Export Promotion Council, the Korea Trade Investment Promotion Agency (KOTRA), and the Korea Traders'

Association. General trading companies, the precursors to chaebols, were also promoted to maximize scale and scope in international trade. The phenomenal expansion in exports was attributable not only to state policy, but also to private entrepreneurs. Korean entrepreneurs were successful in exploiting the country's comparative advantage, and capitalizing on opportunities arising in world export markets independently of foreign multinationals.

The success of Korea's export promotion strategy is evident in an export–GDP ratio that increased from 3.9 to 30.3 per cent between 1963 and 1996, and a share of world exports that increased from 0.04 per cent in 1962 to 2.5 per cent in 1996. Export-led development has also resulted in a deepening of Korea's industrial structure. The share of manufactured exports grew from 27 per cent in 1962 to 93 per cent in 1996. Attributable to the industrial policy of the 1970s, the share of heavy and chemical industry in exports expanded from 10.4 per cent in 1962 to 71.7 per cent in 1996 (Lee et al. 2003).

Heavy and chemical industries
In the 1970s, Korea switched industrial policy toward capital and technology-intensive heavy and chemical (HC) industries. The policy task was therefore to mobilize capital, technology, skilled workers, industrial sites and entrepreneurs into the HC industries. To this end, the government implemented four strategic initiatives: a generous incentive scheme, the expansion of educational capacity to supply skilled workers, the establishment of new research institutes, and a huge industrial site at Changwon dedicated to the HC sector (Kwon 1997).

The incentive scheme included not only monetary incentives, as stated earlier, but also protection of the industry from domestic and international competition. The most powerful tool was the allocation of investment funds at preferential interest rates. Between 1973 and 1981, around 50 per cent of all investment funds was allocated to policy loans for the HC sector at interest rates substantially less than those available from commercial banks (Kwon 1997). As a result, capital was rapidly accumulated and intensified in the HC industry sector. Employment in the HC industrial sector grew faster than in the total manufacturing sector. Export composition also changed, with the export share taken by HC industries increasing significantly relative to that of light industries.

Korea's HC industrial policy, although successful in promoting export expansion and economic growth, created a different problem: the concentration of economic power in chaebols, which have expanded and diversified with government blessing. This has raised serious equity problems, retarded the development of small and medium-sized industries, and led to financial sector underdevelopment due to the long period of government control.

High investment and saving

Increases in the gross investment rate fuelled impressive economic growth. The high investment rate was attributable to a high rate of return on capital and low business risk. The rate of return was markedly higher in Korea in the 1970s and 1980s than in developed economies, although slowing over time (Kwack 1994; Pyo 1996). A high return on capital was enabled by low interest rates, low wages until the late 1980s, and the protection of domestic industries from foreign investment. Prices for investment goods also remained relatively low due to preferential tax and tariff arrangements. On numerous occasions, the government encouraged or coerced companies to invest in priority projects by means of subsidized or guaranteed loans (Stern et al. 1995). The state also bailed out a number of troubled projects, thereby reducing the actual and perceived risk associated with private investment. Macroeconomic stability, indicated by moderately low inflation and a stable exchange rate, also reduced investment uncertainty.

Sustained capital accumulation in Korea would not have been possible without significant increases in domestic savings. Korea's gross saving rate was one of the highest in the world. During the 1963–96 period, private savings accounted for 78.3 per cent of national savings; of this, business saving comprised 57.1 per cent (KNSO 2002). The main objective of firms during this period was to expand market share for their products. Consequently, they were less concerned with short-term profits and would retain a high proportion of profits as savings.

Korean household consumption decisions during the rapid growth period were based on relatively stable patterns, and were closely related to current rather than projected future income (Kuznets 1994; Collins 1994). Thus, as income increased, so did savings. The Confucian cultural trait of frugality contributed to the high rate of saving. A large portion of remuneration in Korea is also paid in the form of bonuses, and the marginal propensity to save from bonuses is regarded as high (Song 1994, p. 159). Government policy also contributed to the high saving rate by maintaining macroeconomic stability, high real interest rates on deposits, stable financial institutions, and tax exemptions on credit interest (Nam and Kim 1995). The lack of a social security system also helps explain the high saving rate, with welfare generally regarded as a family concern in Korea.

Between 1963 and 1996, investment exceeded domestic saving except in the four-year period from 1986–89. This excess was financed by foreign savings in the form of commercial loans attracted to Korea by government guarantees. FDI accounted for only a minor portion due to government restrictions designed to limit foreign control of the economy.

Human capital development

A remarkable feature of Korean economic development has been the ability to utilize effectively the nation's human resources. Labor demand increased dramatically during the 1960s as a result of the labor-intensive industrialization strategy. As a result, from a labor surplus in the 1960s, Korea was transformed to a labor-shortage economy by 1977 (Kim and Lee 1995). Real wages increased more than productivity, thereby raising real unit labor costs. By contrast with this increase in wages ahead of productivity, real interest rates on loans remained artificially low until the early 1980s. The resulting increases in the wage–rental ratio led companies to substitute capital for labor, a trend that continued after 1987 (Kuznets 1994, p. 68).

Supply of human resources increased rapidly through demographic growth in the labor force, advancement of education, and the mobilization of underemployed farm workers. Between 1963 and 1996, the labor force increased by 2.9 per cent per year. Labor inputs also increased from an average 47.2-hour working week in 1963–65 to 56 hours in 1994 (Kuznets 1994, p. 9). In 1996, Koreans worked an average 49.2 hours per week compared with the Asian average of 44.8 hours (*Korea Herald* 1997).

Korea's flexible and efficient labor market was a key element in the rapid growth of employment and the economy (Kim and Lee 1995; Kuznets 1994, p. 4). Under authoritarian regimes emphasizing high-growth policies, anti-competitive arrangements such as minimum wages, labor protection laws and union monopolies did not exist. Market forces largely determined wages and employment. However, the 'competitive-looking' labor market was, in reality, under strict government control. Management rights were promoted at the expense of labor, union activities were suppressed, and wage guidelines imposed. Taking the government's lead, management applied an authoritarian approach to labor relations. The state often intervened to resolve disputes, leading to a lack of labor–management skill among businesses. The situation changed dramatically with political democratization and the weakening of government control. In conjunction with the late 1980s labor shortage, numerous disputes across 1987–89 demonstrated that past Korean labor practices could no longer work.

Korean education levels have also increased remarkably. Highly valued historically under Confucianism, education is regarded as directly linked to social status and material success. These attributes are considered in terms of the family rather than the individual, and parents commonly dedicate large sums to their children's education. Most Koreans entering the workforce have received at least 12 years of education. Tertiary education has also expanded exponentially. Enrolments increased from 123 000 in 1965 to 1.9 million in 1996, a 9.3 per cent annual growth rate. Heavy social demand for higher education has led to the enforcement of a strict quota system, inevitably leading to fierce competition for university entrance among pupils in primary and secondary schools. The Korean education system has, however, experienced a number of problems. Questions have been raised as to the quality of tertiary education and the ability of science and technology, and business and vocational courses to cope with the ever-increasing demand for skilled labor (Kim 1995). Due to the emphasis on competitive examinations, the education system has been criticized for encouraging rote learning at the expense of critical thinking and analytical skills.

Cultural traits
A large literature exists on the relationship between traditional Confucian culture and economic development (Lee 1995). Confucianism emphasizes harmonious yet hierarchical human relations among citizens who are in turn held to be diligent, disciplined and hardworking, well educated, frugal, responsible, loyal to authority, and oriented toward social cohesion (Morishima 1982; Cho 1994). This value system is supportive of economic growth (Jones and Sakong 1982). Park (1995) argues that the Confucian value works only if certain political and economic preconditions are met, including free enterprise, competition, international trade, suitable institutions, and a stable and growing middle class. Cho (1994) adds that a misguided focus of social development policy had bred the major negative Confucian influence – distinct social stratification and antipathy to manual labor and business. Cho (1994) then argues that these negative Confucian values have lost their strength as the economy has developed and a middle class has emerged.

Technology development
The accumulation of technological capability is another important factor in Korea's economic success. Confucian socio-cultural traits have been conducive to the development of education and technological capacity. The role of the business sector has also been critical. Potentially risky initiatives have combined effectively with the centralized, hierarchical management style of Korean businesses to expand technological capability. Unlike Western companies, family-controlled chaebols are not under constant pressure to deliver shareholder profits, and therefore have been able to reinvest in longer-term technological development. Chaebols were also well positioned to identify, negotiate and finance foreign technology transfer, and to gain captive markets for new products. Business risks for chaebols could also be hedged against existing enterprises within the conglomerate.

The state also played a crucial role in technological improvement. In the 1960s and 1970s, in its catch-up stage of development, Korea found it relatively easy to import foreign technology. As the economy advanced, the development of an indigenous technological development capacity became imperative. The government launched a national R&D program to strengthen capacity, with various tax and financial incentives, resulting in an increase in R&D expenditure as a percentage of GDP from 0.77 per cent in 1980, to 2.3 per cent in 1990. Despite these advances, Korea still faces enormous challenges in this area. Compared with the advanced industrial economies, the ratio of R&D expenditure to GDP is still low. Science and technology facilities at universities are also regarded as dated and inadequate, with high student–staff ratios.

1.3 THE 1997 FINANCIAL CRISIS AND REFORMS2

1.3.1 Causes of the Financial Crisis

After 30 years of almost continuous economic growth, Korea fell into deep financial crisis in November 1997, necessitating an IMF rescue package. Witnessing the emerging crisis and speculating on depreciation of the won, foreign investors and creditors withdrew investments in Korean securities and curtailed short-term loans. Consequently, share prices and the value of the currency plummeted. The Bank of Korea (BOK) made a futile attempt to prop up the won, thereby drastically depleting its foreign reserves. The won depreciated by around 50 per cent and interest rates skyrocketed to over 30 per cent. High interest rates and reduced company profitability precipitated a large number of bankruptcies. This, in turn, induced a banking crisis as foreign debt and non-performing loans escalated. As a result, a number of banks were forced to close. The economy contracted by 6.7 per cent in 1998 with high unemployment and inflation.

One of the important causes of the crisis was continuing high current account deficits, amounting to 4.9 per cent of GDP in 1996 (Kwon 1998). Korea's high current account deficits were attributable to a loss of competitiveness in domestic industries because of high factor costs, including high wages, real interest rates and real estate prices. This overall loss of competitiveness resulted in declines in export earnings and, in turn, increases in insolvency. Insolvent firms then dumped non-performing loans to domestic banks, laying the foundations for the crisis. Another important cause was a sustained overvaluation of the won due to state interference in the foreign exchange market. The managed and overvalued exchange rate system produced the illusion of currency stability, thereby contributing to both excessive foreign borrowing and a loss of international competitiveness.

The excessive expansion and diversification of chaebols through debt capital was another cause of the financial crisis.[3] The concentration of economic power in chaebols was a product of Korea's state-directed industrial and export promotion policy. Collusion with government created the perception that chaebols were 'too big to fail', and would be bailed out if necessary. This reduced expected business risk, leading chaebols to expand through debt capital. Debt capital was also raised by inter-subsidiary loan guarantees. The combination of these factors rendered the chaebols vulnerable to financial crisis. This inherent weakness remained obscured from domestic and international creditors by a lack of transparency and accountability in Korean business operations.

The Korean financial crisis was also attributable to the lack of transparency and accountability of banks and their inefficient supervision. Banking regulations and supervision were fragmented and inefficient with supervisory roles shared between the Bank of Korea and the Ministry of Finance and Economy (MOFE). From the 1960s, banks were one of the main vehicles for tightly controlled government industry policy. The allocation of credits and setting of interest rates was regulated extensively by government. At the same time, the government imposed competition-limiting measures, prohibiting chaebols from being controlling shareholders of banks and shielding banks from international competition. The ownership of Korean banks became so widely diversified that they were regarded as 'entities without owners', and thus accountable only to the government. A strong perception emerged that 'the banks will never fail' because of government protection, leading to moral hazard in the banking sector. The banking sector was also characterized by a lack of independence from chaebols because of their strong relations with government. Chaebols received the bulk of bank credit but did not release consolidated financial statements. This was all indicative of the banking sector's lack of independence, and its lack of prudence in monitoring major debtors. The above combination of circumstances, together with an insatiable demand for funds, ensured that reckless lending to chaebols was bound to arise.

The Korean financial market was significantly liberalized in the early 1990s, allowing banks greater access to international finance. However, regulatory structures did not adapt to this change, and appropriate institutional constraints were not in place, leading to excessive borrowing from offshore capital markets. Reckless offshore borrowing was bolstered by artificially high domestic interest rates in Korea. Financial institutions came to rely heavily on low-interest, short-term borrowings from abroad. Foreign debt was denominated mainly in US dollars because the Korean won was not listed in foreign mercantile exchange markets, nor had hedging tools such as options, swaps and derivatives been developed.

From the late 1980s, adverse changes in internal and external policy environments eroded the effectiveness of state intervention, which in effect became the major underlying cause of the financial crisis. Government control and protection of chaebols led to a lack of transparency and accountability, and encouraged excessive expansion with debt capital. State intervention in financial markets resulted in financial institutions being inefficient, undercapitalized and afflicted by moral hazard. Government protection of domestic industries from international competition resulted in their loss of efficiency and competitiveness. Intervention in the labor market resulted in inefficiency in labor management and labor market inflexibility. Finally, the government failed to introduce appropriate measures in time to stem the financial crisis, despite the presence of emerging symptoms that were evidence of the looming crisis. The 1997 crisis brought the demise of the old paradigm of *dirigist* economic policy.

1.3.2 Structural and Institutional Reforms

The IMF rescue package for Korea consisted of three components:

1. macroeconomic policy;
2. financial sector restructuring; and
3. other structural reform measures.

The macroeconomic policy objective was to restrain aggregate demand by restraining monetary and fiscal policy, thereby reducing current account deficits and maintaining stable prices. Other macroeconomic measures included maintaining a flexible exchange rate without state intervention and restoring an adequate level of foreign reserves. The Korean government initially complied faithfully with restraining macro monetary and fiscal policy. However, the restraining policies resulted in a credit crunch, which exacerbated non-performing loans and raised interest rates. International confidence in the Korean economy was further eroded, thereby inhibiting capital inflows. In September 1998, macroeconomic restraint was relaxed with IMF agreement.

Opening of the Korean market

The crisis forced the Korean government to liberalize its trade and capital accounts to international standards in compliance with Korea's WTO obligations. Capital account liberalization aimed to open the securities market to foreign investors, to allow Korean companies to borrow from abroad, and to eliminate FDI restrictions. The government has made particular efforts to attract FDI, switching its policy emphasis to promotion and assistance from one of restriction and control. Korea has opened a number of sectors, including the service sector and real estate, to FDI and has streamlined complicated administrative procedures. It has also introduced a so-called 'one-stop' service system for inward FDI. M&As, including hostile takeovers, have been promoted in conjunction with liberalization.

Financial sector restructuring

The financial sector has been restructured to increase the banking sector's independence, consolidate and strengthen the supervision of financial institutions, and to eliminate insolvent institutions and recapitalize viable ones. International standards for auditing and disclosure have been adopted to improve transparency and accountability. Management accountability has been enhanced by the establishment of elected boards of directors for financial institutions, who are responsible to their shareholders. Restructuring has also opened the financial sector to FDI, M&As and foreign competition. In the course of banking sector reform, 631 institutions were closed and the remainder recapitalized with 157 trillion won of public funds. Foreign participation in domestic banks' equity capital has increased markedly, with two banks now controlled by foreign shareholders (SERI 2001).

Reform of chaebols

Restructuring of chaebols has been pursued using the 'five plus three point' principles mutually agreed by the chaebols and government. The 'five principles' refer to: management transparency; the eradication of cross-debt guarantees among subsidiaries; financial structure improvements; core business specialization; and improved corporate governance. The aim of the 'three points' was to prevent chaebol domination of the non-bank financial sector, prohibit cross-investment and illegal internal trading, and prevent abnormal wealth inheritance. Substantial progress has been made in accordance with the agreed reform principles. Chaebols have started to provide consolidated financial statements; eliminated cross-subsidiary debt guarantees; reduced debt–equity ratios to 200 per cent; appointed outside directors; removed restrictions on the voting rights of institutional investors; and strengthened the rights of minority shareholders.

Due to the abolition of investment ceilings, and permission for hostile M&A takeovers, foreign capital has substantially penetrated the Korean business sector. Foreign investors will expect management transparency, improved corporate governance and management efficiency, and they are in turn expected to weaken the potential for state intervention and collusion in government–business relations, thereby removing the systematic privileges enjoyed by chaebols. In the course of restructuring, 16 of the 30 largest chaebols were sold, merged or liquidated, discrediting the perception that chaebols were 'too big to fail'. In addition, foreign investors in Korean financial institutions will strengthen their intervention in, and monitoring of, debtor companies. Those lacking in transparency and accountability, or with low profitability and high debt–equity ratios, will have difficulty in raising bank credit. This will force chaebols to concentrate on core competencies and divest themselves of marginal interests.

Reform of the labor market
The amended labor laws of February 1998 enhanced labor-market flexibility and competitiveness by permitting retrenchments of employees for the first time in Korean history. It is expected that the changes will also lead to improvement in labor–management relations, with job security rather than wage increases becoming the core area of labor dispute. Revision of the labor laws has reconfigured the Korean labor market with the number of full-time workers decreasing with a concomitant increase in part-time workers.

Paradigm shift in economic policy
Prior to the 1997 financial crisis, the Korean economic policy paradigm may best be described as extensive state intervention through consecutive five-year plans. Although state intervention was successful until the late 1980s, it was the main underlying cause of the financial crisis. The paradigm then shifted toward a market-oriented economy. This shift was reflected in the liberalization of domestic industry, and in the reform of financial institutions, chaebols, the labor market and public sector. The bulk of the policy tools dedicated to state intervention have been rescinded, with a commensurate reduction in the size of the state bureaucracy.

1.3.3 Recovery from the Financial Crisis

Since early 1999, the Korean economy has made a strong recovery due to a number of factors, including maturity extensions on short-term foreign debt, restored macroeconomic stability, export expansion due to currency depreciation, a more accommodating monetary and fiscal stance from mid-1998, restoration of foreign confidence, and FDI inflows. In addition, the underlying fundamentals of the Korean economy, such as the high savings rate, well-educated workforce and advanced production infrastructure have remained sound. The combination of these factors contributed to a rapid economic recovery by 1999.

1.3.4 Unfinished Economic Reform

Although substantial progress has been made in financial, corporate, labor and public sector restructuring, it is by no means complete (Ahn 2001; Jung 2002). In mid-2000, the economy was considered so fragile that the Kim Dae-Jung administration shifted policy emphasis from reform to growth. In the financial sector, banks that were nationalized through the government bailout still need to be reprivatized to reduce the potential for bureaucratic interference. Many banks are also too small and inefficient by international standards to take advantage of economies of scale. Hence, further amalgamations should be encouraged.

The chaebols' financial structure, although improved, still remains unhealthy. Although debt–equity ratios have decreased below 200 per cent, this was achieved through new stock issues and asset sales and revaluations rather than debt reduction. The degree of founding-family control has not substantially diminished. Running counter to its reform track, the government has also rescued the ailing Hyundai group. Despite prohibitions on bank ownership, chaebols can still own non-bank financial institutions. Labor market rigidity also remains a problem. Korean labor laws still discourage dismissals unless a company is facing a major crisis. Structural reforms of banks and chaebols may not be able to proceed successfully unless labor market flexibility improves and union militancy decreases.

In addition, Korea has not fully opened to the global economy, particularly in relation to inward FDI. Although the FDI regime has been liberalized and streamlined to be consistent with OECD standards, deficiencies remain. These include a lack of transparency and consistency in regulation, policy-making and implementation, bureaucratic intrusion and obstruction, inter-agency turf wars, foreign exchange controls, and restrictions on the legal-service markets (Kwon 2003b).

1.4 PROSPECTS FOR THE KOREAN ECONOMY: GROWTH POTENTIALS

1.4.1 Policy Framework

Prospects for the Korean economy depend above all on economic policy which is in turn predicated on the main policy objectives and policy environments. Under intensifying globalization, the world economy has become further interrelated, integrated and competitive, and is also moving toward a knowledge- and information-based economy. The rise of China to become the paramount economic player in East Asia and a formidable competitor against Korea is another important factor influencing Korean economic policy. Domestically, Korea's demographic development shows trends of declining growth and ageing of the population (Table 1.1 and Chapter 4). Consequently, labor force growth will decline and the social burden of support for the elderly will increase. As prosperity rises, preferences for leisure and quality of life will increase, causing a reduction in the number of hours worked and in the national savings rate. In the absence of government protection together with rising globalization and China's economic prominence, economic risk and uncertainty have increased, lowering the national investment rate. The influence of foreign capital in the Korean economy will continue to rise with its rising penetration in banks, securities markets and businesses.

Under these circumstances, the underpinning principle of Korea's economic policy should be the embrace of market principles and global standards geared toward globalization. This requires a completion of the ongoing process of economic restructuring and reform. The state should provide an environment conducive to the growth of the private sector including both domestic and foreign businesses, while also ensuring openness, transparency and accountability in government policies and regulations as well as in private sector operations. The government needs a strategy to ameliorate slowing demographic growth and an ageing population. To this end, institutional arrangements are required to bolster female participation in knowledge- and information-based industries and to allow entry for both low-skilled and high-skilled foreign workers. In its transition to a knowledge-based economy, Korea has to develop the social capability to develop and adopt new technologies through R&D and an advanced education system. As a member of the global village, homogenous Korean society and culture needs to open up significantly to globalization.

Future Korean governments will place more emphasis on equitable economic development than before. Social development should be an integral element of the new economic strategy. Social programs such as unemployment insurance and other social safety nets should develop in parallel with economic growth, as the financial crisis and structural changes of recent years have eroded the culture of family safety nets and lifetime employment. Issues of equity have taken on greater prominence since the 1997 financial crisis, yet income distribution has deteriorated and household poverty has increased (An and Choi 2003). In the knowledge- and information-based economy, the so-called digital divide will be an emerging phenomenon in Korea. If left unchecked, it will aggravate income inequality and lead to a bipolarization between the underprivileged and the mainstream of society.

1.4.2   Medium- and Long-term Economic Prospects

To assess the prospects of the Korean economy, an analysis of economic growth potential is undertaken in view of the above examination of the Korean economy's transition from success to post-crisis reforms. Economic growth potential depends on external and internal factors. Critical external variables for Korea include the future evolution of the global economy, and geopolitical developments surrounding the North Korea nuclear issue. The most critical internal variable is the implementation of flexible and adaptive economic policy in line with external and internal policy environments. In the medium term, the potential growth of the Korean economy will decline due to slower growth in labor and capital, declines in national savings and investment rates, continuing labor market rigidity, declining population growth, reduced work hours, an ageing population, and an inefficient education system. In addition, it will become increasingly difficult for Korea to attract foreign technology and develop new technologies. Korea is squeezed between China, which is quickly catching up in developing low-tech products, and advanced countries which Korea itself has difficulty catching up with. In order to improve productivity, an economy must expand R&D expenditure and social capability to develop and adopt new technologies. In this context, Korea's potential economic growth rate is estimated at 5 per cent over the 2004–08 period, and 4.9 per cent for the 2004–13 period (Bank of Korea 2003). However, its actual growth could be lower than its potential if the government fails to enact appropriate policy in areas of high-technology and knowledge-intensive industries, or fails to complete the post-crisis institutional and structural reforms.

1.5   CONCLUSION

As a way of assessing business opportunities, this chapter has reviewed Korean economic developments over the last four decades, and provided informed assessment of the medium- to long-term prospects for the economy. During the 1963–96 period, miraculous economic success was achieved against considerable odds. This remarkable economic development was attributable to a number of factors including skilled and abundant labor, high savings and investment rates, high social capability to adopt foreign technologies, conducive external environments, and appropriate economic strategy. However, Korea fell into a serious financial crisis in 1997 as a result of a number of causes, including accumulation of current account deficits, sustained currency overvaluation, a mismanaged, inefficient financial sector afflicted with moral hazard, excessive short-term and foreign-denominated debt, the concentration of economic power in structurally flawed chaebols, and the contagion effects of the crisis. In particular, state intervention, while working well until the late 1980s, lost its effectiveness and became the major underlying cause of the 1997 crisis. Since the crisis, Korea has undertaken comprehensive structural and institutional reforms in the financial, corporate, labor and public sectors, in addition to opening up to the global economy. The paradigm for national economic policy has decisively shifted from state intervention to the development of a market economy.

The economy experienced its most serious contraction of 6.7 per cent in 1998, yet began to recover from mid-1999, recording 5.8 per cent average annual growth over 1999–2005. The rapid recovery is attributable to: restored macroeconomic stability; export expansion; a broad, though incomplete, range of structural reforms; restoration of foreign confidence; and strong underlying fundamentals such as high saving rates, a well-educated workforce, and an advanced production infrastructure.

Turning to a future economic policy framework, this chapter has identified key emerging trends in Korea's policy environments: the intensification of globalization; the rise of China; demographic changes within Korea; declining savings and investment rates; rising foreign influence in the economy; and a growing digital divide. Under these circumstances, the crux of economic development exists in attracting mobile international resources by improving domestic infrastructure and institutions conducive to the growth of the private sector, including both domestic and foreign business, and by developing domestic technology through R&D and educational improvements. In support of this, Korea must embrace market principles, undertake comprehensive liberalization, and provide infrastructure to safeguard the private sector. Korea must also complete ongoing reforms while ensuring openness, transparency and accountability in government policies as well as in operations of the private sector, and adopt an appropriate human resource policy in line with demographic changes and with required science and technology developments.

NOTES

1. According to the Korea Antitrust Act, there were 43 chaebols comprising 672 industrial companies as of 1989 (Song 1994, p. 114).
2. This section draws mainly on Kwon (1998, 2003a).
3. This was manifest in a high debt–equity ratio of 519 per cent of the top 30 chaebols in 1997 (Joh 2001).

REFERENCES

Ahn, Choong-Yong (2001), 'Financial and corporate sector restructuring in South Korea: accomplishments and unfinished agenda', *Japanese Economic Review*, 52 (4), 452–70.

An, Chong-Bum and Kwang Choi (2003), 'Welfare policy in Korea: issues and strategy', in O. Yul Kwon, Sung-Hee Jwa and Kyung-Tae Lee (eds), *Korea's New Economic Strategy in the Globalization Era*, Cheltenham, UK and Northhampton, MA, USA: Edward Elgar Publishing, pp. 192–214.

Bank of Korea (2003), *Quarterly National Accounts*, Seoul: Bank of Korea.

Bank of Korea (2005), *Economic Statistics Yearbook 2005*, Seoul: Bank of Korea.

Bank of Korea (2007), 'Economic statistics system', http://ecos.bok.or.kr/EIndex_en.jsp.

Cho, Lee-Jay (1994), 'Culture, institutions, and economic development in East Asia', in Lee-Jay Cho and Yoon Hyung Kim (eds), *Korea's Political Economy*, San Francisco, CA: Westview Press, pp. 3–41.

Collins, S.M. (1994), 'Saving, investment, and external balance in south Korea', in Stephen Haggard, Richard N. Cooper, Susan Collins, Choongsoo Kim and Sung-Tae Ro (eds), *Macroeconomic Policy and Adjustment in Korea 1970-1990*, Cambridge, MA: Harvard Institute for International Development, pp. 231–59.

Department of Foreign Affairs and Trade (DFAT), Australia (1996), *The Korea Chaebol and the Implications of their Operations for Australian Interests*, Canberra: DFAT.

Joh, Sung Wook (2001), 'The Korean corporate sector: crisis and reform', in O.Y. Kwon and W. Shepherd (eds), *Korea's Economic Prospects: From Financial Crisis to Prosperity*, Cheltenham, UK and Northampton, MA, USA: Edward Elgar Publishing, pp. 116–32.

Jones, Leroy P. and Il SaKong (1982), *Government, Business and Entrepreneurship in Economic Development: The Korean Case*, Cambridge, MA: Harvard University Press.

Jung, Ku-Hyun (2002), 'The Korean model: can the old and new economies coexist?', *Joint US–Korea Academic Studies*, 12.

Kim, Linsu (1995), 'Absorptive capacity and industrial growth: a conceptual framework and Korea's experience', in Bon Ho Koo and Dwight H. Perkins (eds), *Social Capability and Long-Term Economic Growth*, New York: St Martin's Press, pp. 266–87.

Kim, Soogon and Joo-Ho Lee (1995), 'Labour–management relations and human resource development policy', in Dong-Se Cha and Kim Kwang Suk (eds), *Half Century of the Korean Economy* (in Korean), Seoul: Korea Development Institute, pp. 524–65.

Korea Herald (1997), 'South Korea has world's 8th longest workweek', 31 May.

Korea Labor Institute (2003), *2003 KLI Labor Statistics*, Seoul: Korea Labor Institute.

Korea Productivity Center (2004), http://www.kpc.or.kr.

Korea Times (2003), 'Korea outgrows economic development model', 26 October.

Korean National Statistical Office (KNS0) (2002), *Major Statistics of Korean Economy*, Seoul: KNSO.

Korean National Statistical Office (KNS0) (2005), *Korea Statistical Yearbook 2004*, Seoul: KNSO.

Korean National Statistical Office (KNS0) (2006), *Korea Statistical Yearbook 2005*, Seoul: KNSO.

Kuznets, P.W. (1994), *Korean Economic Development: An Interpretive Model*, Westport, CN: Praeger.

Kwack, Sung (1994), 'The rates of return on capital in the United States, Japan, and Korea, 1972–1990', in S.Y. Kwack (ed.), *The Korean Economy at a Crossroad*, Westport, CT: Praeger, pp. 57–71.

Kwon, O. Yul (1997), 'Korean economic developments and prospects', *Asian-Pacific Economic Literature*, 11 (2), 15–39.

Kwon, O. Yul (1998), 'The Korean financial crisis: diagnosis, remedies and prospects', *Journal of the Asia Pacific Economy*, 3 (3), 331–57.

Kwon, O. Yul (2003a), 'Korea's economic policy framework in the globalisation era', in O.Y. Kwon, S.H. Jwa and K.T. Lee (eds), *Korea's New Economic Strategy in the Globalisation Era*, Cheltenham, UK and Northampton, MA, USA: Edward Elgar Publishing, pp. 29–49.

Kwon, O. Yul (2003b), *Foreign Direct Investment in Korea: A Foreign Perspective*, Seoul: Korea Economic Research Institute.

Lee, Kwan-Chun (1995), '"Back to the basic!" New interpretation of Confucian values in Korea's economic growth', *Korea Observer*, 19 (2), 97–113.

Lee, Kyu Uck (1994), 'Ownership–management relations in Korean business', in Lee-Jay Cho and Yoon Hyung Kim (eds), *Korea's Political Economy: An Institutional Perspective*, San Francisco, CA: Westview Press, pp. 469–98.

Lee, Kyung-Tae, N.G. Choi and J.G. Kang (2003), 'Korea's foreign trade strategy in the new millennium', in O.Y. Kwon, S.H. Jwa and K.T. Lee (eds), *Korea's New Economic Strategy in the Globalisation Era*, Cheltenham, UK and Northampton, MA, USA: Edward Elgar Publishing, pp. 50–62.

Morishima, Michio (1982), *Why Has Japan 'Succeeded'? Western Technology and the Japanese Ethos*, Cambridge: Cambridge University Press.

Nam, Sang Woo and Jun-Il Kim (1995), 'Changes in macroeconomic policy and macroeconomies', in Dong-Se Cha and Kwang Suk Kim (eds), *Half Century of the Korean Economy* (in Korean), Seoul: Korea Development Institute, pp. 121–78.

Park, Sang-Seek (1995), 'Culture and development: the Korean experience', *Korea and World* Affairs, 19 (3), 510–21.

Pyo, Hak Kil (1996), 'The East Asian miracle or myth: a reconciliation between the conventional view and the contrarian proposition', *Republic of Korea Economic Bulletin*, 18 (3), 2–23.

SERI (2001), *Three Years after the IMF Bailout*, Seoul: Samsung Economic Research Institute.

Song, Byung-Nak (1994), *The Rise of the Korean Economy*, New York: Oxford University Press.

Stern, Joseph J., J.H Kim, D.H. Perkins and J.H. You (1995), *Industrialization and the State: The Korean Heavy and Chemical Industry Drive*, Cambridge, MA: Institute for International Development and Korea Development Institute.

2. An assessment of political risk of Korea: inter-Korea economic relations, politics and state–business relations

2.1 INTRODUCTION

Country risk is an important part of international business as it relates to the likelihood of changes in the business environment detrimental to the profitability of a business enterprise in a country. Three typical types of country risk include ownership, operational and transfer risk (Shenkar and Luo 2004, p. 184; Hodgetts and Luthans 2003, p. 288). Ownership risk refers in essence to expropriation or forced divestment of assets, and operational risk to any changes in government policies and procedures that directly constrain the management and performance of a firm. Transfer risk stems from government policies that limit the transfer of production factors such as capital and dividends from the country. As Hoti and McAleer (2004) argue, country risk has become increasingly important in practical international business, attested to by the existence of several commercial country risk rating agencies.[1]

In the empirical measurement of country risk, particularly by commercial agencies, a variety of variables have been employed as indicators (or dependent variables). Among them, debt default or debt rescheduling has been most often used (Hoti and McAleer 2004).[2] Causes (or independent variables) of country risk include political, economic and financial risk. Political risk, in turn, includes a range of variables such as political stability, democratic accountability, external conflicts, government–business relations, corruption and social stability (Hoti and McAleer 2004; Dichtl and Koglmayr 1986). Economic and financial risk refers to economic and financial mismanagement – such as high inflation, high budget and current account deficits, high foreign debt and unstable exchange rates. As the issues related to economic and financial risk will be dealt with in different chapters, this chapter will focus on political risk, and proceeds as follows.

In the following section, Korea's *sui generis* external conflict with North Korea will be addressed. An analysis of political and military conflicts between the two Koreas is beyond the scope of this book. Instead, this chapter examines inter-Korea economic relations, as they are highly indicative of political conflicts. That is, insofar as economic relations progress well between the two Koreas, political and military conflicts may not materialize between them. Section 2.3 examines recent developments in Korean politics as an indicator of political stability and democratic accountability. Section 2.4 examines government–business relations in Korea in the recent past. This will shed light on the likelihood of government and bureaucratic intervention in business operations. From a cursory review of the literature, no empirical study has been found on measurements of country or political risk of Korea alone in the public domain. Although indices for Korea's country risk are available from private commercial agencies, they are not available publicly nor used for this chapter. Thus, section 2.5 examines indices of Korea's country or political risk that are publicly available such as those from the OECD, the Belgian Export Credit Agency and the World Bank. Finally, section 2.6 includes a summary and conclusion.[3]

2.2 ECONOMIC RELATIONS BETWEEN NORTH AND SOUTH KOREA

A critical issue on the Korean peninsula is how to maintain peace and prosperity, which depends in turn on a host of geopolitical variables such as the six-party talks on nuclear non-proliferation, counterfeiting and the ensuing banking sanctions on the North. Although an analysis of these geopolitical variables is beyond the scope of this book, it can be argued that there is little likelihood of another war in the peninsula. South Korea and the US signed a Mutual Defense Treaty on 1 October 1953 with two specific purposes:

1. prevention of the renewal of communist aggression in South Korea; and
2. US assurances of South Korea's security by means of formal commitment (Koo and Han 1985, p. 9).

Since 1978, defense ministerial meetings have annually affirmed the US commitment to shield Korea under its 'nuclear umbrella' (*Korea Herald* 2006). This amounts to annual warnings to North Korea against possible military provocation. Under these circumstances, North Korea would not dare to challenge militarily the alliance between South Korea and the US. This chapter discusses inter-Korea economic relations, which have an important bearing on peace in the peninsula. Increasing inter-Korean economic interactions would provide a disincentive for North Korea to engage in political or military provocation for fear of damaging its crucial economic linkages with the South. This section focuses on trade, FDI and tourism between the two Koreas.

Inter-Korean economic relations commenced in 1988 and expanded throughout the 1990s predominantly at the initiative of South Korea. The 'Sunshine Policy' of the Kim Dae-jung administration from 1998 intensified the impetus for inter-Korean economic relations. The Sunshine Policy was predicated on the view that mutual economic interests could provide the basis for reconciliation between the two Koreas. The Roh Moo-hyun government from 2003 to date has continued with its own 'Peace and Prosperity Policy' toward North Korea which is in line with the Sunshine Policy.

From its inception in 1945, the North Korean economy has remained a conventional centrally planned economy with property rights residing primarily with the state, resources allocated by the planning mechanism, and prices, wages, trade, the budget and banking all under strict government control. From the beginning of the 1990s, the economy started to decline as other command economies in Europe collapsed, trade relations deteriorated and foreign aid from socialist countries reduced drastically. Over the nine-year period 1990–98, the North's economy contracted by an annual average of 3.7 per cent (Table 2.1).[4] North Korea experienced food shortages from the beginning of the 1990s; a situation caused by structural inadequacies and heightened by a series of natural disasters in the mid-1990s. North Korea experienced a serious famine over the 1995–98 period, in which starvation was estimated to have claimed between 1 million to 2.4 million lives (Noland et al. 2001).

Table 2.1 Economic growth of South and North Korea (1990–2004) (%)

	1990–98	1999	2000	2001	2002	2003	2004
N. Korea	−3.8/yr	6.2	1.3	3.7	1.2	1.8	2.2
S. Korea	+5.7/yr	10.7	8.5	3.8	7.0	3.1	4.6

Source: KIEP (2004).

As shown in Table 2.1, the North Korean economy has recorded positive growth rates annually, although minimal, since 1999. This growth is attributed to China's aid, and increased economic cooperation with South Korea. Despite its positive growth over 1999–2004, the North Korean economic size remains much smaller than that of South Korea. As shown in Table 2.2, the size of the North Korean economy, measured by GDP purchasing power parity (PPP) was estimated to be US$40 billion in 2006, compared to US$1180 billion for the South Korean economy. The South Korean economy is 29.5 times larger than the North Korean economy, while the population of South Korea is only twice as large as that of North Korea. Per capita GDP (PPP) was US$1800 in the North, while it was US$24 200 in the South.

Table 2.2 Comparison of economic size between South and North Korea

	South Korea (a)	North Korea (b)	a/b
Population (2005)	48.5 million	22.4 million	2.1
GDP (PPP) (2006)*	US$1.18 trillion	US$40 billion	29.5
GDP/capita (2006)*	US$24 200	US$1 800	13.4

Note: * 2006 estimates.

Source: CIA US (2007).

North Korea undertook an economic reform in 2002.[5] After bitterly experiencing a series of economic and social predicaments – such as shortages of household necessities, foreign capital and energy, lack of incentives for workers and enterprises, accumulating budgetary deficits, loss of confidence in the central planning system, growing deterioration of social and political order, and fading citizens' trust in the government, the North Korean regime could not help but introduce a market mechanism and open the economy in 2002, in a genuine attempt to revive its moribund economy. The reform measures include decentralization of the planned economy, price-setting in line with the market mechanism, the establishment of private markets, elimination of the rationing system, maintenance of purchasing power through wage rationalization based on merit, autonomous enterprise management based on profitability, and an open-door policy. Although Pyongyang has claimed that the reform seeks to take advantage of the market economy's efficiency while maintaining the principles of a planned economy, the reform is very significant because it is the first systemized measure to approve market functions, and it is a movement toward the co-existence of a planned and a free market economy.

North Korea will encounter serious difficulties in pursuing the reform such as high inflation, a widening gap between rich and poor, and dwindling socialistic collectivism. Nevertheless, it is inconceivable that the North Korean regime will reverse the economic system to the centrally planned system prior to 2002. The reform will work as a catalyst for further reforms. Over time, the private economy will grow more rapidly than the overall economy, and people's individualism will rise making it increasingly difficult for the regime to control the economy. Rather, it is highly likely that North Korea will carry on with further economic reforms.

Once an appropriate institutional environment is established, economic relations between the two Koreas will increase, taking advantage of their economic complementarities and cultural homogeneity. The two Koreas signed the 'Four-Point Agreement for Inter-Korean Economic Cooperation' in December 2000 that contains agreements related to investment protection, double taxation, commercial dispute settlement and clearing settlement (J.W. Lee 2004). The Roh administration in South Korea has been committed to implementing the Four-Point Agreement. In conjunction with its 2002 reform, and renewed international isolation after the October 2002 nuclear crisis, Pyongyang began to pursue inter-Korean economic cooperation with greater urgency (Ahn 2003; KIEP 2004, p. 230).

2.2.1 Inter-Korea Trade, FDI and Tourism

Inter-Korean trade expanded from US$18.7 million in 1989 to US$697 million in 2004 (Table 2.3), making South Korea the North's second-largest trading partner after China by 2002 (KIEP 2004, p. 199). Inter-Korean trade consists of two components: commercial and non-commercial trade (Table 2.4). South Korea's commercial exports to the North are comprised of textiles, electronic, agricultural and chemical products, while North Korea's exports to the South are predominantly made up of agricultural, forestry and fishing products, textiles, steel and mineral-based commodities. In 2004, approximately 50 per cent of commercial trade involved processing on commission, whereby South Korean firms supply obsolete, labor-intensive machinery and raw materials to the North for low-cost processing. Goods are then 'exported' back to the Republic of Korea (ROK) as finished products (Choe 2003; Oh 2003). The non-commercial trade component flows almost exclusively from South to North Korea.

Table 2.3 Inter-Korean trade volume (1999–2004) (unit: US$1 million)

Direction	1999	2000	2001	2002	2003	2004
South to North	211.8	272.8	226.8	370.2	435.0	439.0
North to South	121.6	152.4	176.2	271.6	289.3	258.0
Total	333.4	425.2	403.0	641.8	724.3	697.0

Sources: Bank of Korea (2005); KIEP (2004, p. 33).

Table 2.4 Inter-Korean trade by type (2002–04) (unit: US$1 million)

Type	2002	2003	2004
Commercial	354.6	419.5	347.8
Non-commercial	322.8	336.0	340.1
Total	677.4	755.5	687.9

Source: calculated from Ministry of Unification (MOU) (2005).

FDI, which flows exclusively from South to North Korea, has not expanded as quickly as inter-Korean trade. Until the 1998 Sunshine Policy, both governments maintained restrictions on direct investment in North Korea. As part of the Sunshine Policy, Seoul has removed many restrictions on inter-Korean FDI, and in 1999, Pyongyang granted Hyundai-Asan exclusive rights to develop the Mt Kumgang Tourism District for South Korean visitors (Lee and Yoon 2003). Beyond this, there was little development in FDI until 2000 when the 'Four-Point Agreement' on investment was signed. Since then, large-scale investment projects such as the Mt Kumgang Tourism District, Kaesong Industrial Complex, and the development of associated inter-Korean transport infrastructure have been established (Lee and Yoon 2003). North Korea has also recently implemented a number of general measures to encourage the growth of FDI.

The Kaesong Industrial Complex project is particularly important. The ultimate aim of the project is to construct an industrial park of 26.4 million square meters in Kaesong. The project has good prospects for success given the economic logic of combining low-wage North Korean labor with technology, management skill and marketing ability from South Korean companies. The Kaesong Industrial Complex has become a showcase of inter-Korean cooperation (J.W. Lee 2004). For South Korea, visible success is necessary as such success may lead to a dramatic expansion of North Korea's reforms and opening to the outside world. From Pyongyang's perspective, the failure of Kaesong would mean a disastrous loss of the last development option available through its promotion of Special Economic Zones (SEZs) (J.W. Lee 2004). By February 2005, 15 South Korean companies were operating at Kaesong, and 300 South Korean managers at the complex employed a total of 1800 North Korean workers. For the first time since the partition of the Korean peninsula, electricity supply was connected from the South to a number of firms operating at Kaesong on 16 March 2005.

Inter-Korean tourism is centered on the scenic Mt Kumgang in North Korea's southeast, which was opened to South Korean tourists as a showcase of the Sunshine Policy. Although operated by a private firm, the South

Korean government has partially subsidized the Mt Kumgang project. Originally, South Korean tourists visited through a sea route that ceased in 2004 after the east coast road to Mt Kumgang was opened from December 2002. As of June 2005, 1 million South Korean tourists had traveled to the site (Korea.net 2005).

2.2.2 Implications for Country Risk

Future developments of North Korea's 2002 economic reform and inter-Korea economic relations are mutually intertwined. The prospects for North Korean economic reform are constrained by the volatile international climate that surrounds Pyongyang. Until the nuclear issue is resolved, North Korea's economy may remain fragile and dysfunctional, and the chances of a successful transition to a market economy, as in the Chinese case, will be limited. However, Pyongyang has proven since 2002 that a gradual movement toward the co-existence of a planned and market economy has taken place. The assessment for inter-Korean economic relations is much more positive. The volumes of trade, FDI and tourist numbers have all been steadily increasing in recent years despite the nuclear crisis. Given the high political and economic stakes involved for both North and South Korea, it is likely that high levels of inter-Korean economic cooperation will be maintained. Increasing inter-Korean economic interactions will discourage the North from engaging in political or military provocation for fear of further damaging its economy. Given the low likelihood of another war on the Korean peninsula, chances of external conflicts involving South Korea are quite minimal.

2.3 RECENT DEVELOPMENTS IN KOREAN POLITICS

Political stability refers to the perception of the likelihood that the government in power will be destabilized or overthrown by some unconstitutional and/or violent means, whereby the continuity of policies and democratic accountability are adversely affected (Kaufmann et al. 2003). As mentioned earlier, political stability and democratic accountability are important variables for political risk for business (Hoti and McAleer 2004), which hinge, in turn, on the level of democratic development. This section examines political developments in Korea over the last 50 years and the structure of government prescribed by the latest Constitution. The salient characteristics underlying Korean politics will then be analyzed, providing important implications for Korea's political risk assessment.

2.3.1 Evolution of Korean Politics

Over its long history, Korea was governed by dynasties until the Japanese occupation in 1910. Japan governed Korea as a colony until the end of the Second World War in 1945. Thus, Korea did not have any experience of governing itself as a modern independent state until 1945. Upon liberation from Japanese colonial rule, external forces divided Korea into two. The former USSR occupied Korea north of the 38th parallel of latitude, while the US occupied Korea south of the 38th parallel. The original plan had been to withdraw all occupation forces from Korea as quickly as possible; however, Cold War tensions and rivalries prevented the formation of a unified Korea. The Soviets established a communist government in North Korea, resulting in the formation of the Democratic People's Republic of Korea in 1948, while in the same year the US established a capitalist democracy in South Korea with the formation of the Republic of Korea. The resulting differences in political and economic structures drove the two Koreas further apart, and efforts to reunify Korea broke down.

In June 1950, North Korea launched an unprovoked full-scale invasion of the South, triggering a three-year fratricidal war. The entire peninsula was devastated by the conflict. Many other countries became involved in the war including the USSR and China as allies of the North, and the US and others under the command of the UN to defend the South from North Korean 'aggression'. The war, which left almost 3 million Koreans dead and millions of others homeless and separated from their families, was ended in 1953 by an armistice agreement, establishing the DMZ between the two sides. However, the political realities of the Cold War caused the ceasefire line to harden into permanency, and it still divides Korea today.

Korea (the Republic of Korea) has a democratic form of government based on the separation of powers and a system of checks and balances. Sungman Rhee was elected as the first President of the Republic in 1948 and governed the country throughout the Korean War and ensuing difficult times until 1960 when he stepped down in response to strong opposition from students and citizens against his authoritarian and corrupt government. In the same year, the Chang Myon government was established under a parliamentary system, but was removed by a military *coup d'état* led by General Park Chung-hee in 1961. After running the country under a military junta for two years, General Park was elected as President and led the economic development of the so-called 'miracle of the Han River'. President Park carried on an authoritarian regime until he was assassinated in 1979, and Chun Doo-hwan was elected president in 1980 for a seven-year term after a short transition period under martial law. In the 1987 presidential election, Roh Tae Woo was elected for a five-year term. Both Chun and Roh were former generals and close associates of General Park.

The democratic advances made during the Roh administration set the stage for the election of Kim Young Sam in 1992, the first president in 32 years who had not served as a general in the army. Subsequently, Kim Dae-jung, the leader of Korea's first opposition party, was elected president in 1997 in the first-ever peaceful transfer of power from the ruling to an opposition party in Korean constitutional history. In December 2002, Roh Moo-hyun was elected unexpectedly from the same political party as Kim Dae-jung under the banner of political reform and, in particular, the elimination of ingrained political regionalism through more participatory politics.

Lacking a majority in the National Assembly, President Roh was initially unable to implement his political program. As his approval ratings plummeted, and amid accusations of corruption and unconstitutionalism, Roh's Millennium Development Party (MDP) split into factions. A new political party aligned with Roh, the Uri Party (UP), emerged from the turmoil. The remaining MDP members joined the conservative Grand National Party (GNP) in voting to impeach the President. After three months of political turmoil in 2004, the first ever effort to impeach a Korean president was rejected by the Constitutional Court (Fukuyama et al. 2005; Hahm and Kim 2005). Public disaffection with the impeachment proceedings was manifest in the results of the April 2004 parliamentary election (Park 2005, p. 86). Roh's centre-left Uri Party won a resounding victory over the GNP, gaining his party a parliamentary majority by winning 152 seats out of a total of 299.

2.3.2 Constitution and Government

The Constitution of the Republic of Korea was first adopted in 1948, and has been amended nine times over the last five decades. The first eight amendments were made largely for the political expediency of the then presidents. The ninth amendment was approved by referendum in 1987 through collaboration by the ruling and opposition parties. The constitutional amendment of 1987 provided for the direct election of the President for a single five-year term and for the institution of a system of local autonomy for the first time in 30 years. It also established a Constitutional Court to safeguard human rights. This Constitution endures to this day (March 2007), and has ensured the last three peaceful transfers of political power.

The Korean Constitution provides for a liberal democratic political order. It provides for the basic rights and freedoms of the people, the separation of powers, and the rule of law. It also assumes a free market economy by declaring that the state guarantees the right to property and other economic rights, such as the right – as well as the duty – to work, freedom of choice of occupation, and rights to association and collective bargaining. It also encourages the freedom and creative initiative of enterprises and individuals in economic affairs. Unique to Korea, one of the basic principles of the Constitution is the pursuit of a peaceful and democratic unification of South and North Korea.

In accordance with the extant Constitution, Korea has a presidential system of government based on the separation of powers and a system of checks and balances. The government consists of three branches: the legislative, judiciary and executive. The President stands at the apex of the executive branch, serving as the head of state and representing the state in foreign affairs. The President is elected by a nationwide, equal, direct and secret ballot, and is assisted by the Prime Minister and the State Council, both of which are appointed by the President. The President serves a single five-year term, with no additional terms being allowed. This single-term provision is a safeguard to prevent any individual from holding the reins of government power for a protracted period of time.

Legislative power is vested in the National Assembly, a unicameral legislature elected for four-year terms. Five-sixths of the National Assembly members are elected directly by popular vote from individual electoral districts, and the remaining seats are distributed proportionately among parties winning five seats or more in the direct election. In addition to its law-making function, the National Assembly has the right to inspect all aspects of state affairs on a regular basis as a check on presidential and executive power. The President cannot dissolve parliament, while the National Assembly has the powers to recommend the removal of the Prime Minister and the impeachment of the President, Prime Minister and other officials in cases of violations of the Constitution or other laws in execution of official duties.

The judiciary of Korea consists of three levels of courts: the Supreme Court, High (appellate) Court and District Court including the specialized Family Court and Administrative Court. The President with the consent of the National Assembly appoints the Chief Justice of the Supreme Court for a single six-year term. Other justices are appointed by the President on the recommendation of the Chief Justice. The Constitutional Court was established in 1988 as a specialized independent court. Issues touching on the Constitution itself, such as impeachment, the dissolution of a political party or the constitutionality of a law are referred to the Constitutional Court.

According to the Constitution, local governments deal with matters pertaining to the welfare of local residents within the limit of laws regarding local autonomy. A local government is required to have a council, but central law determines the organization and powers of the council. The chief executive and council members of a local government are elected by direct vote for four-year terms.

2.3.3 Salient Characteristics of Korean Politics

The contents of Korea's latest Constitution follow closely the norms in the most civilized countries, and the formal structure of government with a system of checks and balances between the three branches is little different from those of politically advanced Western models. However, factors unique to Korea such as its culture, economic development and external environment have shaped the development of politics in a unique way. Of these, Confucian values, such as an emphasis on personal relationships, hierarchical social structures and respect for authority, have retained their fundamental influence in Korean politics.[6] The Confucian influence on Korean political development can be traced back to the Yi Dynasty. For centuries, government officials were selected through a civil examination system focused on Confucian classics. Successful leaders have transmitted Confucian ideas to subsequent generations through education in an attempt to mould society in line with the Confucian doctrine. Through this process, Confucianism has remained influential in shaping contemporary political development in Korea, despite the imposition of Western democracy from 1948.

Confucianism has contributed to the development of a concentration of political power in Korea. Despite democratic elections and other democratic processes, much of the real power in Korea has been highly concentrated in an interconnected elite group comprised of big business, bureaucrats and politicians all bound together by regional affiliations and educational and friendship ties. This reflects the group society of Korea influenced by Confucianism (Helgesen 1998; K.O. Kim 1988).

As well as being hierarchical, Korea has also been a paternalistic society under the Confucian influence. In Korean politics, paternalistic leadership is highly emphasized and personality is often the decisive factor in selecting leaders. Political leaders are expected to be morally strong, benevolent and knowledgeable, humble-minded, compassionate and virtuous. Such an emphasis on leadership has rendered Korean politics largely personality-based, rather than institutionally based.[7] Nowhere is the importance of personality in Korean politics more obvious than in the political party system. The main political parties in Korea are largely recognized through their leaders. They do not represent the contesting ideologies or policy platforms characteristic of Western countries, nor do they represent different social classes.[8] In addition to being indistinguishable on policy, political parties in Korea are subordinate to their leaders, rather than acting as channels for political dialogue between society and political leaders (Helgesen 1998, p. 250).

The 'personality cult' approach in Korean politics has been reinforced by various political systems and culture. The party leader – not the local party members as in Western countries – nominates candidates for election to the National Assembly. Moreover, party leaders nominate the so-called 'nationwide candidates' of parties for one-sixth of the National Assembly members that are distributed proportionately among parties winning five seats or more in a direct election. Therefore, any party member who is interested in running for national office cannot dare to challenge their party leader. Also, people vote essentially for a person or the personal background of the leader, and legitimate considerations such as 'policies' and 'party' are secondary.

Another influential and visible characteristic of politics in Korea is regionalism. In Korea's family- and clan-oriented society, strong emphasis is placed on one's place of origin; a descendent of a particular place will always belong to that place despite being born in another. Regionalism can thus be seen as a natural outcome of the Korean collective mentality. In the post-war period, successive authoritarian regimes exacerbated the problem through utilizing regionalism as a means of maintaining state power. Dictatorships relied on trust and loyalty, values closely associated with regionalism. Furthermore, the unequal distribution of economic benefits of Korea's rapid economic development among regions further reinforced regionalism and its political influence. Accordingly, regionalism is embedded in Korean politics, and people often make important political decisions based on regional affiliations.

The most explicit example of regionalism is the practice of 'voting along regional lines', as demonstrated in the 1987, 1992 and 1997 presidential elections, and in the 2000 general election (Kwon 2000). If a presidential candidate comes from a particular provincial area, people from the region will support that candidate because he or she 'represents their interests'. Likewise, people vote for the candidates of 'their party' representing their regions in the National Assembly. Since its leader identifies a political party, and the region where the leader was born and raised identifies the leader, the region of a party is identified by the region of the party leader.

Another important feature unique to Korea in the development of democracy is the role of groups comprised of university students and other intellectuals. As a result of its emphasis on education, Confucianism expects intellectuals to understand social conscience and lead society. Thus, Korean society pays respect to university students and intellectuals as the group of 'social conscience' and expects them to stand against social injustices. In effect, over four decades university students together with university professors and other intellectuals stood up against the corruption of successive dictatorships under the banner of democracy, justice and unification of the nation. Eventually, in a watershed event for Korea in 1987, the military regimes gave in to the unremitting demonstrations of students and other intellectuals.

2.3.4 Korean Politics in Transition

Political reform has been the slogan of almost every Korean government over the last three decades. However, they have been consistently unsuccessful in reforming the culturally ingrained political system. Although two civilian presidents (Kim Young-Sam and Kim Dae-jung) did make remarkable contributions to democratization, they have failed to reform the Korean political landscape. Current President Roh Moo-hyun was also elected under the banner of political reform and it remains to be seen the extent to which he will be successful.

Political decision-making has often been ineffective in Korea because of opposition majorities in the National Assembly. Due to the 'personality cult' approach, and regionalism, Korea has developed a political culture of exclusionary politics and has failed to develop a politics of compromise and magnanimity. For instance, through a combination of personality, regionalism, and a culture of elitism, the so-called three Kims (Kim Dae-jung, Kim Young-Sam and Kim Jong-pil), who represented three different regions, wielded overwhelming political power over almost four decades until the dawn of the twenty-first century. Political regionalism has also been reinforced by the staffing policies of consecutive governments, which have appointed their own people in key government posts based on the distribution of election spoils among party loyalists. This type of staffing policy has reinforced regional fissures and regional political antagonism.

Korean politics has also been vulnerable to corruption because of the Confucian expectation that paternalistic leaders will look after their followers. Also, National Assembly members or prospective candidates have to support their party district chapter offices financially. Such requirements are extremely expensive. In this political environment, politicians have collected slush funds from businesses and corruption in Korean politics has been rampant over the last few decades. Two former presidents, Chun Doo-hwan and Roh Tae-woo, and the sons of Presidents Kim Young Sam and Kim Dae-jung have been jailed for corruption charges. At the end of 2003, a dozen National Assembly members were arrested on corruption charges.

After his narrow victory over Lee Hoi Chang of the conservative GNP in the December 2002 presidential election, the challenges and problems facing current President Roh Moo-hyun after taking office in February 2003 became increasingly apparent. In a number of ways, Roh represented a new generation of Korean political leaders. A self-made lawyer and dissident political activist from the 1980s, Roh came from a modest family background and was not part of the prevailing political establishment (Freedman 2005, p. 243). His electoral support base was comprised predominantly of a younger generation of voters who were impressed by Roh's personal reputation for integrity, and who were politically mobilized via new Internet communication techniques. High hopes were held that Roh's victory and participatory reform agenda would mark a break from the entrenched regionalism and corrupt money politics of the past (H.Y. Lee 2004, p. 130).

The Roh administration has been dedicated to a reform agenda emphasizing participatory democracy, substantive social justice measures, and a stronger assertion of Korean nationalism that has periodically caused tension in sensitive US–South Korea relations (Hahm and Kim 2005; H.Y. Lee 2004). It appears, however, that Roh has not been successful in reforming Korean politics. Roh's first year (2003) as president delivered little in the way of positive reforms due to the lack of a legislative majority in the National Assembly, a series of political misjudgments, frequent labor and political protests, and corruption scandals involving some of the President's closest advisors and associates (H.Y. Lee 2004). In his second year (2004), the whole country was engulfed in political turmoil through the impeachment of the President, although the Constitutional Court ultimately rejected the action.

During the Roh administration, political ideology has emerged as the main source of conflict in Korean society, with regionalism and paternalistic leadership eroding substantially (Kang 2005). These ideological conflicts are different from those in Western countries traditionally based on class-oriented or divergent views on the priority of economic values. The ideological characteristics of progressivism–conservatism in Korea are based on dual axes of the 'rejection vs acceptance of the anti-communist ideology' and 'liberalism vs authoritarianism' (Kang 2005). Korea's ideological schisms, fueled by generational differences, are so deep that public opinion is polarized into conservative and progressive positions. The public has tired of ideological issues, resulting in a low 11 per cent approval rating for Roh at the end of 2006 (*New York Times* 2006). In February 2007, 23 members of the Uri Party deserted it, and Roh also resigned from the Uri Party, rendering further political reform during this presidential term (2003–08) highly unlikely.

2.3.5 Implications for Political Risk in Korea

As can be seen from the above discussion, the political situation in Korea has undergone fundamental change over the past five decades. The impeachment crisis in 2004 helped Korean democracy advance and mature, demonstrating to the Korean people the value of viable democratic institutions (Fukuyama et al. 2005). Another optimistic aspect of Korean politics is that a younger political generation has emerged and is poised to lead Korean politics in the future, accelerating political reforms. Citizens enjoy freedom of expression and association, and participate freely in selecting their government. It is therefore highly unlikely that the government in power will be destabilized or overthrown by unconstitutional or violent means. Other facets of government operations have also made significant advances. Civil servants are selected through fierce competition and are respected by the public influenced by Confucian tradition. The quality of public services is highly regarded. As rules and regulations are established through proper democratic processes, the rule of law is reasonably maintained in the society. In sum, political risk in Korea, or the probability of disruption to foreign firms' operations from political forces, is not a cause for serious concern.

2.4 GOVERNMENT–BUSINESS RELATIONS

2.4.1 Evolution of the Government–Business Relationship

Beamish et al. (2000, p. 196) argue strongly that the prevalent type of political risk is government intervention in operations of foreign companies related to foreign ownership and control, financial flows, technical fees, local content and minimum export levels. They go on to argue that assessment of the probability of intervention is far more important than assessing broad political shocks or stability. In this regard, the government–business relationship in Korea is examined to provide an assessment of the political risk of government intervention into the activities of MNEs.

There is a general consensus that Korea maintained a state-led economy during the economic success period (1962–97). Since 1962, economic activities had been geared to the achievement of targets set by consecutive five-year economic plans. The economy had thus been tightly controlled and extensively intervened in by the central government.[9] Extensive state intervention, which occurred in every sector of the Korean economy, was implemented through indirect measures such as credit and foreign exchange allowances, interest rate policies and a plethora of regulations. It is generally regarded that state intervention worked well until the end of the 1980s because of a clear social consensus on policy goals, high organizational capabilities and a cooperative external environment.

Over the high-growth period of the state-led economy, Korea developed its unique style of government–business relations. The most powerful policy instrument for state intervention was the allocation of funds at preferential interest rates to particular industries or companies. The government nourished a limited number of chaebols in pursuit of its economic development strategy by providing a variety of incentives such as funds at preferential interest rates, protection from competition and institutionalized privileges. These privileges included cross-subsidiary loan guarantees, cross-subsidiary ownership, prevention of takeover of chaebols by means of hostile M&As by domestic and foreign firms, and a lopsided corporate governance system in favor of majority shareholders. Under these circumstances, the government–business relations were an unequal controller–follower partnership; the government set the policies, and businesses followed them.

The effectiveness of state intervention changed with environments and institutions. In the post-Cold War period from the beginning of the 1990s, Korea has no longer been treated in a preferential way by advanced Western countries. With the intensification of globalization and increasing economic integration and competition, protection of the Korean domestic market and industries by the state would have become increasingly difficult. In conjunction with political democratization in the late 1980s, the government has also lost its strong policy direction sanctioned by the whole society. Over the extended high-growth period, the relative size and importance of the business sector have been enlarged over time, so that the balance in the government–business relationship has swung remarkably toward business. These changes in government–business relations have rendered government control over the private sector less effective.

Over time, not only did state intervention lose its efficacy, but it also sowed the seeds of the 1997 financial crisis in Korea. The causes of the crisis, which have been extensively investigated in the literature (Cha 2001; Jwa and Yi 2001; Kwon 1998; J.W. Lee 2004), include among others:

1. excessive expansion and diversification of chaebols by debt capital;
2. an inefficient financial sector afflicted by moral hazard;
3. lack of transparency in business operation;
4. low productivity and loss of international competitiveness; and
5. rigid labor market practices.

Each of these causes of the crisis was directly related to state intervention, or in other words, the fundamental factor underpinning all these causes was state intervention.[10]

State intervention rendered the private sector vulnerable to financial crisis. Government control and protection allowed chaebols to become lacking in transparency and accountability, and to expand and diversify excessively with debt capital. State intervention in financial markets led financial institutions to be inefficient, undercapitalized and heavily reliant on short-term foreign borrowings. Government protection of domestic industries from international competition by means of restrictions on imports, incoming FDI and M&As resulted in the loss of efficiency and competitiveness of domestic industries. Government repression and intervention resulted in inefficiency in labor management and the lack of labor-market flexibility. Finally, the government failed to introduce appropriate measures in time to rectify the dysfunction of state intervention and to stem the final crisis in the presence of emerging symptoms and evidence. This signified a demise of the old paradigm of economic policy by means of extensive state intervention.

After a painful realization of the limitation of the old policy paradigm through the financial crisis, the policy paradigm has shifted from state intervention toward a market economy. In particular, Korea has undertaken comprehensive structural and institutional reforms in the financial, corporate, labor and public sectors, in addition to opening its economy internationally. The government liberalized the capital market so as to open the securities market to foreign investors; eliminated restrictions on inward FDI, thereby opening a number of business sectors (including the financial sector) to FDI; and allowed M&As. All this has led domestic businesses to be exposed to international competition. The financial sector has been restructured to increase the banking sector's independence, to consolidate and strengthen the supervision of financial institutions, eliminate insolvent institutions and recapitalize viable ones. International standards for auditing and disclosure have been adopted to improve transparency and accountability.

Drastic reforms have been undertaken for chaebols and the labor market. They include enhancement of management transparency, the abolition of cross-debt guarantees among subsidiaries, financial structure improvements, core business specialization, improved corporate governance, prevention of chaebol domination of the non-bank financial sector, prohibition of cross-ownership and illegal internal trading, and prevention of abnormal wealth inheritance. The labor market has been reformed, whereby retrenchment of workers has been permitted for the first time in Korean history. This reform is expected to improve labor market flexibility and labor-management relations.

2.4.2 Implications for Political Intervention in Korea

As a result of the structural reforms of the economy together with capital market liberalization, foreign capital has substantially penetrated the Korean business sector. Foreign investors will expect management transparency, improved corporate governance and management efficiency, and they are in turn expected to weaken the potential for state intervention and collusion in government–business relations. Also, the crisis and ensuing reforms have removed the perception that chaebols are 'too big to fail'. In addition, foreign investors in Korean financial institutions will strengthen their intervention in, and monitoring of debtor companies. Those lacking in transparency and accountability, or with low profitability and high debt–equity ratios, will have difficulty in raising bank credit. This will force chaebols to concentrate on core competencies and divest themselves of marginal interests.

Although economic reforms have by no means been completed, Korea has made great strides in economic restructuring and opening the economy globally. In terms of formal rules and regulations, it may be argued that Korea's government–business relations have improved on par with other OECD countries. Korea is one of the most liberal of the East Asian countries for FDI (Bishop 2003). Prudential supervision and regulations on the banking sector are consistent with international standards (Nicolas 2006). Foreign banks and securities firms are allowed to establish subsidiaries without any restrictions and to own 100 per cent of Korean financial institutions, and foreign nationals are allowed to become directors of Korean banks.[11] The chaebols' transparency, accountability and corporate governance have also improved to global standards.

Because of cultural inertia, however, the actual practices in government–business relations, and the behavior and attitudes of the people involved, have retarded full advancement to the level of advanced Western countries. There remains a subtle perception of government supremacy in government–business relations, and the superior position of bureaucrats relative to businesspeople. The personal relationship still plays an important role in business as well as government–business relations (Kwon 2006). It should be noted, however, that culture-related practices of business or government–business relations are not as salient to foreign companies, as Koreans usually treat foreign businesses at arm's length – quite different from their treatment of domestic counterparts. Therefore, it is unlikely that political intervention in the operations of foreign MNEs would be a serious concern in Korea.

2.5 MEASUREMENTS OF COUNTRY AND POLITICAL RISK OF KOREA

2.5.1 OECD Country Risk Classification

Only a few empirical measurements of country and/or political risk are available in the public domain, although quite a few estimates are available from commercial agencies. The first is the OECD Country Risk Classification, which is a composite index based on a quantitative assessment of credit risk and a qualitative assessment of political risk. The specific determinants of the OECD's Country Risk Classification Method (CRAM) 'are confidential and not published' (OECD 2007a). Table 2.5 shows that the advanced Western OECD countries such as Australia, Canada, France, Germany, the UK and the US consistently scored the lowest risk rating of 0 for the period (1999–2006) under consideration. Out of the East Asian economies over the same period, Singapore and Japan were consistently lowest-risk countries with a 0 rating, while China, Taiwan and Hong Kong achieved consistent ratings of 2, 1 and 2 respectively. Korea maintained the lowest-risk 0 rating in 1999–2000, and from 2003 to 2006. In 2001–02, Korea declined to a risk rating of 2.

The lower risk rating for Korea over 2001–02 appears to be attributable to a series of global and domestic events. After the dot.com bubble burst and the terror attack on the US in 2001, the global economy slowed down. In the aftermath of the dot.com burst, Korean stock prices on the technology-related KOSDAQ fell sharply and the economic growth rate declined to 3.8 per cent in 2001, compared to 8.5 per cent in 2000. As a way of recovering the economic setback caused by the 1997 financial crisis, the Korean government encouraged credit expansion by providing tax breaks for consumers for payments by credit cards. This expanded the number of credit cards issued and raised consumer debt, leading to a liquidity crunch for the credit card industry or to a 'credit card crisis' in 2002. In addition, the presidential election in 2002 amid huge political scandals raised concerns of political stability. As these global and domestic issues have settled down, Korea's risk rating by the OECD has improved to the level of advanced countries (Table 2.5). The OECD country risk classification is broadly consistent with the qualitative assessment of Korea's country risk in this chapter.

2.5.2 Country Risk by the Belgian Export Credit Agency

Another country risk index is provided by the Belgian Export Credit Agency, an autonomous public authority of the Belgian government. It rates countries on four indices related to export transactions, and three indices related to direct investments, focusing on payment defaults and losses of assets by war, expropriation and intervention. Table 2.6 shows seven categories of country risking ratings. The short-term 'political risk' and 'special transaction' risk indices reflect foreign payment defaults of short-term credit arising from foreign currency shortages, wars, revolutions, natural disasters and government actions. The 'long-term political risk' and 'transfer risk' indices measure the probability of defaults of medium- and long-term credit. The 'commercial risk' index reflects the risk of foreign payment default based on microeconomic and macroeconomic determinants. The 'war risk' index encompasses both the risk of external war and the risk of internal political violence. The 'expropriation risk' indices cover the risks of expropriation and breach of contract by the government, in addition to risks related to the legal system (ONDD 2007a).

Table 2.5 Selected OECD country risk classifications (1999–2006)* (scale: 0–7; 0 lowest risk, 7 highest risk)

Country	1999	2000	2001	2002	2003	2004	2005	2006
Argentina	5	6	6	7	7	7	7	7
Australia	0	0	0	0	0	0	0	0
Brazil	6	6	6	6	6	6	5	4
Canada	0	0	0	0	0	0	0	0
Chile	2	2	2	2	2	2	2	2
China	2	2	2	2	2	2	2	2
Egypt	4	4	4	4	4	4	4	4
France	0	0	0	0	0	0	0	0
Germany	0	0	0	0	0	0	0	0
Hong Kong	2	2	2	2	2	2	2	2
India	3	3	3	3	3	3	3	3
Indonesia	6	6	6	6	6	6	5	5
Japan	0	0	0	0	0	0	0	0
Korea	0	0	2	2	0	0	0	0
Malaysia	3	2	2	2	2	2	2	2
Mexico	4	3	3	3	3	3	2	2
Philippines	3	3	4	4	5	5	5	5
Russia	7	7	6	5	4	4	4	4
Singapore	0	0	0	0	0	0	0	0
Taiwan	1	1	1	1	1	1	1	1
Thailand	4	3	3	3	3	3	3	3
Turkey	5	5	6	6	6	5	5	5
UK	0	0	0	0	0	0	0	0
US	0	0	0	0	0	0	0	0
Vietnam	6	6	6	5	5	5	5	5

Note: * as at 31 December of each year.

Source: OECD (2007b).

*Table 2.6 ONDD risk ratings (January 2007) (scale 1–7, 1 lowest risk,
7 highest; and A–C, A lowest risk, 7 highest risk)*

Country	Export transactions				Direct investments		
	Political risk: short term	Political risk: long term	Political risk: special trans	Comm. risk	War risk	Expro-priation and inter-vention risk	Transfer risk
Argentina	3	7	4	C	2	3	6
Australia	1	1	1	B	1	1	1
Brazil	2	4	3	B	1	2	4
Canada	1	1	1	A	1	1	1
Chile	1	2	1	A	1	1	2
China	1	2	1	C	3	4	2
Egypt	2	4	2	C	3	4	3
France	1	1	1	A	1	1	1
Germany	1	1	1	A	1	1	1
Hong Kong	1	2	1	A	2	1	2
India	1	3	2	B	2	3	3
Indonesia	2	5	3	C	2	4	4
Japan	1	1	1	A	2	1	1
Korea	1	1	1	A	3	1	1
Malaysia	1	2	1	B	1	2	2
Mexico	1	2	1	B	2	1	2
Philippines	2	5	3	B	3	4	4
Russia	2	4	2	C	3	4	3
Singapore	1	1	1	A	1	1	1
Taiwan	1	1	1	B	2	1	1
Thailand	1	3	1	A	3	3	2
Turkey	3	5	3	C	2	2	4
UK	1	1	1	A	1	1	1
US	1	1	1	A	1	1	1
Vietnam	2	5	3	C	4	6	5

Source: ONDD (2007b).

Table 2.6 also shows that Korea's four types of political risk related to export transaction are all rated at the lowest end of the scale and comparable with the advanced OECD countries and Singapore. In particular, the larger developing and transition countries all have a heightened long-term political risk assessment, as do the countries of developing Southeast Asia. For country risk indices related to FDI such as expropriation and intervention risk and transfer risk, Korea again ranks among the advanced OECD countries – Chile, Hong Kong, Mexico, Singapore and Taiwan – with the lowest-risk ranking of 1. For war risk, Korea is given a relatively high ranking of 3, equal to China, Egypt, the Philippines, Russia and Thailand, and only exceeded by Vietnam on 4, although it was argued earlier that the likelihood of another war in the Korean peninsula is quite slim.

2.5.3 World Bank Worldwide Governance Indicators

Another quantitative estimate of country risk is the World Bank governance indicators available from 1996 across countries (World Bank 2007). The World Bank's assessment of countries' quality of governance is measured across six indicators that are directly and indirectly related to country and/or political risk from business perspectives. The first is 'voice and accountability', which refers to the extent to which a country's citizens are able to participate in selecting their government, as well as freedom of expression and association. The second is 'political stability and absence of violence', which measures the likelihood that the government will be destabilized or overthrown by unconstitutional or violent means, including domestic violence and terrorism. The third is 'government effectiveness', which measures the quality of public services, the degree of its independence from political pressures, the quality of policy formulation and implementation. The fourth indicator relates to 'regulatory quality', and measures the ability of the government to formulate and implement sound policies and regulations that permit and promote private sector development. The fifth is 'rule of law', which measures the extent to which agents abide by the rules of society, the quality of contract enforcement, the police and the courts, as well as the likelihood of crime and violence. The sixth indicator is 'control of corruption', which measures the extent to which public power is exercised for private gain (World Bank 2007). Corruption may be related to political risk in the sense that resistance to corruption may foster the probability of disruption to MNEs' operations.

Table 2.7 shows the World Bank's governance indicators for Korea in selected years between 1996 and 2005. It appears that, except for political stability, the World Bank governance indicators remained at more or less stable levels in Korea. Voice and accountability remained within a narrow range from 66.2 to 70 with an average level of 67.8 over the period, indicating a significant advancement of democracy and political freedom, as examined in section 2.3. Political stability has shown a significant

56   *The international business environment in Korea*

improvement in Korea between 1996 and 2005, with the indicator increasing from 40.6 in 1996 to 60.8 in 2005. It is interesting to note that the indicator increased significantly in 2004 over 2003, and this may reflect the enhanced perception of political stability after the impeachment resolution. Government effectiveness remained at a high and stable level, ranging from 70.8 to 81.3. This may reflect the high quality of public servants and their services as mentioned earlier. Regulatory quality, which may reflect government–business relations, remained at around 70, although it fluctuated somewhat. Rule of law declined from 78 in 1996 to 67.8 in 2003, improving to 72.5 by 2005. A dip in the indicator in 2003 may reflect the high incidence of political scandals during the presidential election at the end of 2002. Control of corruption had a high score of 76.6 in 1996, while it remained stable at around 65, indicating that corruption control is not effective in Korea.

Table 2.7   World Bank worldwide governance indicators, Korea (1996–2005) (percentile rank 0–100)

Indicator	1996	1998	2000	2002	2003	2004	2005
Voice and accountability	67.3	66.7	67.6	68.6	66.2	70.0	68.1
Political stability	40.6	43.4	51.9	54.7	51.9	61.8	60.8
Govt. effectiveness	77.6	70.8	76.1	81.3	79.9	78.5	78.9
Regulatory quality	72.1	53.7	67.5	74.9	70.9	73.4	71.8
Rule of law	78.0	71.6	67.8	75.0	67.8	69.2	72.5
Control of corruption	76.6	64.2	67.2	67.2	64.2	59.3	69.0

Source: World Bank (2007).

Table 2.8 presents a comparison of the seven-year averages (1996, 1998 and 2000–05) of the World Bank governance indicators across a selection of states including leading OECD countries, large developing countries, and countries of the East Asian region including Korea's most important trading and investment partners. For all those six indicators, Korea is well behind leading OECD countries such as Australia, Canada, France, Germany, the UK and the US over the seven-year period. Korea is also substantially behind Japan, and is broadly comparable with Taiwan and Malaysia, and in general ahead of the rest of the countries included in Table 2.8. In terms of voice and accountability, Korea is well behind leading OECD countries. It ranks some distance behind Chile and Japan, while it is far ahead of a number of developing countries or those with similar economic development levels to Korea. In terms of political stability, there is a clear upward trend, although the seven-year average is 52.2. Again, Korea is far behind the politically advanced countries, while it is far ahead of a number of comparable countries. It is interesting to note that political stability indicators declined significantly during the period for Australia, France, Germany, the UK and the US. In effect, the indicators for France, the UK and the US in 2005 are substantially lower than that for Korea (World Bank 2007). The low values for these advanced countries may indicate the increased possibility of terrorism in the recent past.

Korea's government effectiveness is a long way behind the leading OECD states and Singapore, marginally behind Japan, Taiwan and Chile, and better than the rest of the countries compared. With respect to both regulatory quality and the rule of law, Korea's ranking is similar for the previous three indicators; it is substantially behind advanced Western OECD countries and Singapore, significantly behind Japan and Taiwan, and ahead of the rest of the countries. In the final World Bank index, control of corruption, Korea is broadly comparable with Malaysia, while ranking well behind the leading OECD countries and Chile, Japan, Hong Kong and Singapore, and slightly behind Taiwan. Yet Korea ranked substantially higher than the developing and transition countries.[12] In sum, it appears that the World Bank governance indicators support the qualitative assessment of Korea's political risk, as presented above. Although Korea's political risk, including political intervention, would be higher than those in advanced OECD countries and Singapore, it is comparable to a number of middle-income countries and better than developing and transitional economies.

2.6   CONCLUSION

Country risk has become increasingly important for international business. Although there is no consensus in the literature on the concept and empirical measurements of country risk, it includes external conflicts, political stability, government intervention in business operations and social stability. For political and military conflicts between the two Koreas, this chapter has examined inter-Korea economic relations, as they are indicative of political conflicts. To assess political stability, this chapter has examined recent developments of Korean politics. For political intervention, government–business relations in Korea have been analyzed, and social stability was not addressed in this chapter as it is not a serious business issue in Korea. Then, publicly available empirical measurements of country risk – including those from the OECD, the Belgian Export Credit Agency and the World Bank – were examined to support or reject the qualitative assessments of Korea's country or political risk.

Table 2.8 World Bank worldwide governance indicators: seven-year averages (1996, 1998 and 2000–05) (percentile rank 0–100)

Country	Voice and accountability average (1996–2005)	Political stability average (1996–05)	Government effectiveness average (1996–05)	Regulatory quality average (1996–05)	Rule of law average (1996–05)	Control of corruption average (1996–05)
Argentina	58.2	41.2	56.6	44.8	42.8	42.8
Australia	96.5	81.5	94.2	94.2	95.6	94.4
Brazil	58.2	39.6	54.9	57.7	46.8	56.2
Canada	91.9	83.0	96.1	91.0	94.5	95.7
Chile	76.1	70.1	87.6	91.0	86.3	89.1
China	7.7	40.7	60.2	41.4	42.6	43.9
Egypt	21.3	27.6	50.6	39.6	55.6	50.0
France	87.9	67.2	91.0	81.9	90.0	90.3
Germany	92.8	78.5	92.5	90.7	93.9	93.5
Hong Kong	50.0	77.2	90.0	97.5	89.9	91.3
India	55.5	19.3	52.5	38.6	55.6	46.4
Indonesia	28.7	9.0	39.5	36.3	21.4	15.8
Japan	77.7	83.3	85.6	78.1	90.2	85.9
Korea	67.8	52.2	77.6	69.2	71.7	66.8
Malaysia	40.1	57.3	78.6	68.2	67.4	68.7
Mexico	50.1	36.1	60.7	67.0	43.4	45.5
Philippine	52.3	24.4	58.1	56.8	40.2	39.0
Russia	32.6	21.2	33.9	32.9	20.6	21.9
Singapore	47.5	87.5	99.4	99.4	96.7	98.8
Taiwan	70.5	67.9	86.4	82.2	78.1	75.5
Thailand	51.7	43.3	65.6	62.8	59.1	47.8
Turkey	35.9	18.7	56.6	61.4	55.0	52.8
UK	92.2	69.2	96.3	97.0	94.7	95.4
US	90.1	63.3	93.0	92.7	92.5	92.5
Vietnam	7.9	55.1	46.0	26.1	33.1	27.3

Source: The seven-year averages were calculated from the yearly indicators from World Bank (2007).

North Korea undertook a drastic economic reform in 2002. Although the prospects for the North Korean economic reform are constrained by a host of geopolitical variables, it is inconceivable that the North Korean regime will reverse its economic system to the centrally planned system. The assessment of inter-Korean economic relations is much more positive. The volumes of trade, FDI and tourist numbers have all been steadily increasing in recent years despite the nuclear crisis. Given the high political and economic stakes involved for both North and South Korea, it is likely that high levels of inter-Korean economic cooperation will be maintained. Increasing inter-Korean economic interactions will discourage the North from engaging in political or military provocation for fear of further damaging its economy. Given the low likelihood of another war on the Korean peninsula, chances of external conflicts involving South Korea are quite minimal.

The political situation in Korea has undergone fundamental changes over the past five decades. In 1993, a civilian president first came to power after three decades of military dictatorship. This was followed by a peaceful transfer of power from the ruling to an opposition party in 1998, and Roh Moo-hyun, a candidate from the centre-left party, was elected in 2002 in Korea's inherently conservative political culture. The impeachment crisis in 2004 for the first time in Korean history helped its democracy advance and mature. Citizens enjoy freedom of expression and association, and participate freely in selecting their government. It is highly unlikely that the government in power will be destabilized or overthrown by unconstitutional or violent means. The quality of public services is regarded highly, and the rule of law is reasonably upheld, as rules and regulations are established through proper democratic processes. Therefore, political risk in Korea, or the probability of disruption to foreign firms' operations from political forces, is not a cause for serious concern.

There is a general consensus that the Korean economy was a state-led one and government intervention in business operations was extensive until 1997. Korea has made great strides in restructuring the financial, business and labor sectors, as well as opening its economy globally in the wake of the 1997 crisis. In terms of formal rules and regulations, Korea's government–business relations in the areas of trade, FDI, and regulations of banks and businesses have improved on a par with other OECD countries. As a result of the reforms, foreign capital has substantially penetrated the Korean business sector. Foreign investors are expected to enhance management transparency further, improve corporate governance and management efficiency, and weaken the potential for state intervention and collusion in government–business relations. Therefore, it is unlikely that political intervention in the operations of foreign MNEs would be a serious concern in Korea.

To support the qualitative examination of Korea's country or political risk, publicly available empirical measurements of country risk were examined. The OECD country risk assessment consistently rates Korea's country risk at the lowest rate, equivalent to the advanced OECD countries, except for two years (2001–02) probably due to the global and domestic economic setbacks during the period. The OECD country risk ratings supports the argument from the qualitative assessment that Korea's country risk, including external conflict as well as political stability, is not a cause for serious concern. The measurement of country risk by the Belgian Export Credit Agency further supports the qualitative assessment of Korea's country risk, except for the possibility of external conflicts.

The World Bank governance indicators are comprehensive empirical measurements of political risks, covering the extent of democratic development, political stability, government effectiveness, regulatory quality, the rule of law and corruption. The indicators support the marked improvement in Korea's political stability. Overall, the World Bank indicators also support the qualitative assessment of Korea's political risk made in this chapter. Although Korea's political risk, including political intervention, would be higher than that of advanced OECD countries, it is comparable to a number of middle-income countries and better than developing and transitional economies.

In conclusion, it has been argued that Korea is a reasonably safe country in which to do business. Serious military conflicts between the two Koreas are highly unlikely. Political risk and intervention in business operations are not causes for serious concern under Korea's fully fledged democracy and its well advanced government–business relations. These arguments are supported by empirical measurements of country or political risk by reliable global organizations such as the OECD and the World Bank.

NOTES

1. The major commercial country risk rating agencies include: the Economic Intelligence Unit, Euromoney, Institutional Investor, International Country Risk Guide, Moody's, Political Risk Services, and Standard and Poor's (Hoti and McAleer 2004).
2. Beamish et al. (2000, p. 201) argue that government intervention with the operations of MNEs – such as forced joint ventures, unilateral contract renegotiations, requirements to increase local value-added, and local ownership restriction – are the most prevalent form of political risk. No empirical study has been found, from a cursory review of the literature, which employs the number of government interventions as the dependent variable.
3. Koreans have a homogeneous ethnic background with no ethnic conflicts. Although there are a few religions established in Korea such as Christianity, Buddhism and Confucianism, Koreans are quite tolerant toward religious differences. There are subtle social stratifications by the level of education and gender, and bipolarization by the level of income and wealth has emerged as a social issue in the recent past. However, none of these have become a serious social issue or concern with regard to economic and business activities. Hence, social stability is not a notable concern for political risk in Korea.
4. It is important to note that economic data on North Korea is extremely limited and prone to error, and should generally be considered as 'indicative' rather than 'authoritative'.
5. For further analysis of the 2002 economic reform of North Korea, see Kwon (2007).
6. For Korean culture and Confucianism, see Chapter 3.
7. This was supported by surveys conducted by Helgesen in 1990 and 1995 that found that good morals and humanistic attitudes are almost unanimously accepted as the most important qualities in politics (Helgesen 1998, p. 251).

8. This belief is supported by a national survey conducted in 1996 by the Institute of Social Sciences, Seoul National University, which found that 72 per cent of respondents reported that the political parties did not differ from one another (Shin 1995, pp. 31 and 37). Kwon (2000) also observed this at the April 2000 election of the National Assembly members.

9. For a further detailed examination of state intervention in the Korean economy, see Chapter 1.

10. For further discussion of Korea's state intervention as the underlying cause of its financial crisis, see Kwon (2003).

11. A number of advanced countries, including Canada, do not allow foreign nationals to be directors of domestic commercial banks.

12. Transparency International compiles the Corruption Perceptions Index. This index is based on data generated from 12 surveys by nine institutions: the World Bank, Economist Intelligence Unit, Freedom House, IMD, Merchant International Group, Political and Economic Risk Consultancy Hong Kong, United Nations Economic Commission for Africa, WEF, and the World Markets Research Centre (TI 2006). Korea's comparative performance on the Corruption Perceptions Index mirrors to a large extent the trends of the Control of Corruption Indicators by the World Bank. For recent changes of the Corruption Perceptions Index for Korea, see Chapter 7.

REFERENCES

Ahn, Yinhay (2003), 'North Korea in 2002: a survival game', *Asian Survey*, 43 (1), 49–63.

Bank of Korea (2005), 'Gross domestic product of North Korea in 2004', http://www.bok.or.kr/contents_admin/info_admin/eng/home/press/pressre/info/NK GDP20042.doc.

Beamish, P.W., A.J. Morrison, P.M. Rosenzweig and A.C. Inkpen (2000), *International Management: text and cases*, 4th edn, Boston, MA: Irwin McGraw-Hill.

Bishop, Bernie (2003), 'Will East Asia follow Korea's lead in liberalizing foreign direct investment policy?' in O.Y. Kwon and W. Shepherd (eds), *Korea's Economic Prospects: From Financial Crisis to Prosperity*, Cheltenham, UK and Northampton, MA: Edward Elgar Publishing, pp. 98–112.

Cha, Dong-Se (2001), 'The Korean economy into the new millennium: reform and revival', in O.Y. Kwon and W. Shepherd (eds), *Korea's Economic Prospects: From Financial Crisis to Prosperity*, Cheltenham, UK and Northampton, MA: Edward Elgar Publishing, pp. 39–59.

Choe, Sang T. (2003), 'North Korea moving from isolation to an open market economy: is it time to invest or to continue observing', *Competitiveness Review*, 13 (2), 60–69.

CIA US (2007), *The World Factbook*, www.cia.gov/cia/publications/factbook.

Dichtl, E. and H.G. Koglmayr (1986) 'Country risk ratings', *Management International Review*, 26 (4), 4–11.

Freedman, Amy L. (2005), 'Economic crises and political change: Indonesia, South Korea, and Malaysia', *Asian Affairs*, 31 (4), 232–49.

Fukuyama, Francis, Bjorn Dressel and Boo-Seung Chang (2005), 'Facing the perils of presidentialism', *Journal of Democracy*, 16 (2), 102–16.

Hahm, Chaihark and Sung Ho Kim (2005), 'Constitutionalism on trial in South Korea', *Journal of Democracy*, 16 (2), 28–42.

Helgesen, Geir (1998), *Democracy and Authority in Korea: The Cultural Dimension in Korean Politics*, Great Britain: Curzon.

Hodgetts, Richard M. and F. Luthans (2003), *International Management*, 5th edn, Boston, MA: McGraw-Hill Irwin.

Hoti, Suhejla and Michael McAleer (2004), 'An empirical assessment of country risk ratings and associated models', *Journal of Economic Surveys*, 18 (4), 539–88.

Jwa, Sung Hee and Insill Yi (2001), 'Korean financial crisis: evaluation and lessons', in O.Y. Kwon and W. Shepherd (eds), *Korea's Economic Prospects: From Financial Crisis to Prosperity*, Cheltenham, UK and Northampton, MA: Edward Elgar Publishing, pp. 73–98.

Kang, Won Tack (2005), 'Ideological clash of progressives and conservatives in Korea', *Korea Focus*, 13 (5), 63–80.

Kaufmann, D., A. Kraary and M. Mastruzzi (2003), 'Governance matters III: governance indicators for 1996–2002', World Bank Research Working Paper 3106, World Bank, http://www.worldbank.org/wbi/governance/pubs/govmatters 2001.htm.

Kim, Kwang-ok (1988), 'A study on the political manipulation of elite culture: Confucian culture in local-level politics', *Korea Journal*, 28 (11), 4–16.

Koo, Y.N. and S.J. Han (1985), 'Historical legacy', in Y.N. Koo and S.J. Han (eds), *The Foreign Policy of the Republic of Korea*, New York: Columbia University, pp. 3–13.

Korea Herald (2006), 20 October.

Korea Institute for International Economic Policy (KIEP) (2004), *North Korea Development Report 2003/04*, Seoul: KIEP.

Korea.net (2005), 'Mt Geumgang tourists exceed 1 million', 16 June, http://www.korea.net/News/News/NewsView.asp?serial_no=20050616020, accessed 23 June 2005.

Kwon, O.Y. (1998), 'The Korean financial crisis: diagnosis, remedies and prospects', *Journal of the Asia Pacific Economy*, 3 (3), 331–57.

Kwon, O.Y. (2000), 'Weaknesses of Korean politics and their remedies' (in Korean), *Korea Economic Daily*, 24 April.

Kwon, O.Y. (2003), 'Korea's economic policy framework in the globalisation era', in O.Y. Kwon, S.H. Jwa and K.T. Lee (eds), *Korea's New Economic Strategy in the Globalization Era*, Cheltenham, UK and Northampton, MA: Edward Elgar Publishing, pp. 29–49.

Kwon, O.Y. (2006), 'Recent changes in Korea's business environment: views of foreign business people in Korea', *Asia Pacific Business Review*, 12 (1), 77–94.

Kwon, O.Y. (2007), 'The North Korean economy and inter-Korea economic relations', mimeograph.

Lee, Hong Yung (2004), 'South Korea in 2003: a question of leadership?' *Asian Survey*, 44 (1), 130–38.

Lee, Jong-Wha (2004), 'Lessons from the Korean financial crisis', in C. Harvie, H.H. Lee and J.G. Oh (eds), *The Korean Economy: Post-Crisis Policies, Issues and Prospects*, Cheltenham, UK and Northampton, MA: Edward Elgar Publishing, pp. 11–24.

Lee, Young-Sun and D.R. Yoon (2003), 'Inter-Korea economic relations: past, present and future', in O.Y. Kwon, S.H. Jwa and K.T. Lee (eds), *Korea's New Economic Strategy in the Globalization Era*, Cheltenham, UK and Northampton, MA, USA: Edward Elgar Publishing, pp. 13–26.

Ministry of Unification (MOU) (2005), monthly 'Overview of intra-Korean exchanges' and cooperation', January 2002–December 2004, http://www.uni korea.go.kr/en/presspublic/presspublic.php?page_code=ue0304&ucd=eng0202.

New York Times (2006), 'South Korea's president sags in opinion polls', *New York Times*, 27 November.

Nicolas, Francoise (2006), 'Post-crisis economic reform in Korea: unfinished business', paper presented at the Conference on *Political Change in Korea since the 97 Asian Financial Crisis: Strategies, Trend and Perspectives*, Seoul, June.

OECD (2007a) 'Country risk classification', http://www.oecd.org/documentprint/ 0,2744,en_2649_34171_1901105_1_1_1_37467,00.html, accessed 7 February 2007.

OECD (2007b), 'Country risk classification', http://www.oecd.org/ech/xcred/, accessed 7 February 2007.

Oh, Seung-yul (2003), 'Hands across the DMZ', *Invest Korea Journal*, September–October, http://www.ikjournal.com.

ONDD (2007a), 'Country risks explanation', http://www.ondd.be/webondd/Website. nsf/fcb407daa2d2c578c 125677f002ccd69/00d08a1833de6495c125676e002bbbaa?OpenDocument&Highli ght=0,explanation, accessed 7 February 2007.

ONDD (2007b), 'Country risks summary table', http://www.ondd.be/webondd/ Website.nsf/AllWeb/Rapport+Annuel/$File/CHART.pdf, accessed 7 February 2007.

Park, Myung-lim (2005), 'Korea's constitutional democracy and President Roh's impeachment case', *Korea Focus*, 13 (4), 82–113.

Shenkar, Oded and Yadong Luo (2004), *International Business*, Hoboken, NJ: John Wiley and Sons, Inc.

Shin, Doh Chull (1995), 'Political parties and democratisation in South Korea: the mass public and the democratic consolidation of political parties', *Democratization*, 2 (2), 20–55.

Transparency International (TI) (2006), 'Corruption perceptions index' (CPI), various years, http://www.transparency.org.

World Bank (2007), 'WGI: worldwide governance indicators country snapshot', http://info.worldbank.org/ governance/kkz2005/mc_table.asp, accessed 7 February 2007.

3. Korean society and culture in transition

3.1 INTRODUCTION

The success or failure in conducting business with people from other cultures depends on how effectively one can use one's skills with them. That ability depends in turn on both job-related expertise and sensitivity and responsiveness to different cultures. Thus, cultural sensitivity and responsiveness are vital to success in international business and can be improved by learning more about the nature of culture and how it affects business practices. In the case of overseas assignments the failure rate – the rate at which the assigned employees return before the assignment period is over – is quite high, ranging from 40 per cent to 70 per cent, largely resulting from an inability to understand and adapt to foreign cultures rather than from technical or professional incompetence (Hill 2005, p. 624; Ferraro 1994, p. 7).

The term 'culture' has been defined in a variety of ways by a large number of scholars in the areas of anthropology and management.[1] Culture is in essence referred to as the learned behavioral pattern shared by the people in a country or a community. In this anthropological sense, culture includes attitudes, behavior, values, norms and beliefs shared by the people (Ferraro 1994, p. 17). It should be noted that the culture of a society is a gross generalization about what most of the people do and think most of the time. Although cultural norms exert a strong influence on behavior, they are hardly iron-clad propositions that can be used to predict with precision how people will respond in any given situation. In other words, some individuals could behave differently from their cultural norms, although most do not. Culture is transmitted from generation to generation through the process of learning and interacting with one's environment rather than through a genetic process.

Culture develops as a way of meeting fundamental universal human needs that must be satisfied (Ferraro 1994, p. 24). These include the basic physiological requirements, reproduction, education, social control and supernatural belief. Thus, the culture of a country is molded by its prevailing religion, geographic surroundings, predominant political and economic systems and language. Therefore, cultures are different across countries, as these determinants differ, and cultures cannot be compared and judged to be right or better. Over its long history as an isolated country within its unique geographic surroundings with its own religions and language, Korea has developed its own unique culture.

Culture is not stagnant; rather it flexes and bends itself to provide optimum responses to changes in the determinant factors of cultures. For instance, growing up in a materially abundant and physically secure environment is more likely to engender a materialistic value system than in an environment fraught with danger and the most basic concerns of survival. Research shows, however, that although culture changes, it does so at a glacial pace over time (Ferraro 1994, p. 18). It follows that Korean culture will change as key determining factors change over time.

Society and culture exist in a symbiotic relationship. Neither would exist without the other, and an understanding of both is necessary in understanding the behavior of individuals within any particular social group. A society can be defined as a group of people in a country or region that share a common culture. In this definition, society is synonymous with the concept of culture. However, society is more than culture in that society can also be defined as the entire set of social arrangements in which humans participate (Waters and Crook 1993, p. 76). Thus, society has its own structure and dynamics such as social class stratification and mobility between social classes. There is no strict one-to-one correspondence between a society and a nation-state. The latter is a political creation. A nation can thus have multiple cultures or societies, such as the French Canadian society and Anglo Canadian society within Canada. On the other hand, a society can transcend national boundaries, such as with Islamic societies. Korean society refers to the people in Korea bound together by a common culture and its own structural organization and dynamics. Korean society is a homogeneous society in the sense that Koreans have a common ethnic background as well as sharing a common, single culture. This chapter delineates salient characteristics of Korean culture and analyses why such singularities in culture have developed. Then, the chapter examines cultural transformations in Korea and assesses the prospects of Korean culture and society.

3.2 WHAT IS KOREAN CULTURE?

Identifying a national culture is not only interesting in itself but is also critically important in doing business with foreign countries. It should be noted that as the idea of a national culture is predicated on the existence of a nation-state with clear boundaries, the diversity, conflicts and changes within nation-states are largely ignored in pursuing the identification of a national culture. Within the realm of international business, national culture is defined as the dominant culture within the political boundaries of a nation-state (Cullen 2002, p. 48). Two models in the literature are widely used to identify and measure national cultures. One is the general anthropological approach introduced by Kluckhohn and Strodtbeck (1961), and the other was introduced by Hofstede (1980). The first stresses variations in value orientations, while the latter emphasizes the effectiveness of, and differences between cross-cultural organizations. Korean culture will be analyzed first using the Kluckhohn and Strodtbeck model, and then the Hofstede model.

The value orientations model by Kluckhohn and Strodtbeck (1961) is based on five fundamental questions that identify key elements in the development of cultural values. They are: What is basic human nature? How do people relate to nature? What is the sense of time? How do people conduct activities? What are the relationships of people to one another?

First, innate human nature drives development of cultural values relating to how people deal with others, particularly with subordinates. If innate human nature is assumed to be bad, for instance, a coercive authoritarian leadership will develop. If, however, human nature is regarded as good, a collaborative leadership will develop. With regard to human relationship to nature, cultures develop values about whether nature dominates people or people dominate nature. In this case, possible cultural values include mastery over nature, harmony with nature and subjugation to nature. With regard to a sense of time, cultures can develop past, present and future orientations. Depending on the primary mode of activity, cultures can range from 'being' to 'doing' in their approaches to activities. Within a 'being' culture, people react spontaneously and emotionally to their immediate situations and ascribe the result of their activities to their status. Within a 'doing' culture, people emphasize action and hard work. Finally, with regard to human relationships with other people, cultures develop values regarding how people should interact with each other. Under these circumstances, possible cultural values range from collectivism to individualism.[2]

Although comparison of cultures in accordance with each of the above five questions posed by Kluckhohn and Strodtbeck (1961) has been widely explored in the literature, it is difficult to find studies of specific features of Korean culture that deal directly with these questions. However, there are numerous discourses on Korean culture based on value orientations (Kweon 2003; Han 2003; Yi 2003; Hahm 2003). The salient traits of Korean culture commonly underlying these studies in terms of value orientations include: hierarchical collectivism, patriarchal familism, authoritarianism, status consciousness, secularism and strong nationalism (Yi 2003; Han 2003; Kweon 2003).

Another model used to analyze national cultures is Hofstede's well-known model of national culture. Hofstede's (1980) model is based on four cultural dimensions: power distance, uncertainty avoidance, individualism and masculinity. Later, Hofstede (1991) added the additional dimension of long-term orientation. Power distance concerns the extent to which inequality is seen as an irreducible fact of life. Uncertainty avoidance relates to the extent of tolerance of ambiguity. Individualism–collectivism focuses on the relationship between the individuals and the group. Masculinity–feminism concerns the extent of support for the traditional masculine orientation. Finally, long-term orientation concerns the degree of long-term orientation in a country's culture.

Hofstede (1980, 1991) provides specific indexes for these five cultural dimensions for a number of countries, facilitating comparisons on the basis of these cultural values. For Korea, Hofstede's measurements of the cultural values for power distance, uncertainty avoidance, individualism, masculinity and long-term orientation are: 60, 85, 18, 39 and 75 respectively (Hofstede 1991). According to Hofstede's research, Koreans score moderately high in accepting inequality and a hierarchical society as a way of life, and strongly avoid uncertainty or risk. Also, Koreans are firm believers in collectivism, and have a low proclivity for masculinity. Finally, Koreans have high long-term orientation, particularly when compared to Western countries. Hofstede's analysis of Korean culture is largely consistent with the cultural characteristics identified by Korean scholars, as stated above, although their focus differs. A question then arises as to why Korean culture has developed those characteristics. This question will be investigated through main cultural determinants. By doing so, the salient characteristics of Korean culture will be further explored.

3.3 HISTORICAL INFLUENCES ON KOREAN CULTURE

As reviewed in Chapter 2, Korea has a long history spanning more than 4000 years, punctuated by tragedies, struggles, triumphs and successes. These historic developments have been instrumental in shaping the Korean culture and society of today. Koreans are descendants of a single ethnic group, and after countless rises and falls of tribal communities, three highly centralized ancient kingdoms, Koguryo, Baekje and Shilla, emerged around 57 BC and flourished on the peninsula. Then in AD 668 the Three-Kingdom Era ended, and the peninsula was unified as an independent country under the Kingdom of Shilla.[3]

After continuous struggles with its northern neighbor, China, the Kingdom of Shilla collapsed and was taken over by the Koryo Kingdom. The Koryo era (935–1392) was also marked by periodic external wars with China, the Mongols and Japan. The Koryo Dynasty was replaced by the Chosun (Yi)

Dynasty in 1392, which introduced one of the world's longest continuously ruling royal families, lasting more than 500 years. During the latter few centuries of the Yi Dynasty, Korea was engaged in more or less continuous conflicts with its neighbors, Japan and China.

During the late nineteenth century, European empires reached East Asia. By this time China and Japan had begun opening up to foreign countries. However, Korea maintained its rigorous isolation policy until it was forced to open to foreigners in 1876, earning its nickname of 'the Hermit Kingdom'. Until the beginning of the twentieth century, Korea's three neighboring countries, China, Japan and Russia, jostled with each other to obtain control over the Korean peninsula. Japan defeated China in 1895 and the Russians in 1905 in separate wars, leaving Korea completely under Japan's control. Korea was subsequently occupied by Japan in 1910, and remained a Japanese colony for 35 years until 1945. Although Koreans continuously struggled to liberate their country from Japan, they never succeeded and remained under harsh and relentless colonial suppression. During this period, Japan attempted to destroy Korean culture completely by outlawing the Korean language and even Korean family names. Assimilation efforts ended only with the defeat of Japan in the Second World War in 1945.

Upon liberation from Japanese colonial rule, Korea was divided into two by external forces. The former USSR occupied Korea north of the 38th parallel of latitude, while the US occupied Korea south of the 38th parallel. Cold War tensions and rivalries between the USSR and the US then prevented the fulfillment of the original agreement of withdrawing all occupation forces from Korea and rebuilding an independent and unified country. The Soviets established a communist government in North Korea in 1948, the Democratic People's Republic of Korea, while in the same year the US established a capitalist democracy in South Korea, the Republic of Korea.

In June 1950, North Korea launched an unprovoked full-scale invasion of the South, triggering a three-year fratricidal war. The entire peninsula was devastated by the conflict. Many other countries became involved in the war, including the USSR and China as allies of the North, and 16 countries, including the US, under the command of UN forces, to defend the South from North Korean 'aggression'. The war, which left almost 3 million Koreans dead and millions more homeless and separated from their families, ended in 1953 by an armistice agreement, establishing a Demilitarized Zone (DMZ) between the two sides. However, the political realities of the Cold War caused the ceasefire line of the Korean War to harden into the permanent DMZ which still divides Korea today.

Over this long and tumultuous history, Korea developed strong nationalism. Although surrounded by powerful neighboring countries, Koreans proudly claim a 5000-year independent history as a homogeneous race. Unremitting foreign invasions, incursions and influences over its long history have strengthened Korean nationalism. In particular, at the end of the nineteenth century when Korea became the focus of contention between three powerful nations (China, Japan and Russia) seeking to establish geopolitical 'spheres of influence' in the peninsula, grass-roots nationalist movements emerged as the citizens realized the danger to the nation's independence. During the Japanese colonial period (1910–45), the Japanese tried to eradicate the Korean national spirit and identity. Ironically, Korean nationalism was strengthened by the common bond against the oppression of the Japanese colonial master. Korea's unique culture and society has developed under such strongly prevailing nationalism.

Even though Korea is surrounded by hostile powers and has developed a strong sense of nationalism, Koreans have resisted engaging in military actions to protect their country. Throughout their long history, Koreans have realized that China is too powerful to challenge, and have resigned themselves to living under the umbrella of Chinese protection. It was widely considered that China would not allow Korea to build up military power. Consequently, militarism never gained popularity or social respect. Additionally, military personnel were regarded as being below scholars or civil servants in social stratification during the Yi Dynasty. There has also been no need to develop military protection and logistics for the merchant class, as merchants belonged to the lowest class in Korea during the Chosun Dynasty, and China was the only country with which Korea had extensive trade relations. Thus a number of anthropologists in Korea argue that a prominent trait of Korean culture is contrasted with that of Japanese culture, in that the former is a 'literary culture', while the latter is a 'warrior culture' (for example, Kweon 2003, p. 41).

3.4 RELIGIOUS INFLUENCES ON KOREAN CULTURE

Religion is closely intertwined with culture. Religion has its own beliefs, values and norms that prescribe moral principles for everyday actions. Thus, religious influences are among the strongest shapers of culture, as attested to by the world's ethical systems being based on religions such as Christianity and Islam. This holds true in Korea, where a variety of religions have greatly shaped moral principles, and continue to do so even today.

Unlike some cultures in which a single religion is dominant, Korean society includes a wide variety of religious elements.[4] From the early stages of history until the beginning of the twentieth century, frequent disruptions in Koreans' peace of mind by foreign incursions led them to pursue solace in religious activities. As a result, the population of religious believers expanded rapidly. The rulers of consecutive kingdoms and dynasties employed religious doctrines as legitimization and expedient instruments of their governance. Hence, religious and political functions were combined, whereby religious influences have remained strong throughout Korea's long history.

Historically, Koreans have embraced Shamanism, Buddhism and Confucianism, and in modern times, particularly after the Korean War, Christianity has made strong inroads into the country. Shamanism is a folk religion that has no systematic structure but permeates the daily lives of people through folklore and customs. Korean Shamanism, which existed before the introduction of Buddhism and Confucianism, includes the worship of spirits that are believed to dwell in every object in the natural world, including rocks, trees, mountains and streams as well as celestial bodies. Shamanism gradually gave way to Buddhism and Confucianism, both of which have more sophisticated religious structures. However, Buddhism and Confucianism did not result in the abandonment of Shamanistic beliefs and practices; they assimilated elements of Shamanistic faith and coexisted peacefully. Shamanism has remained an underlying religion of the Korean people and is a vital aspect of their culture (Yi 2003).

Buddhism is a highly disciplined, philosophical religion that emphasizes personal salvation through rebirth in an endless cycle of reincarnation. Buddhism was introduced to the Korean peninsula during the Three-Kingdom Era in the fourth century, and flourished quickly under royal patronage. Not only did Buddhism satisfy the religious needs of individuals, but it was also a convenient ethical standard and an expedient tool for governance. According to Buddhism, to be born as an aristocrat was a reward for merit in a previous life. Moreover, Buddha, as the single object of worship, neatly paralleled the King as the single object of authority. Shilla, which unified the peninsula, regarded faith in Buddhism as a guarantee of the safety of the nation, and its rulers embraced Buddhism as the state religion. The rulers of the succeeding Koryo Dynasty were even more enthusiastic in their support of Buddhism and maintained it as the national religion. Personal and state devotion to Buddhism led to a privileged status for Buddhist monks, who received grants of land and were granted clerical ranks. Thus, Buddhism influenced the government and people's attitudes, behavior, values and mores. However, the state cult of Buddhism began to deteriorate as some of the monks indulged in luxurious lifestyles and intervened in the operation of government.

The founder of the Yi Dynasty tried to remove all influences of Buddhism from the government and adopted Confucianism as the guiding principles of state management and its code of ethics. Confucianism entered Korea around the same time as Buddhism, during the Three-Kingdom Era, and had already influenced Korean society substantially before the Yi Dynasty. Confucianism remained the official ideology for more than 500 years throughout the Yi Dynasty, and made the most significant and everlasting impact on Korean society.

It is debatable whether Confucianism is a religion or not. Religion may be defined as a system of beliefs and rituals through which one is taught a moral system (Hopfe 1987, p. 2). Typically, religions have five elements: the unseen world of spirits, gods, demons; rituals designed for communing with the spirits; the sacred scriptures or gospels; doctrines of an afterlife; and large followings (Hopfe 1987, p. 3). Not many religions in the world meet all these elements. It is contended that the teachings of Confucius were never intended to be a religion and that Confucius was probably an atheist who considered prayers to gods as worthless, while his main concern was the nature of human society. Confucianism does not have sacred writings nor a doctrine of an afterlife. It does not have specific gods, although it refers to 'heaven' as a vague supernatural spirit. However, Confucianism has a set of principles based on Confucius's teachings, certain rituals, and a large number of followers. As mentioned above, religions have their own moral principles which prescribe and proscribe beliefs, values and norms of daily life. In this sense, Confucianism can be considered a religion of some type.

Under a strong Confucian influence over several centuries, Korea developed hierarchical collectivism as a major cultural trait. Confucianism is the ethics prescribed by a natural person, Confucius (AD 551–479) and his pupils. Basically it is a system of ethical principles designed to inspire and preserve the good management of family and a harmonious society. This is the basis of collectivism. Confucianism attempts to achieve these goals primarily by assigning each member of a family and society a particular function. These family and social roles and responsibilities are epitomized by the Five Relationships and the ethical guidelines that govern these relationships. The first relationship is between a ruler and his subject, with the ruler enjoined to treat his subject benevolently and the subject enjoined to be loyal to his ruler. The next is between a father and a son, with the father enjoined to be firm and affectionate in raising his son, and the son enjoined to be obedient and filial toward his father. The relationship between an elder brother and a younger brother is similar, with the elder brother given the responsibility of helping his younger brother and the younger brother given the obligation of respecting his older brother. The next is the relationship between husband and wife, with the husband guiding the wife and the wife being subservient to the husband. The last of the five relationships is between friends. The relationship between friends must be based on trust. These relationships are all hierarchical in nature, except the relationship of friends.

Yet even among friends there exists a subtle hierarchical relationship anchored in various bases such as age, intelligence, wealth, and so on.

The continual inculcation of these relationships as the state code of ethics developed a strong and perhaps a unique kind of group society in Korea, which is vertically structured and hierarchical in nature. Relative social rankings are determined by various factors such as family backgrounds, age, gender, education level and occupation. Under this hierarchical society, loyalty, filial piety, obedience and trust are the primary codes of conduct. At the same time, Confucian ethical principles emphasize the concept of reciprocity. Individuals, regardless of their social ranks, have a duty to reciprocate virtuous and pious deeds of others. These codes of conduct emphasize the consideration of others and de-emphasize the value of individual thought, opinions and ideas that are subjugated to those of the group and society. Under these ethical principles, Koreans developed a strong collectivism under which individuals were constantly reminded that their identity came more from the group they belonged to and the status they held in those groups than from their own individuality.

If groups of people are to survive they must develop established ways of preserving social order. In other words, to survive as a society every society must have a social control system of coercing people to obey the social rules, regardless of its methods (Ferraro 1994, p. 25). Korea developed authoritarianism as its social control system. Throughout Korea's dynastic history, a king stood at the helm of the state. He was the highest authority in the realm and governed the country as an absolute ruler. During the Yi Dynasty, however, the King was constantly surrounded by a court of powerful aristocrats who effectively curtailed his authority. According to the Confucian concept of rulership, the King was supposed to be wise and just, and rule through morality and benevolence rather than through force. The King was constantly reminded of these high ideals of Confucian kingship by his teachers and advisors, who were all Confucian scholars or aristocrats. Only someone of aristocratic status was admitted to the civil service examinations, thereby having a chance to become a government official. Under such a governance system, with a king at the helm surrounded by powerful aristocrats, Korea did not develop feudalism, but instead developed a strong authoritarianism as an important cultural facet.

Confucianism in Korea promoted social stratification, placing aristocrats and scholars at the top, followed by farmers, merchants and artisans, and household servants, in that order. In a vertically structured society with strong authoritarianism, Koreans became keenly conscious of their status within the society, and expected to be treated accordingly by others, thereby developing a cultural trait of status consciousness or face-saving consciousness.

Another salient trait of Korean culture is a strong familism. The aristocracy that dominated Korean public life was a relatively thin, top layer of society, consisting of a few hundred powerful family descent groups. During the Yi Dynasty the descent of an aristocratic group was patrilineal in the sense that the group was traced over generations through male links. Descendants focused on an ancestor who usually had been a high official and identified himself with a surname and an ancestral seat at a particular place. Hence, a prominent place in society could only be achieved through maintaining the family lineage through male heirs. As a result, traditional Korean society placed the utmost importance on family, kinship and filial piety, thereby developing a strong familism as an important trait of Korean culture.[5] Under such culture of strong familism, recording lineage genealogy was critically important for the aristocratic or upper classes of the Chosun Dynasty.

In Korea's traditional society under the strong influence of Confucianism, social status was the major factor in determining one's prospects in life, and the social status was in turn determined largely by family backgrounds. Thus, the family unit took a critically important place for human interrelations in the whole society. Apart from aristocratic family groups, there were two other lower classes: commoners (farmers, merchants and artisans) and household servants due to their lineage. These lower classes had no chance of moving up to the aristocratic level.

Korea developed patriarchal familism and collectivism with regard to women's identity centered on their roles as wife and mother. Women were rarely added to the family genealogical records, and if this honor was bestowed upon them, entry would only be under their husband's name. The main role of a woman in a family was to bear a male heir for the continuation of the lineage and to provide domestic services for her family. Women only had power and status within the domestic arena, and were expected to act at all times with virtue, propriety and decorum.

Education can also be regarded as a determinant of culture. Rather than expecting each new child to rediscover for himself or herself the way of life in society, the society provides an organized way of passing on its cultural heritage from one generation to another (Ferraro 1994, p. 25). In this way countries develop different cultures depending on their education systems. Confucianism stresses education highly. However, the main content of education under Confucianism is not to learn systematic knowledge but to learn Confucian moral principles, disdaining other fields of knowledge (Ahn 1999, p. 281). Over more than 500 years, to become a government official in the Yi Dynasty one had to pass the civil service examination, a test of knowledge of Confucian ethics and literature. This governance system placed a high value on education, and the education system reinforced Confucianism.

Korean language also played an important role in molding and maintaining Korean culture. The language of a country has important bearings on its culture, as it is a means of transmitting and learning culture. Language also reinforces the prevailing culture because it develops in line with the culture. Korean cultural features are well reflected in the Korean language, with expressions differing depending on social status or relational hierarchy. Daily usage of this relational language reinforces the prevailing cultural relations among Koreans. In the same vein, it can be seen that high- and low-context languages are developed by culture at the same time as reinforcing the culture (Ferraro 1994, pp. 41–62).

Although the popularity and direct influence of Confucianism declined during the latter part of the Yi Dynasty, it was revitalized under Japanese colonization, and again after the Second World War. It was used to legitimize the authoritarian rule of the Japanese colonial government and the following military regimes that governed Korea between the early 1960s and the late 1980s. Thus, Confucian cultural features that have been embedded in Koreans' minds over centuries still remain strong today.

Another religion that has influenced the Korean people is Christianity. Although Christianity arrived in Korea in the seventeenth century, it was technically against the law to practice it and there was sporadic Christian persecution until the end of the nineteenth century (Korea Information Service 2000, p. 165). As recently as half a century ago, an allegiance to Christianity was held by only slightly more than one out of every 50 Koreans (Howard 1996, p. 131). According to a 1995 social statistics survey, 50.7 per cent of Koreans followed a specific religious faith, and Christians (both Protestants and Catholics) accounted for 52 per cent of them – or 26 per cent of the total Korean population (Korea Information Service 2000, p. 156). These large numbers are particularly surprising considering the influence of Korea's neighboring countries. In China and Japan, which are both influenced by Buddhism and Confucianism, Christians make up less than 1 per cent of the population.

There are a number of reasons for the rapid increase in Korean Christians. When Protestant missionaries arrived in Korea at the end of the nineteenth century, they presented themselves more as modernizers than as missionaries, establishing modern medical facilities and schools. At that time, the Korean government was facing unprecedented threats to its sovereignty from both China and Japan, and was beginning to realize that it needed Western technology. The King and his officials turned a blind eye to the proselytizing activities of missionaries in order to access knowledge of the outside world and its modern technology. After the Korean War,

Christian churches were some of the most effective organizations in helping Korean War refugees with food, clothing and housing. In gratitude, many Koreans began to consider Christianity more highly. Christianity was increasingly considered by Koreans as part and parcel of the modern world; thus the more education Koreans received, the more likely they were to be Christians. Christianity has now joined Buddhism and Confucianism as an important and permanent religious influence in Korea and is an integral part of modern Korean culture and society. Just as it is impossible to imagine traditional Korean culture without Buddhism and Confucianism, it is also impossible to picture contemporary Korea without Christianity. The three religious traditions, each in their own way, address the religious needs of Koreans, and are likely to continue to coexist and shape Korean culture and society into the foreseeable future.

Christianity has greatly influenced Korean traditional culture and helped Koreans learn about Western culture. Christian missionaries introduced a modern education system, with educational content different from Confucianism. Upon their arrival in Korea, Christian missionaries observed social anomalies such as rigid social stratifications, the subservient social status of women, the slackened moral standards of the society, and the self-indulgent lives of the ruling and upper class of society. Christian missionaries contributed to rectifying these anomalies and forwarding the modernization of Korean society. Christianity has also imbued Koreans with a Protestant work ethic and frugality, which Max Weber has referred to.

3.5 KOREAN INDUSTRIALIZATION AND CULTURE: TRANSFORMATION TO A MODERN SOCIETY

One of the most obvious and immediate needs of a society is to meet the basic physiological requirements of its people. Since no society in the world has unlimited resources with which to produce enough goods and services to meet its people's requirements fully, each society must develop systematic ways of producing, distributing and consuming goods and services. These economic systems have an important bearing on the culture of a country.

Although Korean society had been abating its traditional characteristics after the Second World War, the traditional Korean culture remained more or less unchanged until the 1960s when the economy started to take off. Until the end of the Second World War, the majority of the population were farmers. The majority of farmers were tenants working the fields of landowners who were decedents of aristocrats or collaborators to the Japanese colonial ruler. Over half of the tenants owned no land whatsoever (Howard 1996, p. 102). This kind of industrial structure reinforced the rigidly hierarchical society under traditional culture. The Land Reform Act, passed in 1949 and put into operation in 1950, redistributed the land to tenant families. This land reform abated the social class or status divisions to a considerable extent. Yet agriculture was not mechanized and was run on a family basis, with the roles of men and women clearly defined. Men undertook the major 'outside' field work, while women took on minor 'inside' work such as tending the vegetable garden, raising silkworms, spinning and weaving cloth, as well as bearing and nurturing children. In such a society, the family was all-important as the basic social and economic unit. This helped maintain Korea's patriarchal familism.

Even the legal system supported Korea's patriarchal familism. The family organization was clearly defined by the Civil Code, which ensured continuity of a family through succession from the existing head of the family to his eldest son or to his adopted son. The eldest son inherited the major portion of his parents' wealth, and what remained was distributed among the remaining sons. A daughter could never be heir to her father, since on marriage she left her family to join that of her husband's. In return, the eldest son alone had responsibility for supporting his parents in old age, and performed ceremonies commemorating the death of his parents and that of other ancestors. The unit formed by a father and his wife and their eldest son, who on his marriage was expected to bring his wife to live under his parents' roof, constituted the core family. Younger brothers were expected to move out of their parents' house after marriage. The extended core household could be comprised of up to four generations.

The transition of traditional Korean society to an industrial society gathered momentum in the early 1960s together with the industrialization of the Korea economy. As industrialization occurred at an unprecedented speed from the 1960s, so too did the transformation of Korean society. The transition to an industrial society took almost two centuries in Western societies, while Korea made the transition within a generation. Industrialization entailed people's mobility, urbanization, rural depopulation, and changes in family structure. Industrialization, in particular the export-led industrialization that started in the early 1960s, required a large number of workers in city-based factories. This demand was largely met by the influx of migrants from rural areas. In 1960, for instance, the urban population comprised 28 per cent of the national total, while it reached 48.4 per cent in 1975 (Howard 1996, p. 103). In 1990, the nation's urbanization rate was 74.4 per cent, which exceeded the average urbanization rate of 72.6 per cent in advanced countries (Lim 1998, p. 82). The farm population shrank from 63.1 per cent in 1963 to 28.4 per cent in 1980, and reduced further to 7.1 per cent in 2004 (KNSO 2006), attesting to an almost complete transformation from an agrarian society to an industrial society over three decades. Young people moved to urban areas because of the poor living standards, low income levels, limited economic prospects for themselves and inferior education opportunities for their children in rural areas. Those remaining in the rural area increasingly comprised the elderly, in particular female elderly.

Such a rapid urbanization also transformed the nature of Korean families. The traditional family was large because two or three generations lived together under the same roof, with married couples raising a number of children. The large traditional family changed to a 'nuclear family' that consisted of parents and unmarried children, with no members of a third generation. This decrease in the size of Korean families was due to a drastic decrease in the fertility rate, resulting from the birth control campaign in the early 1960s, and higher educational achievements by women. Another factor that encouraged smaller families was the rising cost of housing and education for children.

Rising urbanization together with changes in the size and composition of families accelerated the transition of traditional Korean society. In urban areas, economic opportunities were not in line with the traditional social status based on family backgrounds. Thus, social class disappeared in urban society, bringing about a sense of equality. Christianity, which expanded rapidly in urban areas during the 1960s and 1970s, contributed to enhancing this sense of equality.

The traditional values of family have also changed under the industrial society. With increased economic independence without financial inheritance from parents, the relationship between parents and children has weakened. With economic independence, the role of the eldest son, looking after his parents in their old age and performing memorial services for deceased ancestors, has become a dubious honor. The status of women has been gradually enhanced as the number of nuclear families has risen and the central role of the mother in their children's education has become increasingly important. Finally, the Family Law, revised in 1977, enhanced the status of women by ensuring sons and daughters received equal inheritance in the absence of a will. The new law allowed married daughters to receive one-quarter of their siblings' share (Howard 1996, p. 108).

During industrialization, the Korean value system changed remarkably. Prior to the 1960s, people maintained traditional values. Family moral values such as respect for parents and ancestors and care for descendants declined, and other moral values such as decorum, humaneness and morality were emphasized. However, as industrialization and economic development accelerated in the 1960s and 1970s, the value system shifted its emphasis from morality and humaneness to materialism. The new value system emphasizes self-realization, economic security and stability, self-esteem and fierce pursuance of higher social standing.

According to an empirical study by Auh (2000), the value system in Korea has further changed from materialistic values to 'post-materialistic' values. People who experienced material poverty and physical insecurity hold materialistic values such as economic success and high social status. Post-materialistic values emphasize such values as freedom of speech, active involvement in the workplace and community, active political participation, development toward a humane society, and development toward an idea-oriented society. People who hold these values dear are found among those who have experienced material prosperity and physical security in their value-formation period. In Korea, the middle-aged and the old-aged cohorts grew up under the social economic conditions of poverty, colonization and war, while the younger age cohort grew up in a relatively better social economic climate due to Korea's miraculous economic development in the 1970s and 1980s. It is the latter group who espouse post-materialistic values. As the latter age group increases over time, the post-materialistic value system will become increasingly important and is eventually expected to prevail.

3.6 CHARACTERISTICS OF MODERN KOREAN SOCIETY

Even though Korean society has transformed remarkably during the 1960s and 1970s, it is still considered collectivist in comparison to Western society. Korean society retains a strong Confucian tradition, which is consistently manifested in the strong devotion to the family and in the emphasis on hierarchy and vertical relationships, although modified to adapt to modern conditions. The emphasis on family and group associations forces individuals to suppress their own needs and desires, transcending their own self-interest and priorities for the sake of groups. This negates individuality and pressures individuals to conform to the goals of the group. Koreans can also be regarded as quite nationalistic, discriminating against foreign goods and companies, and Korean society has until recently been closed to foreigners.

Although Koreans are family-centered people, other bases of group associations have developed in the world and are evident in contemporary Korean society. These include the schools Koreans attend, the regions they are brought up in, and the companies they work for. The ties of friendships among fellow students and alumni members are extremely strong, and alumni associations exist among graduates from elementary schools, high schools and universities. Formal and informal meetings take place regularly among classmates and alumni members. They help each other and provide favors among themselves, over non-members, in their daily interactions. Thus, the school a Korean attends is critically important for a student's future career and his or her personal life after graduation. This is one of the reasons why competition to enter prestigious universities is so fierce. Affinity among people from the same region is also strong. Koreans have developed strong regional ties over a long history. Although the country is small in size, there are several different dialects in the regions. Koreans can easily identify the region a person was brought up in by their dialect. In business and non-business organizations, people from the same region maintain friendly relationships and offer help to each other. As discussed in Chapter 2, regionalism is also evident in politics in that the major political parties in Korea are organized among regional lines.

Strong nationalism has protected Korean business from foreign competition over a long period of time. Korean nationalism has made Koreans wary of foreigners and there is concern that letting foreign companies enter domestic business is a form of economic colonization. Therefore, strong nationalism has led Koreans to strive for an economically independent nation and they undertake, from time to time, campaigns aimed at preventing Koreans from purchasing foreign products.

Korean business reflects Korean society and family. A business firm is regarded as an extension of the family, and the nature and organization of a firm can be quite similar to those of a family. Corporate familism has always been highly emphasized, focusing on harmonious relationships among its members. Because of the paramount importance of family in terms of trust, companies are traditionally owned by families, and management and ownership have not been separated. As such, the organization is strongly hierarchical, with more ranks to its organization than those in the Western world. Leadership in the business organization is paternalistic, and loyalty from employees is expected. In return, leaders are expected to look after their employees based on the concept of reciprocity. Out of this basic consideration of the business as an extension of a family, business practices of seniority and a lifetime employment system have developed. Additionally, discrimination against women has been most overt and widespread in the business community. Until the late 1980s, female workers were expected to leave the workplace as soon as they got married or became pregnant, and they enjoyed few promotion opportunities. Payment was markedly less for female workers for equal work. All this was reflected in the lower average wage level of female workers, which was less than 50 per cent of the average male wage until the mid-1980s. This gradually increased to 64 per cent in 2002 (Korea Labor Institute 2003).

3.7   KOREAN SOCIETY AFTER THE 1997 FINANCIAL CRISIS

Through the bitter experience of the 1997 financial crisis and the ensuing economic setbacks, Koreans and Korean society have once again become markedly transformed. It had been claimed in the past that while the Korean market was quite open, Korean society remained closed. After the crisis, however, Korean society, as well as its people's mindset has opened up. Koreans have come to realize that foreign investment is indispensable to the process of economic recovery, and their views and attitudes toward foreign business and investment have been changing (*Korea Herald* 1998). They have also realized that their economy is inextricably linked to the global economy and thus global competition is inevitable. In such a tightly knit country as Korea, people's first tendency is to buy Korean products. However, the fact that foreign retail stores have been well received by the Korean general public indicates an opening up of the society.

With increasing globalization, the relentless opening up of the Korean economy and corresponding structural and institutional reforms, Korean businesses have needed to become more competitive in the global market for their own survival. This is forcing Korean companies to change their enshrined business culture. The so-called Korean clan management based on the family is one of the sources of inefficiency of management. It is likely that the Western management system based on professional expertise will replace this clan management. It is increasingly difficult to maintain the corporate familism cherished by Korean firms. It is expected that as Korea strives to direct its economy to being knowledge-based, the knowledge and ideas of workers will become the core resource of companies. Under these circumstances, hierarchical organization of firms and paternalistic leadership will not be consistent with the emerging management system. At the same time, under pressing competition from Western counterparts, Korean firms will also have difficulty in maintaining a seniority and lifetime employment system. In its place, merit-based promotion and lay-offs of workers will likely take place. Accordingly, the loyalty of workers toward their companies and their leaders will diminish over time.[6] These changes in business culture will gradually lead to changes in Korean culture, and Korean society will likely transform from a group society to an individualistic one similar to the Western style.[7]

The family system, which has been the core of Korean culture, will change. The financial crisis together with emerging globalization has raised the level of uncertainty and insecurity in the job market. This has in turn intensified competition in education as well as in the job market. Education has become increasingly more expensive as the demand for foreign language skills

(English) rises in addition to traditional education. All this is bound to disrupt the fabric of Korean families that are already nuclear families. Cho (2005) has found a continuous decrease in the marriage rate and the fertility rate, and an unprecedented increase in the divorce rate. Cho (2005) has also found an increasing rate of international marriages and a rising phenomenon of internationally divided families – the wife typically living abroad with her children and the husband staying in Korea – for children's education.

The social status of women will also change. As the nature of human resources required by business changes from industrial workers to professionals, gender discrimination in the job market will diminish. Since the passage of the Equal Employment Act in 1987, to prevent discriminatory practices against female workers in regard to hiring and promotion opportunities, the number of women entering professional jobs has increased significantly (Korea Information Service 2000, p. 93). For instance, the economic participation rate of women increased steadily from 34.4 per cent in 1965 to 50.1 per cent in 2005 (KNSO 2006). In terms of characteristics of the female labor force, only 2 per cent of the female labor force worked in professional and managerial occupations and 4 per cent in clerical positions in 1975. However, by 1998, 12.6 per cent of female employees were serving in professional and managerial positions, and another 16 per cent were working in clerical occupations (Korea Information Service 2000, p. 92).

Along with the dawning of the twenty-first century, Korea will continue to transform from an industrial society to an information society, as are other advanced countries. Unique characteristics of the information era include multimedia and interactive communications. Traditionally, media existed separately for voice, image and character. Increasingly, pieces of information relating to voice, image and character will be integrated into one multimedia channel, and this will greatly expand the flow of information. Traditional mass media communications such as TV and radio have been one-way communications, with the customers typically being passive receivers and reactors. Once multimedia infrastructure such as the information superhighway is fully developed, multimedia communications will become two-way interactive, whereby citizens will not only receive information and communications from multimedia outlets, but they will also participate in providing information. This has important implications for Korean society. Citizens will be able to deal easily with temporal and geophysical distances and have more choices and options available to them. This will increase their self-empowerment and participation in the community and in political activities. Citizens will base communities on computer networks, which will work as the grassroots for new political and social activities and participation. Numerous citizens' associations have already been created in Korea recently. They are all networked via computers and can significantly influence the political process, as the 2003 election of President Roh attests. In a world of global multimedia communications, defending and maintaining Korean nationalistic and monocultural traditions will become increasingly difficult. Korean society will become more open to foreigners and Koreans will gradually adopt multiculturalism.

3.8   CONCLUSION

Since an understanding of Korean culture is one of the indispensable keys to successful business in Korea and relations with Koreans, this chapter has explored the nature of Korean culture, its underlying determinants and its evolutionary transition through economic industrialization and, further, its transformation after the 1997 financial crisis. For this study, culture is referred to as the learned behavioral pattern shared by the people in a country, and includes attitudes, behavior, values, norms and beliefs. Korea has developed its own unique culture over its long history as an isolated independent country with its own religions, political and economic systems, education and language.

A number of attempts have been made to identify and measure Korean culture. The salient traits of Korean culture commonly underlying the discourses available in the literature include: hierarchical collectivism, patriarchal familism, authoritarianism, status consciousness, secularism and strong nationalism. This chapter has attempted to explicate these traits by means of the determining factors of culture.

Korea has had a long and tumultuous history as an independent country with a homogeneous race. Unremitting invasions and incursions by its powerful neighboring countries over its long history have strengthened Korean nationalism. It is interesting to note that even under such a strong nationalism Korea never developed a warrior culture. Korea has resigned itself to being a protégé of China instead of challenging it militarily.

Although there were a number of influential religions in Korea, Confucianism, which was adopted as the guiding principles of state management and as the code of ethics by the Yi Dynasty over 500 years, has been most prominent in molding Korean culture. Continuous inculcation of the importance of relationships in a society has developed a strong group society in Korea. As it was hierarchical and vertically structured, Korean society developed a societal stratification placing aristocrats and scholars at the top, followed by farmers, merchants and artisans, and finally household servants. Over its long dynastic history, the King and the aristocrats surrounding him wielded authoritarian power. Korean collectivism had familism at its core, which was patriarchal in nature. The education system during the Yi Dynasty and the Korean language reinforced the moral principles of Confucianism. These cultural traits along with the Confucian doctrine were used by the Japanese colonial government and subsequent military authoritarian regimes in Korea for political expediency. Subsequently, Confucian influences on Korean society remain strong even today. Christianity, which was introduced in the seventeenth century, made a significant contribution to transforming the traditional Korean culture.

It was the industrialization of the Korean economy since the 1960s that transformed traditional Korean society into an industrial society. Korea's rapid industrialization entailed rapid urbanization and rural depopulation and changes in social and family structure. Social stratification and traditional patriarchal familism eclipsed markedly. Industrialization has also shifted emphasis in the value system from morality and humaneness to materialism. Continuous economic prosperity has further changed the focus on the value system from materialism to a quality-of-life concept.

Since the beginning of industrialization in the 1960s, Korean society has run across a confluence of its traditional culture with the emerging cultural forces running counter to its former ways. Yet, Korean society retains a strong Confucian tradition in comparison to the West. Strong nationalism and collectivism prevail in Korea, attesting to the glacial pace of cultural transformation. The Korean business sector embraced traditional Korean culture and, as a result, Korean companies have maintained highly vertically structured organizations and have operated businesses with strong corporate familism, whereby lifetime employment and seniority practices have been management norms.

Another epoch-making transformation of Korean culture occurred in conjunction with its 1997 financial crisis. The crisis made the general public appreciate the inevitability of emerging globalization and provided an opportunity to review their value systems. Koreans have come to value foreign business and culture, and extreme patriotism has faded significantly. The Korean economic structure and its institutions have changed markedly to enable firms to survive under rising competition and the incessant rapid changes in the globalization and information era.

Whither Korean culture hereafter? Korean culture is determined by various factors. On the one hand, religious doctrines, language and the education system change only at a glacial pace in Korea. On the other hand, the Korean political and economic systems are adjusting themselves rather quickly in line with global trends as well as to epoch-making changes. Such changes in political and economic institutions could lead to changes in imbedded Korean behavioral patterns. A new Korean culture will rise out of balancing these two sets of forces: one a dragging force and the other a speedily advancing force. The traditional value system will be pulled by the precipitating changes in institutional cultures that are, in turn, dragged by the glacial pace of a psychological cultural move.

NOTES

1. For a variety of definitions of culture, see Ferraro (1994) or any textbooks about international business.
2. For a detailed exposition of value orientations in dealing with these five questions and an application of those value orientations to organization and management, see Cullen (2002, pp. 54–63).
3. The historical information in this section draws on Korea Information Service (2000) and Howard (1996).
4. Chang and Chang (1994, p. 16) argue that the Yin–Yang concept by which Koreans perceive the universe in terms of dual cosmic forces has led to a multi-religion society.
5. Filial piety was directed not only to living parents but also toward deceased ancestors. Filial piety for the latter was shown in the form of annual memorial services on the date of their death.
6. Park and Kim (2005) argue that lay-offs, early retirement and job insecurity in the wake of the crisis has resulted in profound changes in workers' attitudes toward their work and self-identity. They have become more realistic and self-centered and significantly lost their job satisfaction together with their sense of identity based on work and jobs.
7. Park and Kim (2005) point out that the financial crisis has led to a gradual diminution of Koreans' collective consciousness.

REFERENCES

Ahn, Byung-Wook (1999), *Analysis of Human Beings by Analects of Confucius* (in Korean), Seoul: Jayumunhak-sa.

Auh, Soo Young (2000), 'Where are Koreans going? change and stability in values among Koreans and democratization', *Korea Observer*, 31 (4), 497–525.

Chang, Chan Sup and N.J. Chang (1994), *The Korean Management System*, Westport, CT: Quorum Books.

Cho, Uhn (2005), 'The encroachment of globalisation into intimate life: the flexible Korean family in "economic crisis"', *Korea Journal*, 45 (3), 8–35.

Cullen, John B. (2002), *Multinational Management: A Strategic Approach*, 2nd edn, Cincinnati, OH: South-Western College Publishing.

Ferraro, Gary P. (1994), *The Cultural Dimension of International Business*, Englewood Cliffs, NJ: Prentice Hall.

Hahm, Hanhee (2003), 'Korean culture seen through Westerners' eyes', *Korea Journal*, 43 (1), 106–28.

Han, Kyung-Koo (2003), 'The anthropology of the discourse on the Koreanness of Koreans', *Korea Journal*, 43 (1), 5–31.

Hill, Charles W.L. (2005), *International Business: Competing in the Global Marketplace*, 5th edn, Boston, MA: McGraw-Hill Irwin.

Hofstede, G. (1980), *Culture's Consequences: International Differences in Work-Related Values*, London: Sage.

Hofstede, G. (1991), *Cultures and Organizations: Software of the Mind*, London: McGraw-Hill.

Hopfe, Lewis M. (1987), *Religions of the World*, 4th edn, New York: Macmillan Publishing.

Howard, Keith (ed.) (1996), *Korea: People, Country and Culture*, London: School of Oriental and African Studies, University of London.

Kluckhohn, F. and F.L. Strodtbeck (1961), *Variations in Value Orientations*, New York: Harper & Row.

Korea Herald (1998), 'Market and economic viewpoint; the most dismaying market', 10 June.

Korea Information Service (2000), *Facts about Korea*, Seoul: Korea Information Service.

Korea Labor Institute (2003), *2003 KLI Labor Statistics*, Seoul: Korea Labor Institute.

Korea National Statistical Office (KNSO) (2006), *Korea Statistical Yearbook 2005*, Seoul: Korea National Statistical Office.

Kweon, Sug-In (2003), 'Popular discourses on Korean culture: from the late 1980s to the present', *Korea Journal*, 43 (1), 32–57.

Lim, Hy-sop (1998), 'Korean society: current status and future outlook', *Korea Focus*, 6 (5), 78–95.

Park, Gil-Sung and A.E. Kim (2005), 'Changes in attitudes toward work and workers' identity in Korea', *Korea Journal*, 45 (3), 36–57.

Waters, M. and R. Crook (1993), *Sociology One: Principles of Sociological Analysis for Australians*, 3rd edn, Melbourne: Longman Cheshire.

Yi, Jeong Duk (2003), 'What is Korean culture anyway?', *Korea Journal*, 43 (1), 58–82.

4. Configuration of the Korean market in transition

4.1 INTRODUCTION

When assessing the desirability of a foreign country to expand business operations, export companies find market screening particularly useful. Market screening is a form of 'environmental scanning' that companies use to identify markets. Market screening of overseas markets generally proceeds through five key stages. The initial stage involves assessing the 'basic need and potential' of the foreign market, taking into account what is consumed and whether the market has potential for the export company's products. The second stage of screening involves assessing the 'financial and economic forces' of the market, including its size and past and future capacity for growth. The third stage analyzes the 'political and legal forces' in the market, which may hinder or enhance an export strategy. The fourth stage focuses on 'socio-cultural forces' that influence the preferences and expectations of consumers and thus the suitability of a product introduced to that market by an external supplier. The final stage of the screening process investigates the nature of 'competition forces' in the market to assess how competition is likely to influence the new product in this market (Ball et al. 2002, p. 522; Rugman and Hodgetts 1995, p. 296).

This chapter analyzes the receptivity of the Korean market to imports for the period 1990 to 2005, with consideration of the type of information that a MNE might use in the market screening process. [1] This analysis covers a broad range of important areas that concern the Korean market, including its potential, institutional changes and trends; the distribution system; socio-cultural forces; and trends in e-commerce. Since this is a broad examination of the Korean market and provides general guidance, those interested in market screening of Korea for specific products will need further, product-specific analysis. Although there is ample literature on the Korean market, no single study appears to cover comprehensively all aspects of the Korean market that foreign export companies require for market screening.

This chapter proceeds as follows. The next section explores trends in Korean imports to assess the overall size and development of the market and identify areas of greatest growth potential. Section 4.3 discusses institutional (legal and other regulatory) changes related to Korea's imports. Section 4.4 presents an analysis of market trends revealed by demographic and other societal changes and considers the influence of salient characteristics of Korean culture upon market behavior. Section 4.5 discusses Korea's complex and idiosyncratic distribution system, which is a major obstacle for foreign businesses attempting market entry. An emerging facet of the Korean market configuration is the rapidly expanding e-commerce, which is discussed in section 4.6. Section 4.7 presents a summary of this chapter and conclusion.[2]

4.2 KOREAN IMPORT MARKET: TRENDS AND POTENTIAL

One general identifier of basic needs in a foreign market is the level of imports. With rapid economic growth over the last four decades, Korea has become one of the world's major importing nations – the fifteenth-largest in 2006 (CIA 2006). As Table 4.1 shows, between 1990 and 2005 the value of Korea's total imports almost quadrupled from US$69.8 billion to US$261.2 billion. This constitutes an average annual increase of 9.2 per cent, compared to an annual growth rate of 7.6 per cent of GDP in US dollars (Bank of Korea 2006a). Over the period 2001–05, the value of total imports increased by 16.7 per cent per annum. The Korean National Statistical Office introduced the aggregate classifications of primary products, light industrial, heavy industrial and information technology (IT) products in 2001 and these provide a useful overview of recent trends. Imports of primary products increased from US$40.2 billion in 2001 to US$71.7 billion in 2005, an annual average increase of 15.5 per cent. Over the same period, imports of light industrial products increased by an average annual 14.9 per cent per annum from US$9.5 billion to US$16.6 billion. Heavy industrial imports increased most rapidly, from US$91.2 billion to US$172.7 billion, an average annual growth rate of 17.3 per cent.

In terms of both value and growth rate, these aggregate import data suggest stronger demand from Korea for heavy industrial and primary products over light industrial and IT products. In 2005, imports of heavy industries accounted for 66.1 per cent of total imports, followed by imports of primary products at 27.5 per cent, and light industrial products at 6.4 per cent (Table 4.1). As part of heavy industrial imports, IT products increased at an average annual growth rate of 11.3 per cent, from US$28.1 billion in 2001 to US$43.1 billion in 2005.

Table 4.1 Korea imports by commodity (1990–2005) (US$ million)

	1995	2000	2001	2002	2003	2004	2005	%[a]
Total	135 118	160 481	141 097	152 126	178 826	224 462	261 238	7.6
Primary products	n.a.	n.a.	40 294	39 689	46 122	58 109	71 791	15.5
Light industrial	n.a.	n.a.	9 562	11 849	13 069	15 426	16 694	14.9
Heavy industrial	n.a.	n.a.	91 241	100 587	119 634	150 926	172 752	17.3
Information technology	(n.a.)	(n.a.)	(28 114)	(29 877)	(34 555)	(39 137)	(43 132)	11.3
Crude material & fuel	n.a.	n.a.	73 939	76 063	89 519	117 723	142 286	17.8
Capital goods	n.a.	n.a.	51 549	56 399	66 947	81 135	90 662	15.2
Consumer goods	n.a.	n.a.	15 210	18 795	21 075	23 296	26 395	14.8
High-tech[b]	n.a.	48 449	38 887	42 438	50 526	60 126	66 040	14.1

Notes:
[a] Annual average percentage growth rate. The growth rate of total imports is for the 1995–05 period; other growth rates are for the period 2001–05.
[b] The sum of KNSO sub-classifications: office and data-processing machines; telecommunications and sound equipment; electrical machinery and appliances; professional and scientific instruments; and photographic and optical goods.

Sources: Korea National Statistical Office (KSNO) (2005); Korea National Statistical Office (KSNO) (2006a).

Another new aggregate classification of imports of crude material and fuel, capital goods and consumer goods, introduced in 2001, provides another indicator of import trends. As shown in Table 4.1, imports of crude material and fuel grew most rapidly between 2001 and 2005 at 17.8 per cent annually, and accounted for 54.5 per cent of total imports in 2005. Imports of capital goods grew by an annual average of 15.2 per cent over this five-year period, and accounted for 34.7 per cent of the total in 2005. Imports of consumer goods accounted for the smallest portion at 10.1 per cent in 2005, and their annual growth rate over this period was also the lowest at 14.8 per cent. Korea imports substantial amounts of high-technology products including office and data-processing machines, telecommunications and sound equipment, electrical machinery and appliances, professional and scientific instruments, and photographic and optical goods (Table 4.1). Imports of these products increased from US$38.9 billion in 2001 to US$66 billion in 2005, a 14.1 per cent annual growth rate over the period. Import trends based on the aggregate classifications indicate that Korea relies heavily on foreign minerals and energy. As Song and Noh (2006) argue, a high and rising level of imports of heavy industrial products, capital goods and high-technology products suggests that Korea still lags behind the advanced industrial countries in key technologies in heavy and high-technology industries.[3] The size of the Korean market for imported consumer goods, though relatively small, is nevertheless significant, with annual imports of about US$26 billion in 2005 and rising.

Another important type of import in terms of value is agricultural products. Table 4.2 shows import trends of agricultural products and food self-sufficiency ratios between 1990 and 2005. Over this period the volume of Korea's agricultural imports increased from US$3.62 billion in 1990 to US$11.1 billion in 2005, with an average growth rate of 4.9 per cent between 1995 and 2005. As a percentage of Korea's overall imports, agricultural products comprise only a small share of around 4–5 per cent over the period under consideration, indicating that Korea is no longer an agrarian country. Korea's need to import agricultural products is reflected in its low food self-sufficiency ratio. The overall food self-sufficiency ratio has decreased from 53.6 per cent in 1990 to 37.5 per cent in 2004 despite claims from some authors that Korea still pursues a policy of agricultural self-sufficiency (Beghin et al. 2003). By 2004, of all agricultural products, Korea maintained self-sufficiency only in eggs and seaweed. Other agricultural products such as rice, starches and vegetables had self-sufficiency ratios in the 90 per cent range. Korea has very low self-sufficiency ratios in cereals, pulses, oil crops and oils and fats, and so has become a major world importer of oilseeds and coarse grains (Beghin et al. 2003).

Table 4.2 Trends in Korean agricultural imports and food self-sufficiency ratio (1990–2005)

Agriculture:	1990	1995	1997	2000	2001	2002	2003	2004	2005
Imports (US$ billions) [a]	3.62	6.85	7.53	7.31	7.62	8.65	9.35	10.38	11.1
Imports' growth rate	5.5	20.7	–10.2	14.0	4.1	11.9	7.5	9.9	6.5
% of total imports	5.2	5.1	5.2	4.6	5.4	5.7	5.2	4.6	4.2
Food self-sufficiency ratio (%):	1990	1995	1997	2000	2001	2002	2003	2004	2005
Total [b]	53.6	44.9	45.6	41.6	40.5	40.1	37.4	37.5	n.a.
Cereals	43.8	30.0	31.7	30.8	32.2	31.0	28.1	27.6	n.a.
(Rice)	108.3	91.1	105.0	102.9	102.7	99.2	90.3	94.3	n.a.
Starch	100.0	98.7	99.2	98.9	98.6	99.0	97.7	96.6	n.a.
Pulses	24.5	11.7	10.3	8.2	9.2	8.8	8.2	8.1	n.a.
Oil crops	86.3	44.7	43.7	35.2	43.6	37.5	24.3	29.7	n.a.
Vegetables	98.9	99.2	97.0	97.7	98.3	97.7	94.7	94.3	n.a.
Fruit	102.5	93.2	92.0	88.7	88.9	89.1	85.0	85.2	n.a.
Meat	92.9	89.2	92.1	83.9	81.0	82.0	81.2	83.5	n.a.
Eggs	100.0	99.9	100.2	100.0	100.0	100.0	100.0	100.0	n.a.
Milk	92.8	93.3	81.8	81.2	78.9	81.0	81.0	74.2	n.a.
Seafood	121.7	100.4	98.3	87.7	77.9	63.8	61.7	55.4	n.a.
Seaweed	172.8	122.2	119.4	132.6	118.5	121.3	141.5	137.4	n.a.
Oils and fats	8.0	4.8	4.1	3.2	2.4	3.5	2.4	2.5	n.a.

Notes:
a   Calculated from the sum of national accounts classifications: food and live animals; beverages and tobacco; animal and vegetable oils, fats and waxes.
b   Calculated from total energy, protein and fat supplies.

Sources: Korea National Statistical Office (KSNO) (2006a); and Korea Rural Economic Institute (2005).

Table 4.3 *Trends in Korea's services sector and imports of services (1990–2005)*

	1990	1995	1997	2000	2001	2002	2003	2004	2005
% GDP	49.5	51.8	53.4	54.4	56.3	57.5	57.2	55.6	56.3
% GDP (including utilities and construction)	62.9	65.4	67.7	65.4	67.6	68.7	69.5	67.3	67.9
*Annual growth rate %	7.8	8.1	5.1	6.1	4.8	7.8	1.6	1.9	3.0
Services imports: (US$ millions)	1990	1995	1997	2000	2001	2002	2003	2004	2005
Total	10 252	25 806	29 502	33 381	32 927	36 585	40 381	49 928	58 787
Transport	3 998	9 645	10 310	11 048	11 043	11 301	13 613	17 655	20 144
Travel	2 768	6 341	6 988	7 132	7 617	10 465	10 103	12 350	15 406
Education	–	998	1 158	958	1 070	1 427	1 855	2 494	–
Communication	162	642	865	623	742	685	693	636	773
Construction	–	–	–	16	15	24	14	4	6
Insurance	–	255	162	146	374	571	390	461	733
Financial	11	130	74	191	83	70	101	127	235
Computing & information	50	93	66	92	104	124	134	157	183
Royalties & licenses	1 364	2 385	2 414	3 221	3 053	3 002	3 570	4 446	4 560
Other business services	1 697	5 807	8 022	10 328	9 237	9 607	11 049	13 162	15 537
Cultural & recreational	20	98	137	160	206	283	261	376	477
Government	202	412	465	425	454	454	453	554	732

Note: * Average annual percentage growth rate.

Sources: Bank of Korea (2006a); OECD (2006); OECD (2007).

Another important trend in the configuration of the Korean market involves service industries and imports of and for these industries. Table 4.3 shows trends in Korea's service industries between 1990 and 2005. As a percentage of GDP, the service sector comprised 49.5 per cent in 1990, increasing to 56.3 per cent in 2005. If utilities and construction are included, the service sector accounted for 62.9 per cent of GDP in 1990 and increased to 67.9 per cent by 2005. The extent of service sector growth is similar to GDP growth. Between 1995 and 2005, the service sector grew in real terms by 3.9 per cent annually, while GDP grew by 5.4 per cent (Bank of Korea 2006b).

Table 4.3 also shows that imports of services have increased significantly since 1990 in line with the liberalization of the Korean economy and Korea's accession to the WTO in 1995 and to the OECD in 1996. The total import value of services increased from US$25.8 billion in 1995 to US$58.8 billion in 2005, an average annual growth rate of 8.6 per cent over the period. In terms of growth rate, education was the industry leader in services imports. Imports of education services increased by an annual average rate of 10.7 per cent, from being worth slightly less than US$1 billion in 1995 to US$2.4 billion in 2004. Imports of transport, travel and insurance services also grew by about 7, 9 and 11 per cent per annum respectively between 1995 and 2005. Payments of royalties and licenses were substantial and increased from US$2.4 billion in 1995 to US$4.6 billion in 2005, a 6.7 per cent annual growth rate over the period and reflecting the relatively high reliance of the Korean economy on foreign technologies.

4.3   LIBERALIZATION OF THE TRADE REGIME

Since its entry into GATT in 1967, Korea has strongly supported the concept of the open multinational trading system. After consultations with the GATT in the late 1980s, the Korean government began to liberalize some of its markets to accept foreign imports. Yet serious liberalization of the Korean trade regime has been undertaken only through a series of developments since the mid-1990s. First, since its accession to the WTO in 1995, Korea has comprehensively implemented WTO agreements and undertaken unilateral measures to liberalize the nation's trade and investment regime. Second, since its accession to the OECD in 1996, Korea has been required to comply with OECD trade guidelines. Third, the financial crisis in 1997 prompted the government to move quickly with further liberalization of trade. Fourth, since 1998, Korea has accelerated the liberalization of the service sector beyond its commitments to the OECD and the WTO as a way of attracting more foreign investment and enhancing overall economic efficiency (Kim and Kim 2003).

Korea was a major participant in formulating the WTO's 2001 Doha Development Agenda (DDA), and has played an active role in WTO negotiations and trade initiatives in areas such as the liberalization of information technology products, financial services and basic telecommunications services (Yeo et al. 2004).

As a result of this series of moves to liberalize the domestic market, most goods can now be imported freely into Korea without import licenses, and only some selected items require approval (EIU 2003). Goods that are prohibited or restricted on the negative list are normally associated with national security, public health and safety.[4] Except for these, and importantly also for rice, trade restrictions other than tariffs and tariff quotas were removed by 2001, even in the agricultural sector (Yeo et al. 2004). Technical barriers have also largely been eliminated, and the domestic regulatory framework has been made more transparent in line with international standards. Implementation of an immediate release system, an electronic data interchange (EDI) system for both imports and exports, and electronic publication of customs information in English have significantly enhanced and streamlined customs procedures. The Korean government is also committed to phasing out export subsidy programs that fail to conform to the WTO Agreement on Subsidies and Countervailing Measures. Under post-financial crisis IMF conditionality, four prohibited export subsidies were eliminated earlier than scheduled (Yeo et al. 2004).

In accordance with Korea's Uruguay Round commitments, the number of bound tariff lines has been increased to 91.7 per cent of total tariff lines, including 92.6 per cent of industrial products. Tariffs on all agricultural products are bound with the exception of forestry and fisheries products, which remain unbound. By 2001, the average tariff rate was 8.9 per cent. There is also a value added tax of 10 per cent imposed on all imports and domestically manufactured goods. Luxury items attract a further 10 to 20 per cent special excise tax (KOTRA 2006). The average tariff rate that applies the Most Favored Nation Clause tariff on industrial goods is approximately 7.5 per cent. In fostering trade with the world's least-developed countries, Korea has extended its duty-free, quota-free treatment to 80 products since 2000 (Yeo et al. 2004).

For the service sector, numerous regulations and restrictions on incoming FDI were lifted after the 1997 crisis, not only to fulfill Korea's WTO commitments but also to attract FDI into the service sector. By 2000, 471 service sectors had been opened to foreign investment, with only 24 remaining restricted, and these were in sectors with a strong public interest and cultural component, such as news agency activities, radio, TV, water services and gambling (Kim and Kim 2003; Yeo et al. 2004).[5] Ceilings for foreign portfolio investment in stocks were also eliminated, and most of the current account transactions of corporations and financial institutions were liberalized through revisions to the regulations concerning foreign exchange transactions in 2001. Liberalization of inward FDI in the service sector, together with the opening of the securities markets and liberalization of the foreign exchange market, have generated trade in services, which has increased rapidly in the recent past as shown in Table 4.3.

For the agricultural sector, the Korean government had long sought protection from international competition through high trade barriers that included regulations, tariffs, and non-tariff barriers. Non-tariff barriers included quotas, licensing requirements, opaque and inconsistent import-related regulations and customs clearance procedures. However, the government has eliminated most import restrictions since the Uruguay Round and has lowered the level of tariffs in this sector (C.H. Yoo 2003). Of a total 1660 categories of agricultural items, only 16 items remained under some restriction in 2001, raising the import liberalization rate of agriculture to 99 per cent (Kwon and Kang 2000). This compares with a 99.9 per cent liberalization rate for the Korean economy as a whole. Rice is the exception as a food security measure and remains a restricted item with market access of 4 per cent of domestic rice consumption. WTO-prohibited domestic subsidies for agriculture have also been eliminated.[6]

Since the mid-1990s, not only has Korea liberalized its trade regime in line with WTO and OECD requirements, but it has also been exploring free trade agreements (FTAs) with a number of countries particularly in East Asia. Korea appears to have recognized recently that participation in preferential trade agreements is an inevitable and urgently required policy tool for foreign market access and sustainable growth. The major political hurdle to establishing FTAs is the agricultural sector. Hence, the preferred initial partners are those least likely to threaten the domestic agricultural market, such as Japan, Singapore and Chile. Bilateral FTAs may thus be seen as a way to avoid politically damaging pressures on domestic agriculture while still expanding market access and investment opportunities.

In November 2001, Korea made an agreement with China and with the Association of South East Asian Nations (ASEAN) to establish FTAs within a decade. Korea and Japan have undertaken to investigate the economic effects and policy implications of a Japan–Korea FTA (Park 2006). Korea's first FTA, with Chile, took effect in April 2004, followed by FTAs with Singapore and the four-member European Free Trade Association (EFTA) that both became effective in 2006 (WTO 2006). FTA negotiations or joint studies are also under way with the US, Canada, the ASEAN, New Zealand and Thailand (Lee and Park 2005). Negotiations with Japan have stalled in recent times, as some concerns have been expressed about this arrangement. Y.H. Kim (2005) argues that the Korean industrial structure is vertically integrated with Japanese industries in terms of technology, and thus free trade with Japan would lead Korea to specialize in less value-added sectors where Korea has comparative advantage over Japan. Rhyu and Lee (2006), however, have disputed the vertical integration thesis, arguing that since 2000 the competitive nature of the major exports of Korea and Japan signals the disintegration of vertical specialization.[7]

4.4 DEMOGRAPHIC AND CULTURAL CHARACTERISTICS OF CONSUMER MARKETS

4.4.1 Demographic Trends

The potential of a market can be assessed by analyzing consumer trends and behavior, for which demographic trends have important implications. Table 4.4 shows demographic trends in Korea between 1990 and 2005, and projections to 2040. During the three-decade period of rapid economic development and modernization from the early 1960s, Korea completed the 'demographic transition' to low mortality and low fertility rates – a characteristic of the advanced world including most other East Asian nations (McNicoll 2006). Korea recorded a very modest population increase of 5 million (11.6 per cent) between 1990 and 2005, from 43 to 48 million. Population growth had declined from 1 per cent in 1990 to less than 0.5 per cent by 2005, alongside Korea's increasing wealth and consistent with demographic trends in most advanced countries with the exception of the US. These recent trends suggest that Korea's population is likely to remain static at around 48 million with minor variations over the coming decades, as Table 4.4 suggests.

The most striking trend is Korea's rapidly ageing population, with the proportion of those aged over 65 years increasing from 5.1 per cent in 1990 to 10.4 per cent in 2005. By 2040, the proportion of those aged over 65 is expected to reach a massive 41.9 per cent. The generally accepted criterion for an 'aged' population is a share of 14 per cent or more aged over 65 years (Kwon 2003). The developed-country average share was recorded at 14.2 per cent in 2004 (Sagaza 2004, p. S35). Furthermore, the working-age population is expected to decline relative to the total population. The middle cohorts of the 30- to 59-year-old group accounted for 45.5 per cent of the Korean population in 2005 and are expected to decline to 38.1 per cent by 2040. It is axiomatic to point out that such a severe decline in the working-age population and a concomitant increase in the elderly population presents a major challenge to future Korean society, with a range of implications for the configuration and capacity of the Korean market.

Table 4.4 Korean demographic changes 1990–2005 and projections 2005–40

	1990	1995	2000	2002	2004	2005	2010	2020	2030	2040
Population (millions)	42.9	45.1	47.0	47.6	48.1	48.3	49.2	50.0	49.3	46.7
Growth rate (%)	0.99	1.01	0.84	0.55	0.49	0.44	0.26	-0.02	-0.25	-0.68
Age %:										
0–19	36.0	32.0	29.2	27.6	26.2	25.7	23.1	17.3	15.4	14.1
20–35	29.9	28.8	26.5	26.1	25.3	24.7	21.8	19.4	15.6	12.7
35–49	17.9	21.1	23.9	24.8	25.6	25.8	25.9	13.4	20.5	18.8
50–64	11.1	12.2	13.2	13.5	14.2	14.7	18.2	24.1	24.1	21.9
65+	5.1	5.9	8.2	9.0	10.0	10.4	12.9	19.4	29.6	41.9
Households (millions)	11.4	13.0	14.6	15.1	15.5	15.8	16.9	18.2	n.a.	n.a.

Sources: Korea National Statistical Office (2005); Korea National Statistical Office (2006b).

T.H. Kwon (2003) argues that one of the most important features of population ageing in South Korea is its unprecedented pace. To reach a similarly large share of the population aged over 65 years took 175 years in France, 65 years in the US and 40 years in Japan, compared with only 25 years in Korea. The rapidity of population ageing will necessarily require a substantive shift in care responsibilities from private households to the state and society. This has normative implications for the Korean cultural tradition of filial piety and obvious fiscal implications in terms of raising the necessary revenue from a declining working-age population and tax base. If not managed carefully by the government, an ageing population could result in a heavy burden on a shrinking working generation to support the elderly financially, which would lessen the disposable income available to the younger generation. It could also mean that the proportion of older, non-working people within the consumer market will continue to grow.

4.4.2 The Growth of the Middle Class

Korea's rapid economic growth since the 1960s has transformed what was a predominantly agrarian society into a modern industrial society. This has necessarily brought significant change to the occupational and 'class' configuration of Korean society. Long-term trends have seen a reduction in the agricultural workforce and a concomitant increase in those engaged in urban employment. The development of industrial capitalism has resulted in the creation of a large new middle class of salaried employees at the expense of the self-employed and smaller family-owned businesses (Hong 2003). The middle class in Korean society has increased as a percentage of the total population from 20.5 per cent in 1960 to 53 per cent in 2000, although an even larger proportion self-identifies as middle class (Hong 2003). Lett (1998, p. 38) argues that the Korean middle class has acquired some Western cultural elements but also displays some traditional elite characteristics.

The new middle class increasingly possesses a larger amount of disposable income with which to purchase more consumer goods and have a comfortable lifestyle. Pursuit of leisure, and pleasure-seeking activities such as golf, rose dramatically within Korean society after the 1980s (Robinson and Goodman 1996). From the beginning of the twenty-first century in particular, there have been significant increases in overseas travel by Korean tourists, as shown in Table 4.3. Koreans have a rate of almost 99 per cent ownership of household items such as refrigerators, color TVs and washing machines, a rate comparable to Japanese ownership (Reid and Lee 1998). With relative increases in income, there has been an increase in food consumption in Korea across the board (Austrade 2004).

The middle class places a high priority on education and parents will make great sacrifices to ensure their children receive the best education they can afford. Lett (1998) points out that for those entering the labor market in the 1990s, a college degree was a prerequisite for most jobs considered to be suitable for people of middle-class status. Self-employment does not require a college degree, but many entrepreneurs were college educated nonetheless. The emphasis on education is reflected in the rapid growth of the international education sector within imported services (Table 4.3).

4.4.3 Position of Women in Society

As the Korean economy changed significantly while undergoing post-war development and modernization, so did the position of women in society. The changing composition of Korea's industrial structure has resulted in greater participation of women in education and in the labor force. In 1965, women accounted for 35 per cent of the workforce. This increased to 47 per cent in 1999 and to 50 per cent in 2005 (KLI 2006), a figure approximately 10 per cent lower than in advanced OECD countries.[8]

Even with more women joining the paid workforce, there is still discrimination against females in Korea's labor market. Women hold the greater proportion of positions as clerks, service and sales workers, agricultural and fishery workers, and unskilled workers (Hong 2003), but only a small portion of professional positions. In 2001, only 7 per cent of managers in Korea were women, compared with 35 per cent in Canada, 33 per cent in the UK, 22 per cent in Mexico, 19 per cent in China and 11 per cent in Egypt (Kang and Rowley 2005). N.C. Lee (2005) argues that progress in improving the status of women has not kept pace with Korea's economic development due to the deeply rooted Confucian male-oriented cultural tradition and patriarchal family system. G. Yoo (2003) points out that wage and gender ratio differentials are partly the result of a gender gap in human capital. On average, women have fewer years of schooling than men and, on average, much lower rates of tertiary education. In terms of college education, women are represented more highly in humanities courses whose graduates are less preferred by Korean employers. To the extent that the gender gap in human capital endowment is a product of education, it appears to be rooted in Korean culture that inclines parents to favor males over females for higher and specialized learning.

Regardless of the gender discrimination against female workers, the increasing entry of women into the labor force has important implications for the Korean consumer market. The perception that women are responsible for looking after the family is still dominant in Korea, as in most countries. The major shoppers in Korea are women, with many housewives and employed women purchasing family necessities. Women are also usually responsible for their children's education. Some observers have speculated that earning an independent income by participating in the paid workforce will strengthen women's economic power in the domestic sphere, although this claim remains spurious while there is no data to support it.

4.4.4 Socio-cultural Factors

The potential of a product in a market is particularly influenced by cultural factors, which shape both consumer preferences and expectations. Characteristics of traditional Korean culture including hierarchical collectivism, patriarchal familism, authoritarianism, status consciousness, risk-aversion, group conformity, high power distance, secularism and strong nationalism are generally well known.[9] Korea's rapid industrialization and modernization since the 1960s has profoundly transformed the nation's traditional socio-economic structure. Industrialization entailed rapid urbanization, concomitant rural depopulation, and significant changes to social and family structure. Social stratification has loosened and patriarchal familism has declined substantially. Industrialization and modernization have shifted emphasis away from Confucian morality and concern for humanity to greater levels of materialism. Continuing economic prosperity has further changed the focus from material consumption to concern for quality of life. Nevertheless, Korean society retains a strong residual Confucian tradition, and strong nationalism and collectivism still prevail to a significant level.

In what is still Korea's status- and face-conscious hierarchical society, formalities are observed assiduously among people of different social status according to age, social reputation and/or organizational rank. These formalities include conduct toward others, dress codes, and ways of addressing and conversing with others. Another important aspect of familial collectivism and a status-conscious society is competitive dedication to improving the relative status of self and family. Prestige has been of the utmost importance within this cultural conditioning.

In their quest for status and prestige, most Koreans are particularly conscious of their appearance, and are thus willing to pay a lot of money to look their best. As Korean society has become more prosperous, people have pursued status and prestige through conspicuous consumption, especially those of the new urban middle class. Koreans are highly brand-conscious as brand names are seen to indicate prestige and to distinguish between upper and lower echelons of society. Group conformity together with brand consciousness make international trends in fashion and other commodities particularly influential in Korea. But whereas Westerners will often buy goods for practical purposes, Koreans generally expect their purchases to serve another purpose as well by bringing them status and prestige. Recognizing these socio-cultural circumstances around consumption, it is suggested that at places where trend-setting consumers shop, a more expensive product will sell more easily since purchasers here assume that high price speaks of the high quality with which they seek to associate themselves.

Over a long period, government policy was largely instrumental in denying Koreans access to foreign goods. This legacy has encouraged Koreans to believe that foreign products are of higher quality and prestige than products made in Korea. This perception of higher quality has enabled foreign brand names and manufacturers to achieve high levels of popularity (Min 2004). Yet despite the popularity of foreign products, Reid and Lee (1998) found that the percentage of foreign brands purchased in Korea was at that time still minimal. Even now there are substantial restrictions on imported luxury goods such as cars through high taxes and prevailing threats of conducting a tax audit of those with foreign products. The strong nationalism that still underscores Korean society has helped to cultivate consumer ethnocentrism, sometimes resulting in subtle campaigns urging Korean consumers to buy domestic products. Although foreign companies seeking market entry in Korea should be aware of the propensity for periodic nationalistic outbursts, they should appreciate that Korean attitudes have shifted from traditional mistrust of foreigners to appreciating foreign brands in recent decades, while young people in particular show great interest in foreign brands.[10]

4.5 DISTRIBUTION SYSTEM

Min (2004) argues that, similar to circumstances in Japan, the structure of the Korean distribution system represents a major obstacle for Western businesses attempting market entry. Foreigners' lack of understanding of Korea's distribution system is attributed to the complex and idiosyncratic nature of this system, which reflects traditional business culture and practices based on personal relationships. Distribution channels in Korea comprise a complicated network of relationship-driven retailers who are often controlled by manufacturers and trading companies. This contrasts with US distribution channels, which are open, independent and margin-driven.

As a reflection of their disproportionate contribution to Korea's long-term economic growth, manufacturers have long controlled Korean distribution channels through exclusive sales networks, vertical integration of the supply chain, and dealing through reciprocity (Min 2004). For example, in the automobile sector there are no sales outlets other than those established and controlled by manufacturers. Half of all clothing retailers offer products by a single manufacturer only. Franchises distribute around 40 per cent of Korean electronics products. In the furniture industry, manufacturers control 70 per cent of wholesale distribution (Min 2004). In the case of chaebols, all elements in the distribution chain are tied together financially as the chaebols' subsidiaries or agents, enabling chaebols to control product distribution from the factory to the consumer. This pattern of control by manufacturers creates few opportunities for outsiders and effectively locks foreign products and their producers out of the country. It is common knowledge that the operations of this type of distribution system provide a major invisible barrier to foreign firms seeking to enter the Korean market.

Even beyond manufacturer control, the Korean distribution system is notoriously complex. There are at least six different types of intermediaries along the distribution channel: trading companies, wholesalers, brokers, distribution vendors and franchisers (Min 2004). Trading companies are typically owned by chaebols and their activities involve imports, trade promotion, foreign brand licensing, government lobbying, market integration, customs clearance, information exchange and technology transfer. Additional layers of distribution, through distribution vendors, franchising stores and the like, are then involved in matching trading companies to retailers or industry buyers with a variety of products. Distribution vendors are large wholesale intermediaries that distribute a wide range of products from trading companies and manufacturers to various types of retailers irrespective of their size. Franchises or chain stores usually stock a single merchandise brand exclusively from a particular trading company or manufacturer and then sell to other retailers or directly to consumers.

Another aspect of the complexity of Korea's distribution system is an unusually large number of small retail stores, a configuration that presents a highly fragmented retail industry of undercapitalized but conveniently located stores (Min 2004). In 1996, before Korea's retail market was effectively liberalized, small 'Mom-and-Pop' stores with fewer than five employees accounted for about 80 per cent of Korea's US$116 billion retail market (J.D. Kim 2003). It is been argued that establishment of small retail stores by retirees is a response to the lack of an adequate social welfare system in Korea, forcing elderly people to continue needing an income in the absence of old-age pensions. The plethora of small retail establishments has provided stable employment for the large segment of Korean society that the government has continued to neglect (Min 2004). In particular, since the 1997 financial crisis, a large number of middle managers have been forced to retire early in their forties and fifties. Under the Korean system of human resource management, as examined in Chapter 9, these people forced into early retirement have little opportunity to return to regular employment and feel they must start operating their own business, which many do through retail stores. Another factor concerns personal preference. As Min (2004) explains, Koreans generally prefer to shop close to home, using the high levels of personalized service provided by small retailers such as free delivery, payment by installments, credit, after-hours service and help with product selection.

This complexity and fragmentation of Korea's distribution system is the main cause of distribution inefficiency. The manufacturer-dominated structure of the Korean retail industry deterred price competition and rendered inordinately high retail prices in Korea. Min (2004) estimates that in 2000, productivity in the Korean retail distribution sector was less than one-fifth of that of the US. The study by J.D. Kim (2003) of the productivity of Korea's wholesale and retail service sector in 1994, in terms of sales per establishment or per employee, found that Korea's productivity was far below that of Japan at that time.

Recently, a non-traditional distribution channel involving direct sales via discounters and membership has gained popularity among price-conscious consumers, particularly since the financial crisis. Wholesale intermediaries are making ever greater use of direct marketing strategies such as home shopping, TV shopping, online shopping, door-to-door sales, in-home parties and mail order. Direct marketing has drawbacks, however, because the free delivery that it offers means that it cannot accommodate large, perishable or very inexpensive items (Min 2004; Coe and Lee 2006).

The complexity and inefficiency of the Korean distribution system can be attributed in essence to government regulations seeking to protect this system from international competition. The Korean retail market was opened to foreigners in stages from 1989. The first stage, from 1989–91, relaxed regulations on the establishment of foreign subsidiaries in Korea and on inward FDI. From 1991 to 1993, foreign retailers were permitted to open stores of up to 1000 square meters although the absolute number of stores was limited to ten per foreign company. From 1993 to 1995, foreign companies were permitted to open up to 20 stores sized up to 3000 square meters each. By 1996, the retail market was close to fully opened to foreign companies (Min 2004; J.D. Kim 2003). After the 1997 financial crisis, the new Foreign Investment Promotion Act (1998) lifted almost all remaining regulations on FDI in the Korean retail market. The effects of the crisis on the property market enabled foreign companies to acquire retail and real estate assets at relatively cheap prices due to the sharp devaluation of the won. Until then, the high price of real estate and rent had been a major disincentive to foreign market entry (Min 2004). The WTO's ongoing Doha Development Agenda (DDA) is expected to liberalize Korea's retail market further (Min 2004).

With liberalization of the distribution sector, foreign discount stores have rushed into Korea. Eliminating restrictions on store size for both domestic and foreign firms has seen the number of super-stores increase rapidly, to reach 207 in June 2002. More than 25 per cent of these stores were established by foreign firms including Carrefour, Wal Mart, Costco and Tesco, together with a proliferation of smaller foreign retailers such as 7-Eleven, Levi Strauss and Gap (J.D. Kim 2003, p. 30). The market share of super-stores has exceeded that of department stores while the market share of traditional retail distribution channels has been steadily in decline (Lee and Choi 2004). Of the five major firms that dominate the super-store market, two are Korean – E-Mart and Lotte Mart – while three are foreign – Carrefour, Samsung-Tesco's Home Plus and Wal-Mart.[11]

The efficiency of the distribution sector has improved following liberalization. The increasing number of super-stores has continued to change the manufacturer-dominated structure of Korean retail, increasing both productivity and price competition. The increasing buying power of the super-stores has shifted price determination to the hands of retailers rather than manufacturers, which has enhanced price competition. Foreign retail firms have also transferred advanced technologies and management skills. As a result of enhanced price competition and management style, sales per employee have in general increased. The price margins of the super-stores and department stores were lowered from 17.8 per cent and 24.2 per cent in 1995, to 13.6 per cent and 21.7 per cent in 1998, respectively (J.D. Kim 2003, p. 32). It is also likely that changes in distribution patterns with the introduction of discount stores may have forced many small stores to specialize their services, and existing domestic retail firms to increase their size to take advantage of the scale effect, thereby contributing to the productivity increment of the distribution sector.

4.6 E-COMMERCE

One rapidly emerging area within the Korean market configuration is e-commerce. E-commerce has exploded in many economies, revolutionizing various business processes including retailing, marketing, production and distribution. Korea is in the midst of this e-commerce revolution. The sales value of e-commerce has expanded much faster than GDP growth in the recent past. The former amounted to 19 per cent of GDP in 2001 and increased to 40.3 per cent in 2004 (KNSO 2006a). Not only are opportunities abundant in Korea for foreign companies to engage in e-commerce activities, but foreign companies can also reduce trade-related costs and increase productivity by undertaking e-trade with Korea.

As shown in Table 4.5, the value of e-commerce in Korea increased from 119 trillion won in 2001 to 314 trillion won in 2004, an average annual growth rate of 38.2 per cent. Business-to-business (B2B) transactions dominate the Internet economy. They accounted for 89 per cent in 2004 and grew at 36.8 per cent over the 2001–04 period. Business-to-government transactions (B2G) accounted for the second-largest proportion of 8.9 per cent in 2004, with a huge average annual growth rate of 57.2 per cent. This figure reflects recent government reforms to enhance the transparency and efficiency of its services and regulatory systems. Business-to-consumer (B2C) transactions comprised the small proportion of 2.1 per cent, but increased at a substantial average annual growth rate of 35.7 per cent over the period. Consumer-to-consumer (C2C) transactions, which are business auctions conducted on sites like eBay, accounted for less than 1 per cent over this period.

Table 4.5 Trends in Korean e-commerce (2001–04) (billion won)

	2001	2002	2003	2004	%*
Total	118 976	177 810	235 025	314 079	38.2
By type					
Business to business	108 941	155 707	206 854	279 399	36.9
Business to government	7 037	16 632	21 634	27 349	57.2
Business to consumer	2 580	50 473	6 095	6 443	35.7
Other	418	427	442	888	28.5
By sector (B2B)					
Manufacturing	86 989	117 974	146 162	197 102	31.3
Utilities	815	1 070	2 289	3 657	64.9
Construction	4 438	5 774	9 664	16 097	53.6
Wholesale and retail trade	14 195	25 730	41 117	51 421	53.6
Transport and commun- ication	2 015	3 721	4 690	6 306	46.3
Other services	489	1 438	2 931	4 816	114.3
By method (B2B)					
Internet	97 321	147 419	199 448	273 563	41.1
Non-Internet	11 710	8 288	7 406	5 836	–20.7

Note: *Annual average percentage growth rate, 2001–04.

Source: Korea National Statistical Office (KSNO) (2006a).

In terms of B2B transactions, the manufacturing sector was the leader in e-commerce transactions between 2001 and 2004, followed by wholesale and retail trade, and then by the construction sector. Table 4.5 data indicates that the Internet is the primary vehicle for e-trade and e-commerce with both growth and volume outstripping other methods of e-commerce. Major commodities transacted through e-commerce include home electronic appliances and telecommunications equipment, computer and computer-related appliances, travel arrangements and reservation services, fashion clothing and related goods (KNSO 2006a, p. 502).

Lee et al. (2003) explained that the leading sectors in B2C transactions are stock trading and Internet banking, and other than the use of retail financial services, there is little evidence of substantial B2C e-commerce in Korea.[12] John and Gorman (2002) pointed out that by March 2002, all domestic and international banks and the Post Office were offering online services, including access to personal banking details, electronic funds transfers, paying bills and credit card loans. The number of Koreans using these online services increased remarkably to exceed 12 million by March 2002, and the number of financial transactions increased by 198 per cent over one year to March 2002 (John and Gorman 2002). Stocks traded online accounted for 66.4 per cent of total stocks traded in 2001, rising to 70 per cent in 2002. The corresponding figure in 1998 was just 3 per cent (Cha et al. 2005). John and Gorman (2002) concluded that growth in e-commerce in financial services is unlikely to slow for some time, but they also forecast a dramatic uptake in Internet-based B2C services in other sectors in the short term.

E-trade has also been actively promoted in Korea, a country with heavy reliance on international trade, as a way to reinforce trade competitiveness. Korea has a high-cost trade structure, basically due to high auxiliary expenses (KITA 2007). E-trade is a way to reduce auxiliary expenses.[13] It has been claimed that auxiliary trade expenses can be reduced by 80 per cent if trade is conducted electronically. Also, the time required to process a trade order from opening a letter of credit to products being cleared through customs can be reduced from four weeks to one (*Business Korea* 2001). In 2000, 18.7 per cent of total Korean exports worth approximately USUS$32.3 billion were handled electronically (KOTRA 2002). This was an increase of 50 per cent from the previous year. Growth in import and export trade via the Internet has been induced largely by government initiatives, in particular through promotion policies and the provision of infrastructure to enable trade (KOTRA 2002). Korea also established the e-Trade Promotion Council under the Ministry of Science and Technology to support the establishment of e-trade infrastructure (KITA 2007).

E-commerce in Korea has grown at an exponential rate due to a number of factors. Internet usage has expanded remarkably in Korea. In 2000, 19 million Koreans used the Internet, accounting for 39.6 per cent of the total population. The number of Internet users increased to 34 million in January 2007, reaching an Internet penetration rate of 67 per cent of the population.

Korea's Internet penetration rate in 2007 was the fourth-highest in the world after Australia, the US and Japan.[14] The rapid increase in the number of Internet users is partly attributable to government policy. To create an environment conducive to e-commerce, the government introduced not only a nationwide education campaign, but also a personal computer (PC) subsidy program that resulted in approximately 1 million Korean households purchasing desktop PCs relatively cheaply (Michael and Sutherland 2002).

A high number of broadband subscriptions has also contributed to the rapid growth of e-commerce. The broadband subscriber rate per 100 inhabitants increased from 17.2 per cent in 2001 to 25.4 per cent in 2005, compared to the OECD average of 15.5 per cent in 2005. In 2006, Korea's subscriber rate grew to 26.2 per cent, as compared to 19.2 per cent in the US and 19 per cent in Japan. In 2006, Korea ranked fourth in the world in subscriber rate after Denmark, the Netherlands and Iceland (OECD 2006).

The Korean government established the national strategy for promoting e-business in 2001 to build e-business networks across industries, strengthen the participation of the public sector, expand the e-business operating base, and globalize the scope of e-business. In line with this strategy, the government has advanced the infrastructure of e-commerce to achieve efficient information communication networks, technology development, and standardization. Korea's telecommunications sector has been steadily liberalized and privatized since the 1980s. From the mid-1990s, the government has pursued a policy promoting establishment of high-speed telecommunication infrastructure as a foundation to build the 'knowledge-based society' (Lee et al. 2003). A number of plans were implemented progressively to construct an advanced nationwide information infrastructure consisting of communications networks, Internet services, application software, computers, and information products and services.

Government policy has also contributed to the growth of e-commerce by adopting a 'hands-off' policy on regulating market entry for Internet services. Any business seeking to provide high-speed Internet access and other online services has been allowed unrestricted entry to the market after a simple registration procedure. The government has also stimulated competition by publicizing the services provided by firms operating in the sector. Demand among the population has also been promoted by concerted government action. IT literacy programs have targeted housewives, the elderly, military personnel, farmers, disabled people and low-income families (Lee et al. 2003). Lee et al. (2003) argue that social pressure to 'keep up with the neighbours', in addition to the traditional Korean emphasis on education, has also helped to increase demand for Internet services. However, as Lee et al. (2003) point out, such strong demand in a deregulated environment has produced too many service providers for the market size and caused overlapping investment, leading to expectations that the industry will undergo restructuring.

The Korean government has attempted to encourage e-commerce through provision of legal and institutional support. It has recognized that consumers need to be protected from commercial fraud, unfair business practices and misleading or fraudulent advertisements and has taken necessary action to help develop the new industry. The government has also set in place institutional frameworks to sustain proper electronic approval processes, e-payment and dispute settlement systems, and protection of intellectual property rights and personal information. It has established necessary Acts and regulations in accordance with global legislation that was put in place very recently (MOCIE 2003).

Although there are some areas of concern, the prospects of e-commerce in Korea are bright. The biggest problem in Korea's regulatory environment for e-commerce is the considerable overlap between responsible ministries. Two ministries (the Ministry of Commerce, Industry and Energy, and the Ministry of Science and Technology) and a large number of Acts are directly involved in the administration of e-commerce. Nonetheless, the technical and regulatory infrastructure for e-commerce is well established, the government promotes e-commerce as a strategic industry consistent with its drive toward a knowledge-based economy, and consumers are inspired to join the e-commerce bandwagon. It is thus very likely that e-commerce in Korea will continue to boom and in the process induce further transformation of the way business is conducted in Korea. Choi and Suh (2004) project that e-commerce will rapidly increase in scale to account for more than 30 per cent of private sector consumption expenditure within the next 30 years. Already there are strong opportunities for foreign firms in e-retailing in the B2C sector through providing electronic infrastructure for the industry and in conducting e-trade in the B2B sector.

4.7 CONCLUSION

This chapter has analyzed a broad range of information on Korea's market configuration from 1990 to the present from the perspective of export market screening. The period under consideration coincides with Korea's efforts to open the national economy, integrate with the global economy, and move from a manufacturing to a knowledge-based economy. During this period of rapid and major change, which included the 1997 financial crisis and responses to it, Korea's market configuration has been in a process of transition. This chapter has identified a number of trends in the evolving configuration of Korea's import market.

Over the period from 1995 to 2005, Korea's total imports increased rapidly at 9.2 per cent per year, substantially higher than the 7.6 per cent growth rate of GDP in US dollars. This indicates that Korea's overall demand for imports is quite income-elastic, suggesting rising market potential for foreign products. The Korean economy has moved away from traditional manufacturing and agriculture toward services and information industries (as explored in Chapter 1). The Korean economy is heavily reliant not only on foreign minerals, energy and agricultural products, but also on heavy industrial, capital and high-technology products, because its key technologies lag behind those of other advanced countries. This is borne out by Korea's strong import demands for these products. Although relatively small, the size of the Korean market for imported consumer goods amounts to about US$26 billion a year and continues to rise. As the Korean agricultural sector has stagnated, the food self-sufficiency ratio declined from 53.6 per cent in 1990 to 37.5 per cent in 2004. During this period, agricultural imports increased accordingly. In contrast, the service sector has expanded over time particularly rapidly in Korea. Imports of services – including education, insurance, transport and travel – have increased significantly since 1990 in line with liberalization of the Korean economy.

In recent years Korea has also undertaken liberalization of the nation's trade regime. The requirements for Korea to gain membership of the WTO and OECD, and soon thereafter the unforeseen consequences of the 1997 financial crisis, were all important drivers of the reform and liberalization. From 1998, the service sector has been liberalized and import levels have grown considerably. As of 2001, 99.9 per cent of the Korean economy was opened to trade, with a 99 per cent liberalization rate for the agricultural sector. Since 1998, tariffs have been reduced, prohibited subsidies have been eliminated, customs clearance procedures have been streamlined, and transparency improved in trade-related areas. From the mid-1990s, Korea has also explored free trade agreements with a number of countries, particularly in East Asia. Korea has already established FTAs with Chile, Singapore and the four-member European Free Trade Association (EFTA). FTA negotiations and joint studies are under way with a number of countries.

The potential of the Korean market has been assessed in this chapter by analyzing consumer trends and behavior for which demographic trends, changes in social structure, and culture have important implications. Demographic change is an important trend in Korea's market configuration. Korea's population remains static at about 48 million, while the growth rate has declined to less than 0.5 per cent. The most striking trend in the demographic data is Korea's rapidly ageing population, which expands the demand for goods and services for the elderly. The size of the middle class has increased relative to the total population. With rising disposable income, those in the middle class seek activities for leisure and pleasure such as playing golf and foreign tours. They are keen to have the best possible education for their children, including study abroad. The social position of women has been changing, particularly as their participation in the labor force has risen steadily and enhances their economic status in the domestic sphere as well as in society at large. Women are generally still responsible for looking after their families including children's education, despite their involvement in the paid workforce. They are thus still the major shoppers and have a strong voice in family financial matters.

Another trend in Korea's market configuration is the influence of Korean culture. Despite major changes in the recent past, Korean society retains a strong Confucian tradition, and social stratification and hierarchical collectivism still prevail to a significant degree across Korean society at large. In Korea's status- and face-conscious hierarchical society, Korean people attempt to maintain or enhance their status and prestige through conspicuous consumption of products with brand names. The group conformity of Korean collectivism together with brand consciousness make international trends in fashion particularly influential in Korea.

Another important aspect of Korea's market configuration is the structure of the nation's distribution system, which for a long time was a major obstacle to foreign businesses seeking market entry. Korea has a complicated distribution system characterized by manufacturer control of distribution channels and with a large number of intermediaries in the distribution channels. The Korean distribution sector has been liberalized since the financial crisis, and the retail market has been opened to foreign competition. A number of large foreign retailers have entered the market. Foreign and domestically owned super-stores are gaining market share at the expense of numerous small local businesses, and these developments have improved both productivity and price competition within the distribution sector.

One remarkable trend in Korea's market configuration is the rapid rise of e-commerce. In line with Korea's transition away from manufacturing toward a knowledge-based economy, businesses and consumers are becoming much more technology focused, and e-commerce has expanded accordingly. Presently, the bulk of e-commerce transactions are B2B and B2G, with growth in B2C transactions particularly strong in the financial sector. Korea is the world leader in take-up of high-speed broadband Internet services, and the technical and regulatory infrastructure required for e-commerce is now well established. Thus, e-commerce is highly likely to expand further, and in the process will help to transform the paradigm of business practices. These circumstances present strong business opportunities for foreign firms involved in this area.

As this chapter has made clear, the Korean market has great potential for foreign exports, with many new trends emerging over time. Since the late 1990s, the Korean market has opened more widely to foreign products. In particular, the Korean markets for capital and high-technology products as well as minerals, energy and agricultural products are highly promising. Added to this are rising markets for foreign services. Foreign companies can participate in seizing the bounty of opportunities now available in Korea through the traditional trade approach or through e-trade, with strong prospects for benefit if market screening has been conducted thoroughly.

NOTES

1. Korea as a target country for FDI is dealt with in Chapter 5.
2. The second stage of market screening, which involves assessments of financial and economic conditions, is addressed in Chapter 1.
3. Song and Noh (2006) argue that although Korea may have reached near parity with the other advanced industrial countries in manufacturing and production technologies, key technologies in heavy and high-technology industries continue to lag behind. They found that Korean R&D expenditure has been concentrated in short-term product development programs rather than in industrial development capabilities and that Korean enterprises in the high-technology field emphasized marketing skills over technical skills in new product development.
4. Applications can be made to import restricted goods and these require a case-by-case screening and approval process (KOTRA 2006).
5. Yeo et al. (2004) argue that the most significant and meaningful liberalization measures since 1996 have been introduced in the service sector.
6. Beghin et al. (2003) argue firmly that Korea has maintained a commitment to agricultural deregulation, although data revealing the extent of institutionalized agricultural regulation substantially undermine their contention.
7. Mansourov (2005) argues that the stall in the Korea–Japan FTA negotiation is at least partly attributable to Japan's official failure to acknowledge its legacy of colonizing Korea, as manifested in visits by the Japanese Prime Minister to the Yasukuni Shrine commemorating Japan's war dead, and the ongoing dispute over the content of Japanese history textbooks.
8. A recent survey shows that 60 per cent of housewives claimed they preferred to stay at home to look after their children and other household matters (http://blog.naver.com/neobrain2004/10003836960, accessed 12 February 2007).
9. For further details of Korean culture in relation to business in Korea, see Chapter 3.
10. An exploratory study by Chung and Pysarchik (2000) found that among the younger generation of Korean consumers, their purchase of imported products was not influenced significantly by Confucian cultural appreciation but was based simply on utilitarian calculations of price and quality.
11. For further information on foreign super-stores, see Lee and Choi (2004) and Coe and Lee (2006).
12. Michael and Sutherland (2002, p. 28) note that financial services are the dominant B2C transactions within the Asia-Pacific.
13. With completion of the e-trade system in 2005, Korea is able to save an estimated US$14.5 billion in auxiliary trade expenses – 24.5 per cent of total trade expenses (KITA 2007).
14. Internet World Statistics (2007).

REFERENCES

Austrade (2004), 'Korea profile', http://www.austrade.gov.au/australia/layout/0,,0_S2-1_CLNTXID0019-2_-3_PWB177063-4_doingbusiness-5_-6_7_,00.html.

Ball, Donald A., McCulloch Jr, Wendell H., Frantz, Paul L., Geringer, J. Michael and Michael S. Minor (2002), *International Business: The Challenge of Global Competition*, 8th edn, New York: McGraw-Hill Irwin.

Bank of Korea (2006a), 'Economic statistics', http://ecos.bok.or.kr/EIndex_en.jsp.

Bank of Korea (2006b), *Quarterly National Accounts*, 27 (4).

Beghin, John C., Jean-Christopher Bureau and Sung Joon Park (2003), 'Food security and agricultural protection in South Korea', *American Journal of Agricultural Economics*, 85 (3), 618–32.

Business Korea (2001), 'Removing the e-trade barriers', Seoul, 18 (11), 48–50.

Cha, Soon Kwean, Minho Kim and Ronald McNiel (2005), 'Diffusion of Internet-based financial transactions among customers in South Korea', *Journal of Global Marketing*, 19 (2), 95–111.

Choi, Yeong C. and Hi-youl Suh (2004), 'A taxation model: the Korean value added tax on electronic commerce', *Review of Business*, 25 (2), 43–50.

Chung, Jae-Eun and Pysarchik, Dawn T. (2000), 'A model of behavioural intention to buy domestic versus imported products in a Confucian culture', *Marketing Intelligence and Planning*, 18 (5), 281–91.

CIA (2006), 'CIA World Factbook, 2006', http://www.photius.com/rankings/economy/imports_2006_1.html.

Coe, Neil M. and Yong-Sook Lee (2006), 'The strategic localization of transnational retailers: the case of Samsung-Tesco in South Korea', *Economic Geography*, 82 (1), 61–88.

The Economist Intelligence Unit (EIU) (2003), *Country Commerce Report: South Korea*.

Hong, Doo-Seung (2003), 'Social change and stratification', in Doh Chull Shin, Conrad P. Rutowski and Chong-Min Park (eds), *The Quality of Life in Korea: Comparative and Dynamic Perspectives*, Dordrecht, Netherlands: Kluwer Academic Publishers, pp. 39–50.

Internet World Statistics (2007), 'Korea, Internet usage stats and marketing report, Internet world statistics', www.internetworldstats.com/asia/kr.htm.

Kang, Hye-Ryun and Chris Rowley (2005), 'Women in management in South Korea: advancement or retrenchment', *Asia Pacific Business Review*, 11 (2), 213–31.

Kim, June-Dong (2003), *Inward Foreign Direct Investment into Korea: Recent Performance and Future Agenda*, Seoul: Korea Institute for International Economic Policy.

Kim, June-Dong and Jong-Il Kim (2003), 'Korea's liberalization of trade in services and its impacts on productivity', in O.Y. Kwon, S.H. Jaw and K.T. Lee (eds), *Korea's New Economic Strategy in the Globalization Era*, Cheltenham, UK and Northampton, MA, USA: Edward Elgar Publishing, pp. 63–79.

Kim, Young-Han (2005), ,The optimal path of regional economic integration between asymmetric countries in the North East Asia', *Journal of Policy Modeling*, 27 (6), 673–87.

KITA (2007), 'E-trade in Korea', http://global.kita.net.

KLI (Korea Labor Institute) (2006), *Labour Statistics 2006*, Seoul: Korea Labor Institute.

Korea National Statistical Office (KNSO) (2005*)*, *Korea Statistical Yearbook 2004*, Seoul: KNSO.

Korea National Statistical Office (KNSO) (2006a), *Korea Statistical Yearbook 2005*, Seoul: KNSO.

Korea National Statistical Office (KNSO) (2006b), *Population, Household*, http://kosis.nso.go.kr.

KOTRA (2002), 'General trade information: current status of e-trade, http://www.kotra.or.kr/eng/file/sub2_5.jsp.

KOTRA (2006), 'General trade information: current status of exports and imports', http://www.kotra.or.kr/eng/file/sub2_1.jsp.

Kwon, O.Y. and Chang Yong Kang (2000), *Recent Developments in Korean Agriculture: Implications for Australia*, Brisbane, Australia: Griffith University.

Kwon, Tai-Hwan (2003), 'Demographic trends and their social implications', in Doh Chull Shin, Conrad P. Rutowski and Chong-Min Park (eds), *The Quality of Life in Korea: Comparative and Dynamic Perspectives*, Dordrecht, Netherlands: Kluwer Academic Publishers, pp. 19–38.

John, Yong J. and G.E. Gorman (2002), 'Internet use in South Korea', *Online Information Review*, 26 (5), 335–44.

Korea Rural Economic Institute (2005), *2004 Food Balance Sheet*, Seoul: Korea Rural Economic Institute (KREI).

Lee, Heejin, Robert M. O'Keefe and Kyounglim Yun (2003), 'The growth of broadband and electronic commerce in South Korea: contributing factors', *The Information Society*, 18, 81–93.

Lee, Jung-Hee and Sang-Chul Choi (2004), 'The effects of liberalization in retail markets on economy and retail industry in Korea', *Journal of Global Marketing*, 18 (1/2), 121–31.

Lee, Namchul (2005), 'Human capital accumulation and labor force participation in Korean women', *Journal of the America Academy of Business*, 7 (2), 63–8.

Lett, Denise P. (1998), *In Pursuit of Status: The Making of South Korea's 'New' Urban Middle Class*, Cambridge, MA and London: Harvard University Asia Center.

McNicoll, Gregory (2006), 'Policy lessons of the East Asian demographic transition', *Population and Development Review*, 32 (1), 1–25.

Mansourov, Alexandre Y. (2005), 'Northeast Asian vortex: regional change, global implications', *Korean Observer*, 36 (3), 511–52.

Michael, D. and G. Sutherland (2002), *Asia's Digital Dividends: How Asia-Pacific's Corporations can Create Value from E-business*, Singapore: John Wiley & Sons.

Min, Hokey (2004), 'The Korean distribution system: an overview with implications for Korean market entry', *Journal of Marketing Channels*, 12 (2), 5–25.

MOCIE (Ministry of Commerce, Industry and Energy) (2003), 'E-commerce in Korea', Ministry of Commerce Industry and Energy, http://www.mocie.go.kr/eng/policies/ecommerce/ecommerce1.asp.

OECD (2006), 'OECD broadband statistics to June 2006', www.oecd.org/document/9/0,2340,en_2649_34223_37529673_1.

OECD (2006), 'OECD statistics', http://www.oecd.org/statsportal/.

OECD (2007), 'OECD statistics', http://stats.oecd.org/wbos/default.aspx?datasetcode=TIS.

Park, Chang-Gun (2006), 'Japan's emerging role in promoting regional integration in East Asia: towards an East Asian integration regime (EAIR)', *Journal of International and Area Studies*, 13 (1), 53–72.

Reid, D. and Y. Lee (1998), 'Strategic business development in South Korea: a post-IMF crisis perspective', *Financial Times Business*, Singapore.

Rhyu, Sang-young and Seungjoo Lee (2006), 'Changing dynamics in Korea–Japan economic relations: policy ideas and development strategies', *Asian Survey*, 46 (2), 195–214.

Robinson, Richard and David Goodman (1996), *The New Rich in Asia: Mobile Phones, McDonald's and Middle-class Revolution*, London: Routledge, pp. 187–91.

Rugman, A.M. and R.M. Hodgetts (1995), *International Business: A Strategic Management Approach*, New York: McGraw-Hill.

Sagaza, Haruo (2004), 'Population ageing in the Asia-Oceanic region', *Geriatrics and Gerontology International*, 4, S34–S37.

Song, Michael and Jeonpyo Noh (2006), 'Best new product development and management practices in the Korean high-tech industry', *Industrial Marketing Management*, 35, 262–78.
World Trade Organization (WTO) (2006), 'Regional trade agreements: facts and figures', http://www.wto.org/english/tratop_e/region_e/summary_e.xls.
Yeo, Taekdong, Young Man Yoon and Kar-yiu Wong (2004), 'Post-crisis foreign trade and foreign investment in Korea: Korea's recovery and challenges ahead', in Charles Harvey, Hyun-Hoon Lee and Junggun Oh (eds), *The Korean Economy: Post-Crisis Policies, Issues and Prospects*, Cheltenham, UK and Northampton, MA, USA: Edward Elgar Publishing, pp. 197–220.
Yoo, Chul Ho (2003), 'Korea's agricultural strategy in the globalization era', in O.Y Kwon, S.H. Jaw and K.T. Lee (eds), *Korea's New Economic Strategy in the Globalization Era*, Cheltenham, UK and Northampton, MA, USA: Edward Elgar Publishing, pp. 133–54.
Yoo, Gyeongjoon (2003), 'Women in the workplace: gender and wage differentials', in Doh Chull Sin, Conrad P. Rutowski and Chong-Min Park (eds), *The Quality of Life in Korea: Comparative and Dynamic Perspectives*, Dordrecht, Netherlands: Kluwer Academic Publishers, pp. 367–85.

5. Foreign direct investment in Korea: changes in the regime and prospects

5.1 INTRODUCTION

Until the 1997 financial crisis, Korea was regarded as the worst place to invest among Asian countries (Booz.Allan & Hamilton 1997, p. 28; *Far Eastern Economic Review* 1998). To protect domestic industries Korea restricted incoming foreign direct investment (FDI) by placing on investors a heavy burden of laws and regulations. A number of sectors were closed to FDI by law until the early 1990s. Even in those areas where FDI was permitted, the administrative regulations and procedures for FDI were complex and lacked transparency. Other aspects of Korea's economic structure, society and culture were not conducive to incoming FDI either. The labor market lacked flexibility, thereby raising labor costs to one of the highest among Asia's newly industrialized countries (NICs). The real estate sector was closed to foreigners and overhead costs were among the highest in Asia (Cha 2001; Jwa and Yi 2001; Kwon 2001).

The formal restrictions on FDI and environmental disincentives were reflected in the flagging level of FDI in Korea. According to the United Nations Conference on Trade and Development (UNCTAD's) *World Investment Report 2002*, inward FDI in Korea over the 1990–97 period amounted to less than 1 per cent (0.96 per cent) of its gross fixed capital formation, while the proportions for the world and East Asian countries were 4.7 per cent and 7.4 per cent, respectively. The inward FDI stock in Korea as a percentage of current GDP in 1995 was 2 per cent, compared to the proportions of 10 per cent and 18.9 per cent for the world and East Asia respectively (UNCTAD 2002).

Since 1997, however, Korea has liberalized the FDI regime up to the level of other OECD countries and switched its policy emphasis on FDI from 'restriction and control' to 'promotion and assistance'. Korean society and the business community as well as the government have sought to improve the Korean business environment. As of 2002, 99.8 per cent of all business sectors were open to foreign investment – a level on par with that of other OECD economies (Sohn et al. 2002). The labor market was reformed to improve its flexibility, and the real estate sector has been opened to foreigners. The government has streamlined the complicated administrative procedures for FDI by dismantling or relaxing more than 50 per cent of restrictions (Kwon 2001). In addition, it has introduced the so-called 'one-stop' service system for inward FDI. As a result, FDI in Korea increased substantially over the three-year period from 1998 to 2000.

Notwithstanding the rapid increases in FDI over the three-year period (1998–2000), the magnitude of FDI in Korea is still small by international comparison. Furthermore, as shown shortly, FDI in Korea fell sharply for the three consecutive years from 2001 to 2003, and then increased in 2004. In particular, Korea fared relatively poorly in attracting FDI as compared to the world and East Asia. The Korean government has undertaken a series of policy measures in an apparent all-out effort to attract FDI. How, then, should this relatively low magnitude of FDI in Korea and recent sharp declines be explained? What additional or alternative measures should the Korean government undertake to increase FDI inflows to a level comparable internationally? This chapter attempts to address these vexing questions.

In order to grasp the seriousness of the issues under consideration, section 5.2 examines recent developments and major characteristics of FDI in Korea in light of global trends in FDI. This is to identify trends in FDI inflows which would in turn suggest some factors underlying the sluggish FDI in Korea. As several studies in the literature stress the importance of host-government policies in determining the quantity and quality of FDI (Stoever 2005), there is no doubt that government policy has been the most critical factor for FDI in Korea. Thus, an overview of the FDI regime and its changes after the 1997 crisis is provided in section 5.3. Section 5.4 includes a broad exploration of the literature in both English and Korean to identify causes of the sluggish FDI inflows in the recent past.

Although a number of studies are available in the literature on FDI in Korea (Kim and Choo 2002; Kim and Kim 2003; Kim 2003; Sohn et al. 2002; Cherry 2006; Stoever 2005; Thurbon and Weiss 2006), most of these were undertaken by Korean scholars in Korea from a domestic perspective, or by foreign scholars from an academic perspective largely based on secondary sources of information. There is no in-depth study of the issue from the perspective of foreign business people who have actually undertaken FDI or operate business in Korea. The views of foreign business people who have investment and business experience in Korea are critically important because it is these people that Korea must convince if it seeks to attract FDI. It is thus important to investigate the recent developments of FDI in Korea from the perspectives of foreign investors and business expatriates. To this end, Kwon (2004) has conducted a comprehensive survey of business people in Korea. Major findings of this study are included in section 5.5 and compared with the factors identified in the literature for the sluggish FDI in Korea in the recent past. Finally, section 5.6 contains conclusions of the study and recommends strategies for attracting FDI in Korea.

5.2   RECENT DEVELOPMENTS IN FDI IN KOREA

Inflows of FDI in Korea have increased remarkably since the 1997 crisis in response to the liberalization of the FDI regime and improvements in the business environment. As shown in Table 5.1, FDI in Korea leaped from US$2.8 billion in 1997 to US$5.4 billion in 1998, and further to US$9.3 billion in both 1999 and 2000. However, the magnitude of FDI in Korea is still small when compared to other countries, indicating a low contribution of FDI to the Korean economy. In 2000, FDI in Korea accounted for 7.1 per cent of gross fixed capital formation, while the corresponding figures for the world and East Asia were 20.8 per cent and 14.8 per cent respectively (Table 5.1). In the same year, the ratio of FDI stock to GDP was 8 per cent in Korea, while it was 19.6 per cent and 37 per cent, respectively, for the world and East Asia (Table 5.2).

Furthermore, as shown in Table 5.1, FDI in Korea fell sharply in 2001 and remained sluggish until 2003. During this three-year period (2001–03), the FDI ratio to gross fixed capital formation also declined and was remarkably lower than those for the world and East Asia. Similarly, the ratio of FDI stock to GDP was also markedly lower than the corresponding ratios for the world and East Asia (Tables 5.1 and 5.2). In 2004, FDI increased to US$7.7 billion (Table 5.1). Nonetheless, FDI in Korea amounted to 3.8 per cent of gross fixed capital formation in 2004, while the corresponding figures for the world and East Asia were, respectively, 7.5 per cent and 9.7 per cent (Table 5.1). The ratio of FDI stock to GDP was 8.1 per cent in Korea as of 2004, compared to 21.7 per cent and 26.2 per cent, respectively, for the world and East Asia.

FDI in Korea played only a minor role in increasing the levels of value added and employment. In 1999, the level of value added by foreign affiliates as a percentage of GDP was 3.1 per cent in Korea compared to 18.4 per cent on average in 33 developing countries. In the same year, employment of foreign affiliates accounted for only 2.2 per cent of total employment in Korea, while the ratio was 4.8 per cent for the average of 33 developing countries (UNCTAD 2002, p. 275).[1]

Korea has attracted less FDI than could be expected given the size of its national economy. In recent years the UNCTAD has put forward an inward FDI performance index, which is the ratio of a country's share in global FDI flows to its share in global GDP. Countries with an index value greater than 1 attract more FDI than may be expected on the basis of relative GDP. According to this index, Korea scored poorly – one of the lowest scores in East Asia. The values for Korea were 0.5 and 0.6, respectively, for the 1988–90 and 1998–2000 periods, ranking it 93rd and 87th among 140 countries over the respective periods (UNCTAD 2002, p. 25). In the 1998–2000 period, Korea ranked the third-lowest among East Asian countries, followed by Taiwan and Japan. The FDI performance index for Korea increased more or less steadily to 1.09 in 2004, ranking 109th among 140 countries. However, East Asia outperformed Korea significantly with an index of 1.821 in 2004 (Table 5.3).

Table 5.1 FDI inflows in Korea and East Asian countries (US$ billion and %)

	1990–96 (average)	1997	1998	1999	2000	2001	2002	2003	2004
FDI (US$ billion)									
Korea	1.2	2.8	5.4	9.3	9.3	3.5	3.0	3.8	7.7
World	253.8	478.1	686.0	1079.1	1393.0	823.8	716.1	632.6	648.1
East Asia*	51.8	96.3	90.1	105.3	138.7	97.6	86.3	94.7	137.7
FDI/GI (%)**									
Korea	0.9	1.7	5.7	8.3	7.1	3.1	1.9	2.1	3.8
World	4.4	7.4	10.9	16.5	20.8	12.8	10.6	8.3	7.5
East Asia	7.1	10.0	11.0	12.2	14.8	10.3	8.2	7.7	9.7

Notes:
* East Asia includes South, East and Southeast Asia.
** GI denotes gross fixed capital formation.

Source: UNCTAD (2005).

Table 5.2 Inward FDI stocks as a percentage of gross domestic product (%)

	1980	1985	1990	1995	2000	2001	2002	2004
Korea	2.1	2.3	2.1	1.9	8.1	9.5	9.2	8.1
World	6.7	8.4	9.3	10.3	18.3	21.2	22.3	21.7
East Asia	27.9	24.9	20.9	21.1	30.7	37.2	37.9	26.2

Source: UNCTAD (2005).

Table 5.3 Inward FDI performance index and potential index

	1990	2000	2001	2002	2003	2004
Korea's performance	0.81	0.93	0.98	1.09	1.16	1.09
Korea's potential	21	19	19	19	20	–
East Asia's performance	–	1.193	–	–	1.523	1.821

Source: UNCTAD (2002, 2005).

Korea has clearly failed to attract FDI to its full potential. According to the UNCTAD inward FDI potential index, estimated through a set of key measurable factors that are expected to affect inward FDI, Korea fared reasonably well, ranking 19th and 18th, respectively, among 140 countries in the periods 1988–90 and 1998–2000, although Korea's ranking declined slightly to 20th in 2003.[2] By comparing the rankings on the performance and potential indices of inward FDI, the UNCTAD designates Korea as one of the 'below-potential economies', with a weak FDI performance because of government policy, a tradition of low reliance on FDI, political and social factors, and weak international competitiveness (UNCTAD 2002, p. 32).

Another aspect of FDI in Korea is that foreign affiliates do not undertake significant R&D activities in Korea as compared to its total business R&D expenditure. As shown in Table 5.4, over the five-year period from 1998 to 2002, foreign affiliates contributed to total business R&D expenditure in Korea by only 1.38 per cent. Over the same period the corresponding figure for China was 20.5 per cent (UNCTAD 2005).[3] In this respect, Korea fares poorly compared with Japan. Over the 1998–2001 period, R&D expenditure by foreign affiliates amounted to 1.33 per cent of total business R&D expenditure in Korea, compared to the corresponding figure of 3.2 per cent in Japan (UNCTAD 2005). Part of the benefit of FDI to the host economy is the diffusion of advanced technology through the R&D activities of foreign MNEs in the host country (Cherry 2006). In this respect, the contribution of FDI to the Korean economy would be of a relatively small extent.

In summary, on the basis of the World Investment Reports by the UNCTAD, Korea has performed quite poorly in attracting FDI, compared to East Asia and the world. Except for a couple of years following the 1997 financial crisis, FDI inflows in Korea have remained sluggish in recent years and, as compared to domestic gross investment and GDP, have been significantly less than those of neighboring countries in East Asia and the world. This indicates that Korea has clearly failed to attract FDI to its full potential. Contributions of FDI to domestic value added and employment were relatively low in Korea. Similarly, contributions of FDI to R&D are relatively less in Korea than in China and Japan.

The trend of FDI inflows based on a notification (approval) basis is consistent with the trend of FDI inflows on an arrival basis that is shown in Table 5.1. As shown in Table 5.5, which is comprised of FDI data on a notification basis from the Korean Ministry of Commerce, Industry and Energy (MOCIE), FDI in Korea rose from US$3.2 billion in 1996 to US$7 billion in 1997, continued to increase to US$15.5 billion in 1999, and then slightly declined to US$15.2 billion in 2000. It then declined remarkably in the next three consecutive years (2001–03) to US$6.5 billion in 2003. Finally, FDI inflows increased to US$12.8 billion and US$11.6 billion, respectively, in 2004 and 2005.

*Table 5.4 R&D expenditure by foreign affiliates to total business R&D
expenditure, 1997–2003: Korea, China and Japan (%)*

	1997	1998	1999	2000	2001	2002	2003
Korea	0.4	0.5	1.5	1.6	1.7	1.6	–
China	–	18.0	19.2	21.6	21.7	22.0	23.7
Japan	1.3	1.7	3.9	3.6	3.4	–	–

Source: UNCTAD (2005).

In terms of industries, more than 60 per cent of FDI in Korea was traditionally undertaken in the manufacturing sector (Table 5.5). Over the three-year period 1998–2000 immediately following the crisis, FDI in the manufacturing sector took more than half of the total due to 'fire sale' of assets immediately following the crisis. However, since then the FDI share in the manufacturing sector has declined, while that in the services sector has increased. Over the five-year period 2001–05, in particular, the service sector accounted on average for about 67 per cent of FDI, while the FDI share of the manufacturing sector declined to 30 per cent. Lately, FDI has been mainly concentrated in finance and insurance, electronics, wholesale and retail sales, industrial services, telecommunications and automobiles (MOFE 2006). In particular, FDI in finance and insurance accounted for 24.8 per cent and 33.9 per cent of the total FDI inflows, respectively, in 2004 and 2005 (KIEP 2006). It should be noted that decreases in FDI in the manufacturing sector over the 2001–03 period accounted for almost all the decreases in FDI in Korea. This may reflect the structural change in the Korean economy and the opening of the service sector after the financial crisis. At the same time, the decline in FDI in the manufacturing sector may indicate the loss of international competitiveness of the sector in the recent past. Primary industries – agriculture, fisheries and mining – have continued to attract an insignificant amount of FDI, except for 2002.

Table 5.5 FDI by industry on a notification basis (US$ million and %)

	1962–95	1997	1998	1999	2000	2001	2002	2003	2004	2005
Primary industries	60	55	179	54	3	7	16	6	1	3
	(0.3)	(0.9)	(2.0)	(0.3)		(0.1)	(0.2)	(0.1)	(–)	(–)
Manufacturing	10 616	2 348	5 735	7 129	6 649	2 911	2 337	1 698	6 217	3 076
	(60.1)	(33.7)	(64.8)	(45.9)	(43.7)	(25.8)	(26.7)	(26.2)	(48.6)	(26.6)
Services	6 998	4 568	2 938	8 359	8 565	8 369	6 740	4 765	6 574	8 485
	(39.6)	(65.6)	(33.2)	(53.8)	(56.3)	(74.1)	(73.0)	(63.9)	(51.4)	(73.4)
Total	17 675	6 971	8 853	15 542	15 217	11 286	9 093	6 469	12 792	11 564
	(100.0)	(100.0)	(100.0)	(100.0)	(100.0)	(100.0)	(100.0)	(100.0)	(100.0)	(100.0)

Sources: MOCIE (2006); KIEP (2006).

Table 5.6 shows recent trends of FDI by investment type. The share of M&A type of FDI has increased more or less steadily over the period 1999–2005 at the expense of that of greenfield FDI (Table 5.6), although Korea obviously prefers the latter to the former (Cherry 2006). In particular, over the three-year period 2003–05, M&As accounted for about 45 per cent of total FDI (Table 5.6), and most M&As were in the form of purchasing existing shares (KIEP 2006). This indicates that recently about 30 to 40 per cent of FDI in Korea has been undertaken in the form of purchasing a certain percentage of shares in existing firms with the intention of gaining managerial control. The rising share of the M&A type of FDI at the expense of greenfield FDI may raise concern about the rising level of concentration which may lead ultimately to streamlining, plant closure and job losses. Over the period 1999–2005, most greenfield investment was in the form of investment in operational facilities – not for new factories (KIEP 2006). This shows that Korea is no longer a target country for FDI in factories for manufacturing purposes. Table 5.6 also shows that over the period from 2000 to 2005, on average 58 per cent of FDIs were larger than US$100 million.

Table 5.6 FDI in Korea by investment type and size on a notification basis (US$ million and %)

	1999	2000	2001	2002	2003	2004	2005
M&A	2 333	2 865	2 649	2 084	2 943	6 169	5 267
	(15.0)	(18.8)	(23.5)	(22.9)	(45.5)	(48.2)	45.5)
Greenfield	13 208	12 354	8 637	7 009	3 526	6 621	6 294
	(85.0)	(81.2)	(76.5)	(77.1)	(54.5)	(51.8)	(54.5)
Total	15 542	15 219	11 286	9 093	6 469	12 792	11 564
	(100.0)	(100.0)	(100.0)	(100.0)	(100.0)	(100.0)	(100.0)
Below US$100 million (%)	n.a	37.5	37.5	34.6	51.2	41.9	47.5
Above US$100 million (%)	n.a	62.5	62.5	65.4	48.8	58.1	52.5

Source: KIEP (2005, 2006).

Table 5.7 shows that the bulk of total inward FDI to Korea between 1999 and 2005 originated from a limited number of countries. Although there were some variations in total FDI inflow by country, about two-thirds of FDI in Korea was from the US, Japan, the UK, Germany and the Netherlands. Over the same period, FDI flows from the US comprised the largest proportion on average with about 29 per cent of FDI in Korea.

Table 5.7 FDI by country source (%)

	1999	2000	2001	2002	2003	2004	2005
US	24.1	18.6	34.4	49.4	19.2	36.9	23.3
Japan	11.3	15.6	6.9	15.4	8.4	17.7	16.2
UK	3.1	0.5	3.8	1.3	13.5	5.0	20.0
Germany	6.2	10.2	4.1	3.1	5.7	3.8	6.1
Netherlands	21.4	11.3	10.9	5.0	2.5	10.2	9.9
Others	33.9	43.8	39.9	25.8	50.7	26.4	24.5
Total							
(US$ million)	15 542	15 219	11 286	9 093	6 469	12 792	11 564
(%)	(100.0)	(100.0)	(100.0)	(100.0)	(100.0)	(100.0)	(100.0)

Source: KIEP (2005, 2006).

Some trends in FDI inflows based on a notification basis have been discerned in Korea. Although fluctuating somewhat, the share of FDI in the manufacturing sector has declined substantially, while the share of the service sector has increased in the recent past. This indicates that Korea has been losing its competitive advantage as a production site. Consistent with this, the share of greenfield investment, particularly in new factories, is falling, while that of the M&A type of FDI is rising. Increases in the M&A type of FDI may raise some social concerns about the taking over of prosperous domestic companies by foreigners, as well as plant closures and job losses.

As examined above, soon after the 1997 financial crisis, inward FDI increased substantially and has become an increasingly important component of the Korean economy in recent years. This has been attributed, most of all, to the changes in the FDI regime and a series of policy measures to attract FDI. Nonetheless, Korea has clearly failed to attract FDI to its full potential or to a level comparable internationally. Contributions of FDI to the Korean economy in terms of value added and R&D appear to be relatively low compared to other comparable countries. At the same time, the support of the general public for FDI has faded, as social concern arises about foreign control of domestic industries. In this regard, the evolution of the FDI regime in conjunction with the crisis will be examined in the following section.

5.3 THE KOREAN FDI REGIME

5.3.1 FDI Policy before the 1997 Financial Crisis

Unlike trade, for which international rules exist under the GATT and WTO, there has been no significant progress made on investment-related multilateral rules for FDI. In the absence of international guidelines, Korea pursued a singular FDI policy that restricted and discouraged inward FDI over a long period of time until the mid-1980s. From the mid-1980s, however, Korea began to liberalize the FDI regime under rising pressure from trade partners, thereby opening more business categories for FDI and relaxing restrictive regulations. Also, the FDI permission system was changed from a 'positive system' to a 'negative system', where FDI could enter any industry except those with specific prohibitions.

Over the period 1990–97, Korea further liberalized its FDI regime with the launch of the WTO and its admission to the OECD in 1996. The approval system of relevant government organizations for FDI was replaced by a reporting system. Non-hostile M&As were allowed, and long-term offshore borrowings with terms of five years or longer were liberalized. However, the basic position of the government toward FDI was passive and restrictive, except for high-technology areas. Under the anti-FDI policy, a number of sectors were closed to FDI by law until the mid-1990s. These included most service industries (distribution including wholesale and retail industries, communications, transport, banking and financing, insurance, trust, real estate, investment consulting and business services), the agricultural sector, and heavy and chemical industries. Even in those areas that permitted FDI, the administrative regulations and processes for FDI were complex and lacked transparency.

The Korean economic structure and socio-culture were not conducive to incoming FDI either. The Korean economy was heavily concentrated in a handful of large chaebols that enjoyed various types of institutionalized advantages over foreign firms (Kwon 2001). The Korean labor market was not flexible and unions were renowned for their militant tactics. Restrictive zoning laws raised real estate prices extraordinarily high and foreigners were prohibited from purchasing real estate. Korean society had been xenophobic, and had failed to appreciate the economic benefits of FDI. Korean business culture had not been congruous with foreign investors, and Koreans in general preferred to work for domestic firms rather than foreign firms. As a result, Korea was regarded as the worst place to invest among Asian countries until 1997 (*Far Eastern Economic Review* 1998).

From this brief survey of government policy toward incoming FDI and the business environment in Korea prior to the 1997 crisis, we have observed both structural and social impediments to foreign interests that sought to enter the Korean market. The consequences of Korea's restrictive policy toward FDI and the business environment have been huge. The sudden economic crippling borne out of the 1997 financial crisis was an inescapable watershed, signaling unmistakably that both the structure and the principles that had supported Korea could not be sustained. As a consequence, Korea had to make a shift in policy principles not only for FDI but also for other areas. Business environment and management also had to undertake fundamental changes.

5.3.2 Liberalization of the FDI Regime after 1997

Since the onset of the 1997 financial crisis, Korea has switched its policy emphasis on FDI from 'restriction and control' to 'promotion and assistance' and has undertaken a series of policy measures and all-out efforts with the highest policy priority to improve the business environment to attract FDI (MOFE 2006). With the enactment of the new Foreign Investment Promotion Act in 1998, replacing the Foreign Capital Inducement Act of 1966, Korea has liberalized its FDI regime to the standard among OECD members (Bishop 2001). The new Act has opened more business sectors (including the service sector) to FDI, making the liberalization rate 99.8 per cent in terms of the number of business sectors opened for FDI. It has also eased the complicated administrative procedures by dismantling or relaxing more than 50 per cent of extant restrictions (Kwon 2004; Kim et al. 2004). The new Act has eliminated discriminatory laws and regulations against foreign investors in the Korean real estate market and permitted M&As (including hostile M&As) by liberalizing the capital market. The new Act has also provided a variety of tax and other incentives for FDI. Some restrictions on FDI remain in the agricultural, media and telecommunications, transport and power generation sectors (Bishop 2001; Kwon 2004).

A crucial facilitating factor for the liberalization of FDI was the government's 'dismantling or relaxing' of more than 50 per cent of the complicated administrative regulations associated with foreign investment, along with the establishment of the Korea Investment Service Center, as a 'one-stop shop' for inward FDI (Kwon 2004).[4] The centre offers consultation, advice and assistance to investors, an investment ombudsman, intellectual property rights protection, and best international practice in accounting and corporate governance standards (Cherry 2006). In addition, the Korean government has pursued the 'active promotion' and 'aggressive solicitation' of inward FDI, and has eliminated the ceilings on foreign equity ownership. It has also expanded the number of Foreign Invested Zones where foreign investors would be eligible for a number of further incentives (Kwon 2004; Cherry 2006).

The business environment has also improved remarkably since 1997. As a result of chaebol reforms, part of the institutionalized privileges bestowed on chaebols and the collusive government–chaebol relations have been eliminated. Corporate governance and the management transparency and accountability of Korean firms have improved. Penetration of foreign capital into the Korean business sector has reduced government intervention in business operations. Reform of the Korean labor market has substantially improved its flexibility. Management practices have substantially changed toward the Western style.

In the wider and less tangible arena of Korean society and culture, perceptions of FDI have also undergone significant change since 1997. Once suspicious of perceived foreign control through capital inflows, Korean society has come to appreciate the value of FDI in aiding the recovery of the crisis-stricken economy and in sustaining economic prosperity. In conjunction with changes in Korean society toward FDI, preferences for domestic companies and products and discrimination against foreign firms have also declined among ordinary Koreans. This makes it easier for foreign firms to recruit and retain competent local staff.[5] How, then, would the relatively low magnitude of FDI in Korea, as examined above, be explained? What should Korea do further to attract FDI to the level comparable to those of neighboring countries and commensurate to its economy? The following section attempts to address these vexing questions.

5.4   CAUSES OF SLUGGISH FDI IN KOREA

5.4.1 Macro and Global Effects

As shown in Table 5.1, FDI inflows in Korea surged over the three-year period (1998–2000) following the crisis. This was largely attributable to hasty sales of assets by a number of financially troubled or bankrupt companies to pay down their debts and improve their financial health. The drastic change in the FDI regime, as examined above, buoyant global economic conditions, rapid increases in world FDI flows, and a steep decline in the value of Korean currency have also contributed to the surge in FDI. The initial surge in investment after the financial crisis has waned, partly due to the recovery of the Korean economy from the crisis, but also to decreases in the number of troubled companies available for sale. As a result, FDI in Korea fell sharply in 2001 and remained sluggish for the three consecutive years from 2001 to 2003 (Table 5.1). From the perspective of foreign investors, the sharp fall in FDI inflows during this period was also attributable to global events such as the slowdown in the world economy, marked decreases in world FDI flows (Table 5.1), the 11 September 2001 terrorist attacks and the emergence of China as an attractive destination for global capital (Cherry 2006).

5.4.2 Loss of Korea's Location Advantages

Although the fall in FDI inflows in Korea can be attributable to both the demand and the supply side, it appears that Korea has been losing its indigenous competitiveness in attracting FDI. According to Dunning (1980, 1998, 2000), three key determinants for FDI are location advantages, ownership advantages and internalization advantages. Kwon (2004) has found from a comprehensive survey of foreign business people in Korea that foreign firms chose to pursue FDI in Korea to capitalize on the emerging business opportunities in Korea by means of their firm-specific advantages. Ha (2002) has found empirically that location advantage is one of the key determinants for FDI in Korea. The loss of Korea's location advantages can be attributable to a number of recent developments in Korea.

First, public support for FDI has faded (MOFE 2006; Cherry 2006). As the Korean economy began to recover from the financial crisis, the social consensus on the necessity and benefits of FDI and globalization for the economy has weakened. Negative views of inward FDI, such as foreign control of domestic industries, have revived after remaining dormant for a while soon after the crisis. Furthermore, institutional and public support for the sales of assets of Korean companies has fallen, as many of the early deals were viewed and criticized as 'fire sales' where assets were sold at well below their perceived value. The negative view of inward FDI is reflected in the relentless resistance of unions to FDI, and in Koreans' prejudice against foreign companies and products (Kwon 2006). Koreans' nationalistic mindsets are revealed by the outlandishly disruptive and militant participation of Korean farmers, union members and students in anti-globalization protests at a number of international meetings in the recent past such as the WTO meetings in Seattle in 1999, in Cancun, Mexico in 2003, and in Hong Kong in 2005, and at the Asia-Pacific Economic Cooperation (APEC) meeting at Busan, Korea in 2005. As public support for FDI fades, the government has begun putting the brakes on its liberalization program for FDI, such as its reluctance to force further reforms in corporate governance and the labor market, and the provision of financial support for unviable Korean businesses (Stoever 2005). Thurbon and Weiss (2006) point to new regulations or guidelines introduced to restrain foreigners' takeover of Korean banks and companies and to prevent the wholesale outflow of profits from the Korean economy.[6]

Second, Korea's regulatory reform was incomplete and deficient. Although the number of regulations decreased markedly, Korea's regulatory environment is still regarded as excessive and complex. Significant regulatory reform and deregulation has occurred post-1997 under the proviso that all regulations which hinder competition and the market are to be eliminated except for those required for the preservation of the environment, public safety or health (Yang 2004; Choi 1999; Jeong et al. 2002). As a result, of the 11 125 existing regulations, 5430 (48.2 per cent) had been removed and 2411 (21.7 per cent) revised by the end of 1998. Of the remaining 6820 regulations, 503 (7.4 per cent) were eliminated to leave 6317 regulations in 1999 (Jeong et al. 2002). Despite about a 50 per cent reduction in the number of regulations, many Koreans still do not feel that the regulatory burden has been lifted significantly in day-to-day economic affairs. The most common criticism of the regulatory reform process is that it has focused more on quantity rather than quality (Yang 2004). Yang (2004) also points out that the regulatory review mechanism is not empowered to reject laws passed by the National Assembly, so that new laws allow interest groups to increase regulations. The OECD (2000) points to excessive regulations, lack of transparency in regulations, varying interpretation of domestic regulations, discrimination against foreign competitors, slow implementation and cumbersome administrative procedures as crucial problems in Korea. This may be reflected in Korea's poor performance in public institutions as assessed by the World Economic Forum (WEF), with Korea ranking 42nd out of 65 countries in 2005 (WEF 2006).

Even though the laws and regulations were liberalized on a par with the OECD average, implementation of the liberalization policy has been lukewarm. Stoever (2005) argues that the Korean government drew back from the liberalization of FDI as soon as the financial crisis eased slightly. According to Thurbon and Weiss (2006), Korea's post-crisis FDI policies represent the government's streamlining efforts to attract FDI and do not indicate any profound shift in national orientation from Korea's erstwhile strategic approach to governing FDI flows. They argue that the Korean authorities still systematically link the promotion of FDI with the goal of the nation's industrial policy by means of incentives geared to the promotion of preferred domestic industries, technology transfers and particular regions. They also point to the new FDI guidelines introduced to restrain foreigners' takeover of domestic banks and outflows of profits, and conclude that the fall in FDI is attributable to still excessive regulations.

Third, the lack of flexibility in the labor market and thorny labor relations are another reason for sluggish FDI. It is common knowledge that unions employ militant tactics and an unyielding posture for their causes with respect to labor issues. Although the labor law allows lay-offs for management reasons, it is in effect impractical to lay off unionized employees because of stringent restrictions and unions' combatant attitudes. According to a World Bank study of labor market flexibility based on conditions of firing, hiring and employment, Korea ranked 51st out of 133 countries (World Bank 2003, cited in Bank of Korea 2004). Korean labor market flexibility was estimated to be much less than that of East Asian countries such as Hong Kong, Singapore and Malaysia. The International Institute for Management Development (IMD) has also estimated Korea's labor market flexibility based on the ease of hiring and firing and the minimum wage rate (IMD 2004, cited in Bank of Korea 2004). The IMD ranked Korea 44th out of 60 countries studied in 2004, with Korean labor market flexibility worse than those of neighboring East Asian countries such as Hong Kong, Singapore, Malaysia, Taiwan and Japan.

Fourth, the relatively high wage rate is another reason for the low level of inward FDI in Korea. Labor costs have risen rapidly in the recent past, surpassing productivity increments. Over the six-year period from 2000 to 2005, the real wage rate increased annually on average by 4.7 per cent, while labor productivity per hour increased by 3.1 per cent (KLI 2006). This raised labor costs in Korea per unit of output in the manufacturing sector faster than those of neighboring countries. Over the period between 2000 and 2004, the labor unit cost in the manufacturing sector in terms of US dollars increased by 6.6 per cent in Korea, while it decreased by 21 per cent, 16.5 per cent and 10.4 per cent, respectively, in Taiwan, Japan and the US (KLI 2006). As a result, over the same period (2000–04), average hourly compensation costs in US dollars in the manufacturing sector increased in Korea from US$8.2 in 2000 to US$11.50 in 2004. This contrasted with decreases from US$6.1 to US$6 in Taiwan and from US$22 to US$21.9 in Japan (KLI 2006).

Fifth, a series of recent developments in Korea related to globalization, deregulation, business and FDI environments and the deterioration of location advantages are reflected in internationally renowned indicators. An indication of Koreans' reluctance to open their mindsets and economy is shown by a low extent of globalization. Dreher (2006) has developed an index of globalization covering the three main dimensions: economic integration social integration, and political integration. In 2000, Korea ranked 40th out of 123 countries in the globalization index (Dreher 2006). It should be noted that the globalization index increased in Korea by 18.2 per cent over the 1990–2000 period, while the indices of most other East Asian countries of similar economic development to Korea were either higher than Korea's as of 2000, or had increased significantly more than that of Korea. Korea's ranking by the Dreher index of globalization improved to 29th in 2006 (SIBCR 2006). However, out of the three dimensions, the index of economic integration appears to be more relevant for the present study (Dreher 2006). This index is calculated by the weighted average of actual flows (such as trade volume, FDI, portfolio investment, income payments to foreign nationals) to GDP and restrictions (such as hidden import barriers, mean tariff rate, taxes on international trade, capital account restrictions).

According to the index of economic integration, the Korean ranking slightly worsened from 62nd in 2000 to 63rd in 2006.

Sixth, Korea's national competitiveness is relatively low compared to neighboring East Asian countries. National competitiveness measured by the World Economic Forum (WEF) and the International Institute for Management Development (IMD) would be indicative of location advantages. According to the WEF Growth Competitiveness Index (GCI), which is calculated based on technology, public institutions and macroeconomic environments, Korea's performance has fluctuated markedly, ranking 17th in 2005, while it ranked 29th in both 2000 and 2004 (WEF 2006).[7] A number of countries in East Asia such as Taiwan, Singapore and Japan outperformed Korea in 2005. The components of the WEF Growth Competitiveness Index show that Korea owes its ranking of 17th in 2005 to its technological prowess. Between 2002 and 2005, Korea's rank in the technology index improved from 18th to 7th, while Korea performed poorly on both the public institutions and macroeconomic environment indices, ranking 32nd and 42nd for the former and ranking 10th and 25th for the latter index. Korea's poor performance in public institutions and macroeconomic environments, particularly as compared to neighboring East Asian countries, signals difficulties in undertaking FDI in Korea. Korea's technological prowess is not an important factor which attracts FDI, as foreign investors are in general the owners of technologies as their ownership advantage. They pursue FDI in Korea to seize upon rising business opportunities in the Korean market (Kwon 2004).

Seventh, another well-known competitiveness index is the one developed by the International Institute for Management Development (IMD). This index is based on economic performance, government efficiency, business efficiency and infrastructure (IMD 2006). The top-ranked 15 economies listed in the IMD are similar to those of the WEF, with the exception of a rapidly improving Hong Kong under the IMD scores. Korea's relative position in the IMD scoreboard improved significantly from 37th in 2003 to 29th in 2005, but declined back to 38th in 2006. A number of countries in East Asia such as Hong Kong, Singapore, Taiwan, Japan, Thailand and Malaysia outperformed Korea. China also significantly outranked Korea in both 2003 and 2004, and again in 2006, with a vastly improved 19th position. In addition, in terms of the ease of doing business estimated by the IMD, Korea ranked 42nd in 2006, with most Asian competitors outperforming Korea. All this indicates a relative deterioration of Korea's location advantage.

In summary, Korea's location advantages for FDI have deteriorated in the recent past. As the pain of the financial crisis has eased, social consensus on the benefit of FDI and globalization has weakened, and the government has begun to put the brakes on its liberalization programs, rendering the institutional and structural reforms incomplete and deficient. Consequently, the Korean regulatory regime is still excessive and incoherent. The labor market lacks flexibility and labor relations are turbulent. Wage rates have increased rapidly, thereby exceeding those of competitor countries in East Asia. This series of recent developments in Korea have been borne out in well-known global indicators. Korea ranks poorly in the indices of globalization and national competitiveness as compared to the East Asian countries with economic development stages similar to Korea. Another important determinant of FDI in Korea would be the perception of Korean FDI environment held by foreign investors. Kwon (2004) has attempted to address this question.

5.5   PERCEPTION OF FOREIGN BUSINESS PEOPLE

Any viable strategy, either by governments or by private firms, to attract or undertake FDI must be based on relevant, accurate market information. One of the most effective sources of information is companies with first-hand experience of undertaking FDI and operating overseas businesses. To this end, a comprehensive survey was undertaken from May to July 2002 of foreign companies that had undertaken FDI and were operating businesses in Korea.[8] In order to supplement the survey and garner additional information, personal interviews were conducted with a number of the responding company representatives and some foreign business expatriates. As Dunning (1980) suggests, the predominant motive of foreign companies to invest in Korea was to capitalize on the emerging business opportunities by means of their firm-specific advantages such as patents, technology, brands, know-how or expertise (Kwon 2004). Foreign business people had a negative view, though moderate, on the importance of the other location-specific variables. They include 'advanced related industries', 'easy access to information and technology', 'abundant skilled workers', 'investment incentives by Korea', 'easy access to parts and materials', 'low production costs' and 'overcoming tariff and other import barriers'.[9] It also appears that foreign investors did not consider Korea as a stepping stone to other Asian markets. This runs counter to the recent Korean campaign to promote Korea as the business hub in Northeast Asia.

Foreign business people pointed out difficulties in setting up investment projects in Korea such as onerous procedures for investment, complex administrative procedures, inadequate protection of intellectual properties, inadequate corporate governance of Korean companies and their opaque financial statements, and militant unions. Interviews with survey participants revealed their view that there was substantial inconsistency in the policies, regulations and administrative procedures between the central and local governments. Some foreign expatriates voiced their concern at the opacity and variability in interpreting and applying regulations at the local government level. They were also aggrieved by interauthority turf wars between fire, police, construction and environmental authorities at both local and regional levels, since these battles delay approval requirements. These survey and interview results vindicate the earlier arguments of Korea's incomplete and deficient liberalization reform and its excessive and complex regulatory regime.

Contrary to a number of arguments that the business environment in Korea had improved (Kim and Choo 2002; Kim 2003; Kim and Kim 2003), foreign business people had in general a moderately negative view of the improvement except for political stability and economic prospects. They did not feel that foreign firms engage in level playing-field competition with Korean counterparts. Foreign business people expressed their negative views on the improvement in Koreans' discrimination against foreigners and foreign products. In personal interviews, participants expressed their view that Koreans are still nationalistic and narrow-minded and do not appreciate racial diversity in the world. This may point to the fading social consensus on the benefits of FDI and globalization, the reviving negative view on inward FDI, and the discriminatory regulations against foreign companies, as examined above.

The survey attempted to identify difficulties encountered by foreign business people in on-site management of businesses in Korea. They pointed out many types of difficulties in the area of government–business relations such as 'lack of transparency and consistency in regulations', 'prevailing cronyism and corruption', 'excessive discretionary power of bureaucrats', and 'excessive government regulations'. These survey findings are consistent with the above argument regarding excessive government regulations. On their business operations and relations with Korean companies, respondents rated 'importance of personal relationships in business' as the most difficult area and 'unfair advantages held by Korean firms, especially chaebols' as the second most difficult area. It appears that foreign business people view chaebols as adversarial competitors. They did not consider that chaebols were competing on a level playing field.

In the area of human resource management, foreign business people agreed strongly with positive aspects of Korean workers such as their being hardworking, with high loyalty to companies and supervisors, willingness to work for foreign companies, collaborative team spirit, and willingness to get trained for new jobs. Foreigners did not consider Korean workers as being highly skilled and efficient, nor possessing high reliability and stability.

Recruiting and retaining efficient local workers, high wage levels and low labor productivity were regarded as areas of concern. Poor English language skills were rated as one of the most serious issues for Korean workers. Overall, these survey findings appear to confirm the reputable nature of Korean workers.

Foreign business people considered that coping with culture and society was difficult for them because of cultural and communication differences, Koreans' prejudice against foreign firms and products, and Korean society being closed to foreigners. Finally, many respondents regarded poor social amenities for expatriates' families as a serious concern. The findings of the survey may indicate that, while the Korean government provides various types of support, incentives and assistance in attracting FDI and streamlining the FDI procedure, it does not perform as well in supporting the on-site operations of FDI projects.

5.6 CONCLUSIONS

The Korean government restricted and controlled FDI up to the 1997 financial crisis, largely because of its historical obsession with protecting domestic industries and management control. The Korean economic structure and socio-culture were not conducive to incoming FDI either. As a result, Korea was regarded as the worst place to invest among Asian nations until 1997. These restrictions on FDI and unhealthy FDI environments were reflected in the flagging level of FDI.

After the 1997 financial crisis, the Korean government has undertaken a paradigm shift in the FDI policy from 'restriction and control' to 'promotion and assistance', and has undertaken a series of policy measures and all-out efforts to improve the business environment and attract FDI. As a result, FDI in Korea increased remarkably over a three-year period 1998–2000. Despite this spurt, Korea still attracted FDI less than a level comparable internationally. In addition, FDI in Korea decreased markedly in 2001, and remained sluggish until 2004 when it finally increased substantially. Notwithstanding the rapid increases in FDI over the three-year period (1998–2000) and a substantial increase in 2004, the magnitude of FDI in Korea is still small by international comparison. In particular, Korea fared poorly in attracting FDI as compared to the world and East Asia. The Korean government has undertaken a series of policy measures in an apparent all-out effort to attract FDI. This begs questions as to why the magnitude of FDI in Korea is still relatively low, and what additional measures are needed to increase FDI inflows to a level comparable internationally.

Korea has clearly failed to attract FDI to its full potential or to a level comparable internationally in the recent past. Contributions of FDI to the Korean economy in terms of value added and R&D appear to be relatively low. The trend in FDI by industry indicates that Korea has lost its advantage as a production site perhaps because of relatively high wage rates and militant unions. Relative increases in the M&A form of FDI in the recent past, together with the relatively low contributions of FDI for the economy overall, might have raised suspicions of FDI as controlling domestic companies and causing company closures and job losses. This might have led the government to drag its feet in carrying out the regulatory reform and expediting implementation procedures of reforms. All of this appears as causes for the sluggish FDI.

There are a variety of causes of the sluggish FDI in Korea identified in the literature in both English and Korean. Korea's location advantages for FDI have worsened in the recent past. No sooner had economic difficulties from the financial crisis eased, than social consensus on the benefit of FDI and globalization weakened, and societal suspicion of FDI about controlling and downsizing domestic companies has come to the fore. In response to changes in social mood with regard to FDI, the government has begun to put the brakes on its liberalization programs, rendering the institutional and structural reforms incomplete and deficient. Consequently, the Korean regulatory regime is still excessive and incoherent, and lacks transparency. Due to its incomplete and deficient reform, the labor market lacks flexibility and labor relations are turbulent. Wage rates have increased rapidly, thereby exceeding those of competitor countries in East Asia. This series of recent developments in Korea has been borne out in internationally renowned indicators of location advantages. Korea ranks poorly in the indices of globalization and national competitiveness, as compared to the East Asian countries with economic development stages similar to Korea.

Another important determinant of FDI in Korea would be the perception of the Korean FDI environment held by foreign investors. Kwon (2004) has attempted to address this question by means of a comprehensive survey of foreign companies that had undertaken FDI and have been operating business in Korea. According to the survey results, foreign firms chose to pursue FDI in Korea to capitalize on the emerging business opportunities in Korea by means of their firm-specific advantages. This indicates the recent slowdown of the Korean economy would be one of the main causes of the sluggish FDI in Korea, although no one has pointed this out in the literature.[10] Foreign firms did not regard Korea as a target country for supply-seeking investment. They did not consider Korea as having competitive production costs, nor of being a stepping stone to gain market access to other Asian countries.

The survey results indicate that foreign investors encountered various types of difficulties in establishing FDI projects in Korea. Although formal entry barriers such as the approval process and FDI-restricted industrial sectors have been dismantled to OECD standards, there remain difficulties in setting up investment projects and on-site management. These difficulties arise not only from excessive, complex and opaque government regulations, excessive bureaucratic power and bureaucratic stonewalling, but also from unique Korean business cultures, unfair advantages held by domestic firms, and cultural and societal differences. The survey findings are not only consistent with the causes of failing FDI in Korea examined through the literature, but they also provide additional pieces of information regarding the slow FDI in Korea. Besides, the survey findings reflect the views of foreign business people who have investment and business experience in Korea. They are critically important because it is these people that Korea must convince if it seeks to attract FDI.

Some studies have attributed recent decreases in FDI to external factors such as economic stagnation in the world, particularly in the US and Japan; the 11 September 2001 terror attack; and the emergence of China as an attractive destination for global capital (Kim 2002, 2003; Cherry 2006). However, the present study shows that to attract further FDI, Korea should undertake not only an across-the-board liberalization of the FDI regime, but also further regulatory reforms and an enhancement of public awareness and understanding of the benefits of FDI and globalization. It should also improve the operational environment for foreign businesses. Although the FDI regime has been liberalized and the entry procedure has been streamlined substantially, the present study clearly indicates that there is substantial room for improvement in the areas of government regulations and policy implementation, both at the central and local levels of government. To improve the poor quality of the domestic business environment, not only should excessive government regulations and bureaucratic power be removed, but unfair advantages bestowed on domestic firms, continued rigidities in the labor market and living conditions of foreign expatriates should also be improved. Korean society and Koreans in general need to become more open and amicable to foreigners and foreign business operations in Korea.

The challenges confronting foreign firms that have been examined through survey research are the perceptions of survey respondents. The people of Korea may disagree profoundly with the respondents' claims. Nevertheless, since the respondents have first-hand experience of FDI in Korea, and it is these types of investors that the Korean government is trying to attract, the survey findings point to a number of areas that government policy should reconsider in its bid to increase inward FDI.

NOTES

1. Later issues of the World Investment Reports (2004 and 2005) by the UNCTAD do not include data on the levels of value added and employment by foreign affiliates.
2. The factors used in estimating the UNCTAD inward FDI potential index included: the rate of growth of GDP; per capita GDP; share of exports in GDP; telephone lines per 1000 inhabitants; commercial energy use per capita; share of R&D expenditure in gross national income; share of tertiary students in population; country risk; exports of natural resources as a percentage of the world total; imports of parts and components of electronics and automobiles as a percentage of the world total; exports in services as a percentage of the world total; and inward FDI stock as a percentage of the world total. The index is an unweighted average of the normalized values of these variables (UNCTAD 2005).
3. The relatively high ratio of R&D expenditure by foreign affiliates in China may be attributable to its relatively low level of domestic business R&D expenditure.
4. The Korea Investment Service Center was renamed Investment Korea in 2004 with more autonomy (Cherry 2006).
5. For further details of the change in the Korea FDI regime soon after the 1997 crisis, see Kwon (2001), Kim and Choo (2002), Kim (2003), Kwon (2004), Kim et al. (2004) and Cherry (2006).
6. In 2003, the Bank of Korea halted the privatization of domestic banks until local buyers are found. In 2005 the Financial Supervisory Commission (FSC) suspended the voting rights of investors purchasing 5 per cent or more of stocks in Korean companies for five days to allow the target company time to deal with the threat of takeover. The FSC also introduced in 2005 a guideline requiring that Korean nationals comprise at least 50 per cent of the boards of all local banks. In the same year, there was also a spate of surprise tax audits on foreign investment funds (Thurbon and Weiss 2006).
7. The technology index is comprised of innovation, information and telecommunications technology, and technology transfer. The public institutions index is made up of judicial independence, property rights protection, impartial operations of government contracts, and the extent of corruption and organized crime. The macroeconomic environment index is made up of macroeconomic stability, country's credit rating and government wastage.
8. For details of the survey, its procedure and findings, see Kwon (2004). Although the survey was conducted in mid-2002, the results would still be valid at the time of writing (2007) because there has been no significant change in regulations, policy and the business environment related to FDI in Korea over the last few years.
9. The OECD (2000) points out the unnecessary trade restrictiveness which is indicative of the difficulty in overcoming tariff and other import barriers.
10. The Korean economy grew at a rate of 4.5 per cent per year from 2001 to 2005, which is substantially lower than the annual growth rates over the earlier period of rapid development.

REFERENCES

Bank of Korea (2004), 'Korean labour market inflexibility and future agenda' (in Korean), *Monthly Bulletin*, August, 23–53.

Bishop, Bernie (2001), 'Barriers to foreign direct investment in Korea and Australia', in O.Y. Kwon and W. Shepherd (eds), *Korea's Economic Prospects: From Financial Crisis to Prosperity*, Cheltenham, UK and Northampton, MA, USA: Edward Elgar Publishing, pp. 266–80.

Booz.Allen & Hamilton (1997), *Revitalizing the Korean Economy toward the 21st Century*, Seoul: Booz.Allen & Hamilton.

Cha, Dong-Se (2001), 'The Korean economy in the new millennium: reform or revival?' in O.Y. Kwon and W. Shepherd (eds), *Korea's Economic Prospects: From Financial Crisis to Prosperity*, Cheltenham, UK and Northampton, MA, USA: Edward Elgar Publishing, pp. 39–59.

Cherry, Judith (2006), 'Killing five birds with one stone: inward foreign direct investment in post-crisis Korea', *Pacific Affairs*, 79 (1), pp. 9–27.

Choi, Kwang (1999), 'Public sector reform in Korea', *Korea Focus*, 7 (5), 66–77.

Dreher, Axel (2006), 'Does globalization affect growth? Evidence from a new index of globalisation', *Applied Economics*, 38 (10), 1091–110.

Dunning, John H. (1980), 'Toward an eclectic theory of international production: some empirical tests', *Journal of International Business Studies*, 11 (1), 9–31.

Dunning, John H. (1998), 'Location and multinational enterprises: a neglected factor?' *Journal of International Business Studies*, 29 (1), 45–66.

Dunning, John H. (2000), 'The eclectic paradigm as an envelope for economic and business theories of MNE activity', *International Business Review*, 9, 163–90.

Far Eastern Economic Review (1998), 'Asian executives poll', 18 June, p. 36.

Ha, Jong-Wook (2002), 'A study of the patterns of FDI in Korea' (in Korean), *Review of International Management*, 6 (1), 1–22.

IMD (International Institute for Management Development) (2006), *World Competitiveness Yearbook 2006*, Lausanne: IMD.

Jeong, Hakyung, Dae-Ki Kim, Kookhyun Kim and Jeff Rinne (2002), 'South Korea', World Bank Administrative and Civil Service Reform Country Reform Summaries, http://www1.worldbank.org/publicsector/civilservice/rsSouth Korea.pdf, accessed 26 July 2005.

Jwa, Sung Hee and Insill Yi (2001), 'Korea financial crisis: evaluation and lessons', in O.Y. Kwon and W. Shepherd (eds), *Korea's Economic Prospects: From Financial Crisis to Prosperity*, Cheltenham, UK and Northampton, MA, USA: Edward Elgar Publishing, pp. 73–98.

Kim, June-Dong (2002), 'Inward foreign direct investment into Korea: recent performance and future tasks', *Joint US–Korea Academic Studies*, 13, 195–220.

Kim, June-Dong (2003), 'Inward foreign direct investment into Korea: recent performance and future agenda', Discussion Paper 03-01, Seoul: Korea Institute for International Economic Policy (KIEP).

Kim, June-Dong and Yong-Il Kim (2003), 'Korea's liberalisation of trade in services and implications for Australia', in O.Y. Kwon, S.H. Jwa and K.T. Lee (eds), *Korea's New Economic Strategy in the Globalization Era*, Cheltenham, UK and Northampton, MA, USA: Edward Elgar Publishing, pp. 63–81.

Kim, Soyoung, Sunghyun H. Kim and Yunjong Wang (2004), 'Macroeconomic effects of capital account liberalization: the case of Korea', *Review of Development Economics*, 8 (4), 624–39.

Kim, Wan-Soon and M.J. Choo (2002), *Managing the Road to Globalization: The Korean Experience*, Seoul: Korea Trade & Investment Promotion Agency (KOTRA).

KIEP (Korea Institute for International Economic Policy) (2005), *Global Economic Review*, 8 (11), December.

KIEP (Korea Institute for International Economic Policy) (2006), *Global Economic Review*, 9 (8), September–October.

KLI (Korea Labor Institute) (2006), *2006 KLI Labor Statistics*, Seoul: KLI.

Kwon, O. Yul (2001), 'Korea's international business environment before and after the financial crisis', in O.Y. Kwon and W. Shepherd (eds), *Korea's Economic*

Prospects: From Financial Crisis to Prosperity, Cheltenham, UK and Northampton, MA, USA: Edward Elgar Publishing, pp. 245–65.

Kwon, O. Yul (2004), 'Causes for sluggish foreign direct investment in Korea: a foreign perspective', *Journal of the Korean Economy*, 5 (1), 69–96.

Kwon, O. Yul (2006), 'Recent changes in Korea's business environment: views of foreign business people in Korea', *Asia Pacific Business Review*, 12 (1), 77–94.

MOCIE (Ministry of Commerce, Industry and Energy) (2006), database, www.mocie.go.kr.

MOFE (Ministry of Finance and Economy) (2006), 'FDI vision 2015 and implementation strategy', *Economic Bulletin*, 28 (11), 40–47.

OECD (2000), 'Regulatory reform in Korea: enhancing market openness through regulatory reform', Paris: OECD, http://www.oecd.org/dataoecd/25/34/2956205.pdf, accessed 2 August 2005.

SIBCR (Swiss Institute for Business Cycle Research) (2006), 'KOF index of globalisation', http://www.kof.ch/globalization.

Sohn, C.H., J.S. Yang and S.B. Kim (2002), 'Liberalization measures in the process of Korea's corporate restructuring: trade, investment and capital account market opening,' Discussion Paper 02-11, Seoul: Korea Institute for International Economic Policy (KIEP).

Stoever, William A. (2005), 'Restructuring FDI policy in emerging economies: the Republic of Korea case', *Thunderbird International Business Review*, 47 (5), pp. 555–74.

Thurbon, Elizabeth and Linda Weiss (2006), 'Investing in openness: the evolution of FDI strategy in South Korea and Taiwan', *New Political Economy*, 11 (1), 1–22.

UNCTAD (2002, 2004, 2005), *World Investment Report 2002, 2004, 2005*.

WEF (World Economic Forum) (2006), *The Global Competitiveness Report 2005–2006*, New York: Palgrave Macmillan.

Yang, Junsok (2004), 'Public sector reforms', in Charles Harvie, Hyun-Hoon Lee and Junggun Oh (eds), *The Korean Economy: Post-Crisis Policies, Issues and Prospects*, Cheltenham, UK and Northampton, MA, USA: Edward Elgar Publishing, pp. 120–42.

PART II

Business operation and management in Korea

6. Business negotiation in Korea: cross-cultural aspects

6.1 INTRODUCTION

All business transactions involve some degree of negotiation. Negotiation is the process of discussion and bargaining between two or more parties over opportunities and/or disputes to reach an outcome acceptable to those parties. Since negotiation involves interaction and communication, it is critical for parties to understand the culture – particularly communication style, behavior, attitudes and values – of their counterparts in order to negotiate successfully. This is particularly true in international business where parties usually bring very different understandings and approaches to the negotiating table.

The importance, the difficulty and the careful planning required for successful negotiation in international business can hardly be overemphasized. 'Right' products, technology and prices are simply not enough to achieve success in international deal-making; international business negotiations can fail even under the most favorable business conditions. The consequences of business negotiation failure can be enormous. Graham (1981) argued that the main source of the US trade deficit with Japan was the poor performance of US business negotiators against their Japanese counterparts.

International business negotiation is by definition intercultural negotiation. As Lewicki et al. (2004, p. 204) argue, cross-cultural negotiations are much more complex and more difficult than intra-cultural ones. International business negotiations require not only sensitivity, but also understanding of the culture of foreign counterparts, informed analysis of their negotiating principles, strategies and tactics, communication and interpersonal skills for engaging effectively with foreign counterparts. Increasing globalization has expanded the scope and extent of international business, making cross-cultural negotiations even more vital in both the global and domestic economies. There are no fixed rules and formulas for effective business negotiation across different cultures, since negotiation is as distinctive as the people and cultures involved.

In conducting international business with Koreans, a clear understanding of the business negotiation principles, strategies and tactics that are usually employed by them is critical. It appears, though, that no adequate attention has been paid to this issue; there is a paucity of systematic studies explaining Korean business negotiation in the English language literature, although several 'how-to' books are available. The English language literature on cross-cultural negotiation with Asian nations has focused mainly on China and Japan.[1] Tung's 1990 study is now somewhat dated as Korean business culture has changed substantially from that time, and particularly after the 1997 financial crisis. Song et al. (2004) have surveyed and interviewed Korean senior managers to identify the factors that contribute to success or failure in business negotiations by Koreans, yet they have considered only the Korean perspective and not the perspective of foreign counterparts. Their findings are useful but limited, since they are not discussed in the context of systematic theoretical underpinnings or with attention to negotiation ethics, both of which are necessary for deep and accurate understanding. The several Korean-language studies of business negotiation have not been well incorporated into the knowledge and literature on international business negotiation in Korea.

The purpose of this chapter is therefore to examine the most important factors that concern Korean approaches to business negotiation, drawing from the literatures in English and Korean to synthesize disparate knowledge from various sources and provide a course of action for effective negotiation with Korean business partners.[2] The chapter adopts a cross-cultural perspective on business negotiation in Korea, since this is critical in both the process and the outcome of negotiation.[3] To put these issues into context, a few of the well-known models of international business negotiation are briefly reviewed, based on which international business negotiation in Korea will be analyzed.

6.2   MODELS OF INTERNATIONAL BUSINESS NEGOTIATION

Of the numerous models proposed for analyzing international business negotiation, two models are regarded as most relevant for examining international business negotiation with Koreans, and they are reviewed here first as the basis for examination.[4] Graham (1981) is a pioneering work on cross-cultural business negotiations that identifies the process of business negotiations through four stages:

1. non-task sounding;
2. task-related exchange of information;

3. persuasion; and
4. concessions and agreement.[5]

The non-task sounding stage is where negotiating parties come to know each other and begin to establish relationships. In the second stage, parties provide information directly related to the issue under negotiation, such as their needs and preferences. At the persuasion stage, each party puts effort into modifying the views and expectations of the other party in an attempt to sway the other party to their own way of thinking. The final stage involves reaching initial agreement after both sides have made concessions. Graham (1981) and Hodgson et al. (2000) argue that despite the consistency of the negotiation process across cultures, the content, duration and focus of these four stages differ substantially between parties from different cultures.

Weiss and Stripp (1985) identify how culture particularly influences 12 crucial aspects of intercultural negotiations. These are:

1. the basic concept of negotiation;
2. the types of issues that are most significant;
3. selection of negotiators;
4. individuals' aspirations;
5. decision-making in groups;
6. orientation toward time;
7. risk-taking propensity;
8. bases of trust;
9. concern with protocol;
10. communication complexity;
11. nature of persuasion; and
12. form of agreement (explicit and implicit forms).

Weiss and Strip's study aims to make business negotiators aware of culturally based differences that are likely in each of these 12 aspects, and argues that the negotiators' familiarity with these intercultural differences in negotiation enables them to coordinate their own negotiation strategies better.

Although the Graham (1981) and Weiss and Stripp (1985) models are based on different perspectives of negotiation, there are significant interfaces between the two models. Aspects (1), (3), (6), (8), (9) and (10) of the Weiss and Stripp model run across the four stages of the Graham model. The negotiation aspects (2), (4), (5), (7), (11) and (12) of the Weiss and Stripp model all have important bearing on the persuasion, concession and agreement stages of the Graham model. Thus, the model developed by Weiss and Stripp presents the most comprehensive framework for analyzing intercultural negotiations, and is most appropriate for this examination of intercultural negotiation with Koreans. No study is available in the literature that incorporates all these 12 aspects of international business negotiation in Korea.

In recent years, ethics in negotiation has received increasing attention (Lewicki et al. 2004, p. 179). Negotiation by its nature raises ethical issues. Hence, the question of whether there are accepted ethical standards for behavior or tactics in negotiation has been explored not only in a normative sense, prescribing 'should' and 'should not' negotiation behavior, but also in a positive sense, assessing the consequences of unethical negotiation tactics. Research on the ethics of negotiators indicates that although unethical or expedient tactics may yield success in the short run, the same tactics typically lead to diminished effectiveness and disadvantage the unethical party in the long run (Lewicki et al. 2004, p. 199). Recognizing the importance of ethics and of different understandings of ethics in intercultural negotiations, this chapter therefore includes examination of the negotiation ethics of Korean negotiators.

6.3   KOREAN CULTURAL TRAITS RELEVANT TO BUSINESS NEGOTIATION

As discussed in Chapter 3, Korean culture has developed over a long history in isolation from other cultures with *sui generis* religions, political, economic and education systems and language. The salient traits of Korean culture most commonly noted are: hierarchical collectivism, reciprocity and moderation, patriarchal familism, authoritarianism, status consciousness, secularism and strong nationalism (Kweon 2003; Han 2003; Yi 2003; Hahm 2003). Unremitting invasions and incursions by powerful neighboring countries over its long history have served to strengthen Korean nationalism. Confucianism, which was adopted as the guiding principle of state management and the code of ethics by the Yi Dynasty over 500 years, has been one of the most prominent influences on Korean culture. Continuous inculcation of the importance of personal relationships in a society under Confucianism has underpinned the development of a strong group-oriented society in Korea. Collectivism under Confucianism includes reciprocity and moderation, both of which are promoted as an important part of virtuous social behavior. Korean collectivism is supported by Hofstede's estimate of 18 for its individualism, ranking it 43rd out of 53 countries studied.

Collectivism in Korean society is family-centered and hierarchical. Consistent with Confucian hierarchy, Korean society has developed over its long history a hierarchical collectivism and embraced a form of social stratification placing aristocrats and scholars at the top, followed by farmers, merchants and artisans, and menial workers in that order. In a vertically structured authoritarian society where Koreans are made to be conscious of their status and expect others to treat them accordingly, the cultural trait of status- and face-saving consciousness has developed. Hofstede's estimate of 60 for the Korean cultural value of power distance appears to support hierarchical collectivism, with Korea ranking 27th out of 53 countries. Patriarchal familism was at the core of the collectivism in Korean society. Perhaps because of strong familism, Hofstede's estimate of Korean masculinity is relatively low at 39, ranking 41st out of 53 countries. Beyond family, the regions in which people are born and raised serve as an important basis of Korean collectivism. Another basis is educational institutions, and classmates from elementary and high schools and university alumni feel strong mutual affinity.

Koreans are quite risk averse. A history marked by unremitting invasions by powerful neighboring countries, division of the nation between South and North, the fratricidal Korean War, the subsequent harsh politics of a series of authoritarian regimes and recent volatile changes in policies have surely contributed to the high level of risk aversion. This is indicated by a ranking of 16th out of 53 countries on Hofstede's measurement of uncertainty avoidance, with a value of 85. Finally, Koreans have embraced secularism. Confucianism is mainly concerned with the nature of human society, and does not have sacred writings or a doctrine of afterlife. Nor does it have specific gods, although it refers to 'heaven' as a vague supernatural spirit. This type of secular doctrine has helped develop secularism in Korea.

Koreans generally take a long-term perspective in decision-making. Many Korean companies are operated and owned by their founders or by their family members. Strong familism in Korean society bolsters family concern for the futures of their children and grandchildren, which helps to foster long-term vision. Koreans' long-term perspectives are reflected in their high saving rates. According to the Confucian dynamism (long-term orientation) index by Hofstede and Bond (1988), Koreans score a high value of 75, ranking 5th out of 23 countries. As well as being long-term-oriented, Korean people are generally persistent and respect traditional values.

These cultural traits remain strong even today. Christianity, which was introduced in the seventeenth century, has made a significant contribution to transforming traditional Korean culture. Rapid industrialization of the Korean economy since the 1960s has transformed the traditional Korean society into an industrial society. Industrialization has also been accompanied by a shift in values away from morality and humaneness toward materialism. Continuous economic prosperity has further changed the focus of Korea's value system from materialism to quality of life. Nevertheless,

Korean society retains a strong Confucian tradition alongside strong nationalism and collectivism.

The Korean business sector has embraced traditional Korean culture. Influenced by hierarchical collectivism and paternalistic familism, Korean companies have maintained highly vertically structured organizations and strong corporate familism, in which lifetime employment and seniority practices have been management norms. Also decision-making at Korean companies has been based on a top-down system. The 1997 financial crisis has forced transformation of Korean corporate culture and review of the value system underpinning it. Subsequently, Koreans have come to value foreign business and culture more highly than before the crisis, and their patriotism has faded significantly. Korean economic and institutional structure has changed markedly so as to help firms survive under the rising competition and rapid changes constantly under way in the globalization and information era. Yet for all the forces of change at work upon Korean culture, religious doctrines, language and the education system shift at a much slower pace. So there is still significant continuity in contemporary Korean culture and a firm imprint of traditional features in business practices.

6.4 CHARACTERISTICS OF KOREANS' NEGOTIATION PROCESS

There are very few published studies of business negotiation with Koreans. Bowen (1998) surveyed and interviewed foreigners as well as Koreans, guided, although limited in scope, by the Weiss and Stripp (1985) model. He identified similarities and differences between Korean and non-Korean negotiators in their perceptions of negotiation. Although Bowen's study has identified noteworthy features of business negotiation in Korea, it does not explore in detail the cross-cultural aspects of negotiation proposed by Weiss and Stripp (1985), and his discussion of quantitative results lacks conceptual foundation and reasoning. Tung's 1990 study examines a limited number of cultural factors (importance of relationship and long-term view) involved in cross-cultural business negotiation with Koreans. Recognizing the shortcomings of these earlier studies, the present study undertakes an examination of salient characteristics of Korean negotiators including all of the 12 aspects of negotiation proposed by Weiss and Stripp (1985).

6.4.1 Basic Concept of the Negotiation Process

Weiss and Stripp (1985) argue that business people tend to approach business negotiation with one of two basic attitudes or strategies: taking a negotiation as a process in which both parties can gain (win–win, interactive, mutual gains, and so on) or a struggle in which one side wins while the other loses (win–lose, distributive, competitive, and so on).

Koreans tend to show negative and passive attitudes toward negotiation (Lee and Park 2004). They regard the necessity for negotiation as arising from a lack of trust and principle. They view negotiation as a zero-sum or win–lose game and its results as dependent on negotiation power. Korean negotiators tend to view their counterparts as adversaries and seek to win in negotiation (Lee and Park 2004). Koreans developed a predilection for being 'on top' during the period of rapid economic growth period from the 1960s to the 1980s. The Korean education system also encourages fierce, almost cut-throat competition with no prizes for second place. Jones and Sakong (1980) explore these features in their argument that competitive dedication to improving the relative position of self and family is firmly developed in Korea. This attitude leads Korean negotiators to be competitive and aggressive, thereby taking a distributive stance in negotiation (Lee and Park 2004).[6]

Furthermore, career progression has been largely based on the seniority system in the business sector in which failure of any kind means missing a promotion, damaging not only career progression but also personal self-esteem in the hierarchical organization. Thus, the person in charge of the negotiation seeks to win at the negotiation table, viewing a negotiation as a process in which one wins and the other loses. Yet, as Koreans value highly the relationship, reciprocity and long-term view in negotiations, Korean negotiators may propose a proposition of 'I win now – and you win next'.[7]

6.4.2 Most Significant Types of Issues

Wiess and Stripp (1985) identify four types of issues during business negotiation: substantive, relationship-building, procedural and personal or internal. Korean negotiators put great emphasis on personal relationships (Lee and Park 2004). Koreans first seek to develop close, emotional ties with their counterparts. Their embrace of collectivism makes Koreans reluctant to do business with people they do not know, and in whom they tend to place less trust. They also expect favorable terms from trusted personal friends. Thus, they regard gift-giving and entertainment as an integral part of negotiation, as a way of establishing relationships. To establish the relationship as an important basis of mutual trust, Koreans look for mutual friends at the onset of negotiation. In particular, because of their status-conscious and face-conscious culture, Korean negotiators exchange business cards and study the status of their counterparts at their own organizations. Koreans are reluctant to deal with people who they consider to be of a lower status than themselves. Korean companies tend to assign their negotiators equivalent in status to their counterparts. Under this practice of matching negotiators in status, and the top-down decision-making system, the negotiation process will take longer if lower levels of staff are assigned for negotiation.

With respect to substantive issues, Korean sellers tend to follow typical negotiation behavior of making an initial offer of a price much higher than their expected final price – sometimes appearing highly unrealistic – but in anticipation of a counter-offer from their negotiating counterpart. Similarly, buyers begin their offer with a very low price. This may be attributable to commercial practices in which price negotiations usually take place, other than at department stores. It is thus important for foreign negotiators to find out what the Korean counterparts really want to get out of their initial offer, and to have some room for negotiation in their first bid. Koreans are also reluctant to provide information, compared to Westerners who, in most cases, regard information as in the public domain. Yet they are eager to get information from their counterpart, and are reluctant to make an offer until they think they have enough information.[8]

6.4.3 Selection of Negotiators

The criteria for selection of negotiators include negotiating experience, status, gender, ethnic ties, knowledge of the issue, and personal attributes such as affability, loyalty and trustworthiness (Weiss and Stripp 1985). Korea negotiators stress highly the personal attributes of their counterparts (Lee and Park 2004). While Koreans usually delegate the negotiations to their junior staff, they place great value on seniority and status of members of the counterpart, and attempt to assign negotiators equivalent in company status to that of the counterpart. This is attributable to Korean culture in which social status is an important element of relationship and interaction.

With respect to selection of negotiators, Korean companies assign a negotiation team of individuals on the basis of status (gender, age and seniority), education level and knowledge of the issue under negotiation.[9] Korean negotiation teams are large and mainly composed of males, and one of them serves as the head of the team. Junior members do not participate in negotiation sessions; they are at the negotiation table to observe and learn the negotiation process, rather than to participate in it. The expectation of lifetime employment leads companies to teach negotiation conduct to junior staff for the long-term benefit of the company. The paternalistic style of management encourages senior officials to assume personal responsibility for the development of their subordinates. People in much senior positions such as chief executive officers (CEOs), who are the real decision-makers under the Korean top-down decision-making system, generally do not join the negotiation team unless those of the counterpart team have done so. Lawyers are in general not included in the team, to avoid giving an impression of distrust.

6.4.4 Individuals' Aspirations

This particular factor refers to the emphasis that negotiators place on their individual goals and needs (Weiss and Stripp 1985). In collective Korean society, a negotiator is expected to suppress individual desires and goals and act for the good of the company. Pursuing self-interest during business negotiations is perceived as morally wrong and will have significantly negative effects on that person's career.

Since hierarchical collectivism, familism, and status- and face-consciousness are important features of Korean culture, an individual negotiator is concerned with how other members, particularly his superiors, view his behavior. Other than the team leader, individual negotiation team members are reluctant to speak out in front of their team, as suggested in the Korean adage that 'the protruded corner of a stone is chiseled down'. The Korean education system reinforces this attitude, teaching students to obey authority without question. At the same time, the negotiation team leader will attempt to achieve something out of the negotiation that would fulfill his status or save face.

6.4.5 Decision-making in Groups

This variable refers to the system by which decisions are reached within the negotiating teams, and between their teams and the organization they represent (Weiss and Stripp 1985). As mentioned above, business decisions in Korea tend to be made authoritatively through a top-down decision-making system (Paik and Tung 1999). Most companies are owned and managed by the founders and their families, and the owner-manager holds full authority. Even though companies have a long preparation process to take decision-making from the bottom ranks through the middle managers and up to the top, decisions are actually made at the upper levels of management. The top manager may often ask subordinates to go through the preparation process to justify rather than to inform his or her decisions. This type of decision-making process is reflected in negotiation. Since senior management has set the company's position for the negotiations, little responsibility or elbow-room is left for negotiators, who typically state the company's position and simply reiterate the same position in different ways. As a result, as noted by Bowen (1998), Korean negotiators are regarded by foreigners and Koreans themselves as narrow-minded and lacking in flexibility and creativity.

Disruptions to the negotiation process can be frequent, with interruptions by secretaries passing on slips of paper for messages, and some members leaving the table without excusing themselves. These disruptions may be regarded by foreigners as stalling negotiation tactics (Tung 1991). If a senior manager calls upon the members of the negotiation team, they cannot help but respond to the message even though they are in the middle of negotiation. Some members may leave to have consultations with real decision-makers.

6.4.6 Orientation Toward Time

This particular variable is concerned with two opposite attitudes toward time: monochromic and polychromic time orientations (Weiss and Stripp 1985). While most Westerners generally view time as linear, Koreans generally have a non-linear view of time or polychromic attitude, and a long-term time orientation (Paik and Tung 1999). As a result, Korean negotiators' understanding of time and urgency are a great deal more lax than Westerners' views. Koreans do not have an adage that corresponds to 'time is money', and punctuality is not a priority. However, they have learned that Westerners value time, and they try to be punctual with foreigners.

In terms of negotiation, Koreans are very flexible with regard to time, although in general they take less time to finalize deals than do their Japanese and Chinese counterparts (Tung 1991). Nonetheless, Koreans take a longer time than Western counterparts because they need to establish personal relationships with negotiation counterparts. The length of time taken in the negotiation process in Korea usually differs according to the size of company. The decision-making process in a small company is very rapid because usually very senior management will be directly involved in negotiation. In large companies and chaebols, negotiations will take much longer. Most negotiations are conducted by more junior personnel who must consult on the ongoing negotiation process with their senior managers, and are then directed for the ensuing sessions. Once a negotiation has been consummated successfully, it will be viewed as a long-term relationship.

6.4.7 Risk-taking Propensity

Weiss and Stripp (1985) refer to risk-taking propensity in negotiation as the willingness to divulge critical information when counterpart's trustworthiness is questioned, or the willingness to go beyond superiors' directives. Koreans are highly risk averse, and lifetime employment and the seniority system, which are still commonly practiced by large corporations, reinforce the perception for certainty. Under this kind of human resource management, a staff member within an organization will progress step by step more or less automatically, if they do not make a serious mistake. Individual negotiators are also concerned with losing face or reputation and social standing from making mistakes. So, risk-taking is rarely an option, and individual negotiators tend to be reluctant to pursue dynamic and creative positions in negotiation. Furthermore, as senior management usually sets the position to be taken at the negotiation process, Korean negotiators cannot have a great deal of flexibility and creativity.[10]

6.4.8 Bases of Trust

Concerns about trustworthiness are of great importance in negotiation since this determines the disclosure and retention of information. Trust is important in any society for business transactions, and must be earned. Trust is particularly important in East Asian countries as they maintain group societies in which people are more trusting of group members than of others and interact accordingly. Thus, trust fits with the overall emphasis on relationships in oriental group society. As the base of morality is 'shame' in oriental society, as compared to 'guilt' in the Western world under Christianity, the level of trust among the insiders of a group, or among people who know each other, is higher than that with outsiders. Trust or a lack of it generates a self-fulfilling process. A party that does not trust or feel trusted by the counterpart negotiating party has less incentive to behave in a trustworthy manner, while a party that trusts or feels trusted by the counterpart feels obliged to treat the counterpart trustfully.

Because of the preference of Koreans to do business with people they know and trust, Koreans seek to test the trustworthiness of those who they do not know before doing serious business with them. Korean business people believe that establishing a relationship based on trust is an essential first step in the negotiating process. Trustworthiness is assessed and develops on the basis of past experience and record. Thus, Koreans consider that activities beyond business, such as evening entertainments and sports, serve as avenues for learning about the personality and character, including the trustworthiness, of business associates, and for building relationships with them. Trustworthy intermediaries, particularly those with a high social status or those from their own groups, such as family members and classmates, can also play an important role in developing trust and enhancing business relations. For this reason, Koreans seek out any extant connections when they encounter people they do not know in order to find a basis for developing relationship and trust.[11]

6.4.9   Concern with Protocol

This variable is concerned with 'proper' conduct and level of expected formality. In Korea's hierarchical society where 'status' and 'face' have particular importance, formalities are observed assiduously in business life. This is particularly so among people of different social status, according to age, social reputation and rank in an organization. Koreans are taught from an early age how to behave in the relationships of daily life. Under strong Confucian influence, the roles and behavior of individual family members are clearly prescribed by their position within the family, as explained in Chapter 3. Family members within a clan are graded by genealogy within the clan. Roles and behavior among family members are paralleled in the wider society, where it is expected that members of society will respect and follow the protocols determined by their status. These formalities include mannerisms, dress codes, ways of addressing people and ways of discourse. Many Koreans appear to be inquisitive about a person's family and educational background, age and place of origin. In other national cultures these questions may be seen as intrusive, but in Korean society these questions are part of determining relative social status, so that one can behave accordingly. Koreans generally respect those who are older and ranked more highly than themselves, and as a sign of deference, customarily use two hands when giving something to these people.

Consistent with the protocols with which they are most familiar in their daily lives, in business negotiation with foreigners Koreans seek to determine the status of those in the foreign negotiating party so that they can treat them in ways that the Korean team believe to be appropriate. Thus, when Koreans exchange business cards on first meeting with foreign counterparts, they study the cards carefully to find out the team members' respective positions within their company. Korean negotiators may ask quite inquisitive questions about the family and educational background of foreign counterparts at the outset of conversations to determine the relative status of foreigners, so that Korean negotiators can treat the foreigners in line with their perception of this status. Unless they are advised otherwise, Korean negotiators address foreign counterparts by their family names, and wear business suits.

6.4.10   Communication Complexity

Communication complexity is concerned with the degree of reliance on non-verbal communication cues including distance, gaze, gestures, and silence, to name a few. The Korean language is a high-context language such that Westerners who use low-context languages like English regard verbal expressions of Koreans as vague. In their daily discourse, Koreans may skip the noun, object of a verb, or articles in a sentence. Tense in Korean language is much simpler and less precise than English and the plural and singular forms of nouns and verbs are not well distinguished. Koreans comprehend the meaning of otherwise ambiguous sentences by context.

Face-consciousness and an emphasis on harmonious relationships are reflected in Korean conversation. Koreans do not talk in a straightforward manner in an attempt not to offend others. In particular, they are hesitant and cautious in giving negative responses. Instead of saying 'no', they may hedge with a response like 'it is difficult', 'we will think about it', 'we need more information' or 'we will consult our manager'. Even when Koreans answer 'yes', it could be an expression of civility or an agreement that they have heard the speaker, rather than actual agreement with the speaker. In a similar vein, Koreans may prefer not to ask questions about what has been said, particularly in a foreign language, even if they have not understood fully. This means Koreans may understand what is said in a foreign language less than foreign counterparts think, or indeed they may misunderstand and leave with the wrong message. Although Koreans study English intensively from elementary school, their speaking and listening comprehension skills are often significantly lower than their reading abilities. In negotiation, Koreans do not talk directly and immediately about the content, conclusion or problem, which Western counterparts are usually very eager to address and resolve.

In non-verbal communication, Koreans exhibit little facial expression and few hand motions. Unlike the Japanese, Koreans do not respond with long silences to signal their displeasure. While conversing, Koreans usually avoid direct eye contact, which they find uncomfortable. A unique non-verbal expression of Koreans is the so-called *kibun*, which means personal feeling and mood. As Koreans are emotional and temperamental, their feeling and mood will have important bearings on their decision-making or general conduct of negotiation (Tung 1991).[12] Many observers therefore claim that it is essential to understand the *kibun* of the Korean counterpart in business negotiation. Once a Korean negotiator's *kibun* is damaged, that person becomes temperamental and is likely to withdraw from any communication with his counterpart.

6.4.11 Nature of Persuasion

This factor refers to the extent to which negotiators from different cultures use direct experience, logic, tradition, emotion or intuition in persuading the opposing party. The very nature of argument and persuasion runs against the instincts and cultural traits of many Koreans (Lee and Park 2004). The hierarchical and stratified nature of Korean society profoundly influences individual conversational style, such that most Koreans are not accustomed to carrying on systematic, logical arguments and debates. The Korean education system that emphasizes rote learning fails to develop, or discourages, the capacity to sustain discussion and debate. Korean people therefore feel generally uncomfortable with the expression of a different opinion or disposition and do not know how to proceed with discussion to overcome differences and work toward a mutually acceptable compromise. They feel uncomfortable with an extended argument with which they may lose their temper. This life experience inclines them to focus on exposition rather than argument, which gives foreigners the impression that Koreans are not logical in decision-making.[13]

Koreans' understanding of persuasion and compromise also differs from that of Western negotiators in some critical ways. For Koreans, persuasion involves one yielding or capitulating to the other party, thereby losing face. Instead of putting forward a contrary position and attempting to persuade the counterpart in front of people involved in negotiation, Koreans are inclined to use persuasion behind the scenes, for example during breaks between sessions, rather than at the session itself. They will also resist persuasion by foreign counterparts at the negotiation session. Foreign negotiators facing an impasse may therefore find it useful to engage an intermediary who has a good personal relationship with the Korean counterpart. This intermediary will be better placed to persuade the Korean negotiators rather than the foreign party attempting to reason its way out of the impasse.

6.4.12 Form of Agreement

This variable refers to the desired forms of a negotiated agreement, categorized as explicit and implicit forms. Korean people are more familiar with implicit forms. Traditionally, Koreans have been neither familiar nor comfortable with written contracts. Koreans have a historical distrust of legalism. As mentioned above, Korean business style is to do business with people who are known and trusted. Insistence on a written contract is taken to imply that the counterpart cannot be trusted. Koreans therefore regard contracts, even if they are written, as a framework establishing the general principles of the parties' basic wishes and intent, and still leaving much to trust. In this view a contract is not legally or otherwise binding, and details can be worked out over time as the contact is implemented.

Koreans understand that contracts allow flexibility to the contracting parties because they regard a contract as an agreement made under a certain condition at a fixed point in time. They feel that this flexibility allows them to change the contract over time as conditions change (Paik and Tung 1999). The pressure imposed by senior management can also translate into Korean negotiators seeking to force a more flexible position from the other party to the contract. Another very important difference in the understanding of contracts also arises from the aspect of trust. To signal their trust in the other party, Korean negotiators have considered it common courtesy not to check the contract item by item. Under this type of cultural view of contracts, Koreans may request further concessions after the deal has been closed and the contract signed.[14] Clearly the difference between Korean and non-Korean negotiators in understanding legal, fiduciary and other aspects of contracts needs to be identified and addressed by both parties during the negotiation, before legally binding documents are signed.

6.5 ETHICS OF BUSINESS NEGOTIATION IN KOREA

The characteristics of Korean negotiators examined in the preceding section reflect the perception of negotiation held by Koreans and their negotiation culture and styles. This section considers some specific negotiation tactics identified empirically and assesses them by ethical criteria. Ethical issues arise in every negotiation, ranging from the ethical appropriateness of conduct undertaken by a negotiator to the ethical dimension and standards by which the conduct is judged.

Lewicki et al. (2004, p. 185) argue that for practical reasons, most of the ethics issues in negotiation are concerned with standards of truth-telling. That is, how honest, candid, and disclosing a negotiator should be. This view recognizes ethics in what negotiators say they will do, rather than what negotiators actually do. More specifically, Lewicki et al. (2004) argue that attention to the ethics of negotiators has mainly focused on lying behavior. This raises a question as to what constitutes truth-telling or lying. Lewicki et al. (2004) argue that to sustain the bargaining relationship, each party usually selects a middle course between the extremes of complete openness toward, and deception of, the other.

Lewicki et al. (2004) argue that there are six categories of deceptive tactics within this range. These are:

1. misrepresenting one's position to an opponent, such as by making an inflated opening offer (traditional competitive bargaining tactics);
2. emotional manipulation including faking anger or fear;
3. misrepresentation and selective disclosure of information;
4. bluffing;
5. misrepresentation to the opponent's network, such as corrupting the opponent's reputation among their peers; and

6. inappropriate information collection by means of bribery, infiltration and spying.

The first two types of deceptive tactics are generally regarded as ethically appropriate and are likely to be used. The other four categories are generally regarded as unethical, because they violate either standards of truth-telling, or the perceived rules of negotiation. Further, as Lewicki et al. (2004) explain, frequent use of unethical tactics may result in a loss of negotiation power over time, even though it may gain negotiation power in the short run. These criteria will be used to evaluate the ethics of business negotiation in Korea.

Very few studies have examined the ethical aspects of business negotiation in Korea, particularly in the English literature. Bowen (1998) claims that foreigners generally have a high opinion of their Korean counterparts in relation to negotiation ethics. The few exceptions here include Korean negotiators making unrealistic opening offers, requests for more concessions after closing the deal, and the use of time pressure to force concessions. Although the last two factors are not included in the six categories by Lewicki et al. (2004), they appear to be part of traditional competitive bargaining tactics, which are in general regarded as ethically acceptable and so are likely to be used.

Park and Lee (2003) apply the Lewicki and Robinson (1998) model to Korean negotiators to judge the ethics of their bargaining tactics. Their survey results reveal that Korean negotiators feel cognitive conflict between the appropriateness and effectiveness of using unethical tactics but generally give more weight to their effectiveness. Thus, even though they have some concerns for ethics, Korean negotiators will use unethical tactics if they believe these tactics will be effective. This implies some differences between Korean negotiators and Western counterparts in their cognitive structure toward unethical bargaining tactics, suggesting the influence of societal and cultural background on the choices of their negotiation tactics.

Lee and Park (2004) attempt to identify the major factors underlying 30 negotiation tactics that Korean negotiators frequently employ. Then, extending Park and Lee (2003), they attempt to assess the relationship among the perceived ethical appropriateness, effectiveness, and adoption likelihood rating of each of these identified tactics. They identify five primary tactics from 30 commonly used tactics: physical discomfort, traditional competitive bargaining, bluffing, persuasive argument and avoidance. Physical discomfort, which is not part of the model offered by Lewicki et al. (2004), refers to the intention to make the counterpart feel uncomfortable, irritated or annoyed. 'Traditional' competitive bargaining tactics include coercion of the counterpart to make an offer first, pretentious surprise at the offer, allusion to the existence of substitutes, and a large negotiation team. 'Bluffing' refers to exaggeration of one's professional and social position or network. 'Persuasive argument' refers to arguments of coinciding mutual interests and requests of 'I win now – you win next', or additional concessions after closing the deal. 'Avoidance' tactics refers to passive and negative attitudes such as repeated referrals to irrelevant issues and reiteration of counterpart's weaknesses or shortcomings with intention to avoid negotiations.

The ethical appropriateness, effectiveness and adoption likelihood ratings perceived by Korean negotiators for each of the five negotiation tactics identified by Lee and Park (2004) are shown in Table 6.1. Korean negotiators are most likely to employ the traditional competitive bargaining tactics because these are regarded as most ethical and effective. Korean negotiators are likely to employ the tactic of persuasive argument which they rank second for its effectiveness and ethical appropriateness. This indicates that the two most effective and adoption-likely tactics are also ethically the most appropriate. Although bluffing is rated third in terms of ethical appropriateness, its effectiveness is rated fifth, the last out of the five tactics. Thus, it is least likely for Korean negotiators to employ bluffing as a negotiation tactic.[15]

Table 6.1   The ethical appropriateness, effectiveness and adoption likelihood of Koreans' preferred negotiation tactics

	Ethical appropriateness rating	Effectiveness rating	Adoption likelihood rating
Physical discomfort	4th	3rd	3rd
Traditional competitive bargaining	1st	1st	1st
Bluffing	3rd	5th	5th
Persuasive argument	2nd	2nd	2nd
Avoidance	5th	4th	4th

Source: Lee and Park (2004).

The findings of Lee and Park (2004) also indicate that Korean negotiators employ negotiation tactics based on their perceived effectiveness, rather than on their perceived ethical appropriateness. This is shown by the same ranking of the five tactics for the effectiveness and adoption likelihood, in contrast to different rankings for the ethical appropriateness and adoption likelihood. For instance, the physical discomfort tactic may be adopted as its effectiveness and adoption likelihood are rated third, although its ethical appropriateness is rated fourth. Finally, the avoidance tactic is rated fifth in terms of ethical appropriateness and fourth in terms of effectiveness, indicating a low likelihood of its being adopted as a negotiation tactic.[16]

Song et al. (2004) use a survey and interviews of Korean negotiators to investigate the effects of culture and ethics-related tactics on negotiations in Korea. They identify 'sincerity, good faith, and honesty', demonstrated by both Korean negotiators and their counterparts, as the most important attitudinal factors for success in business negotiations in Korea. The second most important success factor is 'cultural awareness', including counterparts' familiarity with Korean business practices and customs. The third success factor is 'the counterpart's attitude', including preparedness and patience, and the fourth factor is past experience.

Song et al. (2004) also identify factors for failure in business negotiations in Korea. Differences in negotiation style, business practice, and social custom and culture are found to be the most important factors for failure, followed by lack of sincerity of the counterpart and communication breakdown in second place, and the absence of clear needs and competitive edge in the product under negotiation in third place. This empirical study highlights clearly that the ethical appropriateness of negotiation tactics on both sides has important bearings on the success and failure of negotiation, and that cultural awareness and preparedness are extremely important for all parties in business negotiation in Korea.

6.6 IMPLICATIONS FOR INTERNATIONAL BUSINESS IN KOREA

The discussion above highlights that to achieve success in business negotiation in Korea foreigners should be fully prepared across the board. In approaching Korean negotiators, it is imperative for foreigners to appreciate the significant differences between the negotiation practices they commonly use and the negotiation practices of Korean negotiators, which are shaped profoundly by Korean society and culture, business culture and communication style. Their negotiation ethics are similarly quite different. Foreign negotiators need to undertake thorough research of the Korean market, competition within the market, and government policy concerning their products. They will further improve their bargaining position if they learn as much as possible about the Korean business environment, organizational structure and decision-making system. In addition, to succeed in negotiating with Koreans, foreign negotiators should appreciate and respect salient Korean culture, negotiation practices and tactics as examined above.

Since trust and relationships are valued highly in business negotiation in Korea, foreign negotiators should realize that building and nurturing relationships is a key to successful negotiation and recognize that through the negotiations they enter a long-term relationship based on trust. Arriving at the negotiation table accompanied or introduced by highly placed Korean consultants or intermediaries is a valuable move for establishing a trusting business relationship. As Koreans spend a considerable time to understand and build a relationship with their negotiating counterpart, it is advisable for foreigners to prepare some pleasantries or praiseworthy remarks for casual talk at the outset of negotiation, rather than attempting to jump straight into the negotiation tasks. As noted earlier, entertainment is regarded as an important way of establishing a relationship, and Westerners should be prepared to be entertained and to reciprocate. Protocol is highly regarded, as is formality in behavior, dress code, ways of addressing people and ways of discoursing with others. Breaches of protocol may hinder relationship-building and hurt the *kibun* of the Korean negotiators.

Understanding Korean negotiators' unique styles of negotiation will certainly help foreigners to achieve success in negotiation. Koreans are renowned as aggressive negotiators who attempt to produce negotiation outcomes of a 'win–lose', or 'I win now – you win next'. The key decision-maker in the Korean team is usually not involved in the actual negotiation process, and the participating negotiators may need to consult fully with the key decision-maker at various stages throughout the negotiation. Indeed, every decision made by a negotiator must be ratified by his superior. As is widely recognized in international business circles, Koreans are risk averse. Besides, for the complex reasons discussed above, Korean negotiators are relatively inflexible and lack creativity. These features mean that business negotiations in the Korean context will take longer to complete than those in Western contexts. This requires patience for success in negotiations with Koreans.

The ethics of business negotiations in Korea are also different from those in other countries. Although Korean negotiators are likely to employ negotiation tactics based on the perceived effectiveness rather than the perceived ethical appropriateness of the tactics, foreigners generally have a high opinion of the negotiation tactics used by their Korean counterparts, with a few exceptions. These exceptions include traditional competitive bargaining tactics such as making unrealistic opening offers, and asking for more concessions after closing the deal. They indicate that foreigners should avoid making too many commitments or concessions until the final stage, and should leave some room for further concession even on the closed deal. Korean negotiators believe that success in business negotiation in Korea requires an ethical approach not only by their own team but also by their foreign counterparts. Foreigners should therefore approach business negotiation in Korea with sincerity and high communication skills, as well as an appreciation of ethical and cultural considerations.

6.7 CONCLUSION

This chapter has examined business negotiation in Korea. Understanding the importance of business negotiation is an integral part of international business. International business negotiation is intercultural negotiation. Cross-cultural negotiation is bound to be more sensitive and complex than intra-cultural negotiation, as it requires cross-cultural communication and understanding of the negotiation cultures, styles and tactics of foreign counterparts. To investigate the complexity of cross-cultural negotiation, a number of models have been considered. The Weiss and Stripp (1985) model which is the most comprehensive and culture-focused was adopted to analyze the negotiation process and practices employed by Korean negotiators. As the ethics of cross-cultural business negotiation are becoming increasingly important, the ethics of specific negotiation tactics have also been examined.

The negotiation process and practices that are dominant in any country are embedded in the culture of that country. As Korean culture is distinctive, so too is its dominant style of business negotiation. The salient traits of Korean culture, particularly hierarchical collectivism, patriarchal familism, authoritarianism, secularism, strong nationalism and long-term orientation, have shaped indelibly the negotiation process and practices that Korean negotiators use. Koreans regard negotiations as the beginning of a long-term trustful relationship which they value highly, and seek to establish such a relationship before they start to negotiate substantive issues. Since status and face matter very much in Korea's hierarchical society, formalities and protocol are assiduously observed. These features inevitably flow into negotiation protocols. Out of concerns with face, Korean negotiators are inclined to seek persuasion behind the scenes. Since Koreans are not familiar with written contracts, their perception of the legal nature of such an arrangement is less binding than Western negotiators understand, and the Korean team may ask for further concessions after closing the deal – ethically acceptable behavior in Korea. Both verbal and non-verbal communication modes of Koreans shape the negotiation process. Thus, it is important to appreciate both the high-context nature of Korean language, and the importance of *kibun* or feelings in non-verbal communication. Korean negotiators have distinctive approaches to negotiation ethics. They are likely to employ negotiation tactics for perceived effectiveness rather than perceived ethical appropriateness. Beyond this consideration, however, Korean negotiators are likely to employ conventional competitive or distributive bargaining strategy and tactics that are similar to and consistent with Western standards.

Just as all nations can be seen to have a distinctive style of business negotiation, this is certainly true for Korea. As argued and demonstrated in this chapter, the dominant style and ethics of negotiation in Korea have many distinctive features that make the Korean model appear to be *sui generis*. Nevertheless foreign negotiators will be able to conduct successful, long-term business relations with Korean companies through knowledge, respect, sensitivity and judicious planning, which are surely the keys to fruitful business negotiations wherever they are conducted.

NOTES

1. Weiss (2004) presents a useful survey of the literature of international negotiation.
2. The author has the benefits of both direct observation of and participation in negotiation. He has been involved in the process of negotiation between Koreans and foreigners as an interpreter, and has personally participated in business negotiations with a number of Korean companies as vice-president of Net Five Com Corporation Ltd, a Canadian company.
3. Factors other than culture that affect international business negotiation such as political and legal aspects, economic systems, government and bureaucracies, ideology, and involvement of other stakeholders including labor unions and industrial associations, are beyond the scope of this chapter.
4. For a detailed review of the literature on international business negotiation, see Weiss (2004).
5. Hodgson et al. (2000, p. 28) reiterate the four-stage negotiation process in every country they have studied. Like the Graham model, models that consider a negotiation to traverse different and sequential stages over time are referred to as stage models (Weiss 2004). There are numerous stage models with different numbers and characteristics of stages.
6. Bowen (1998) points out the aggressive attitude of Korean negotiators, as seen not only by themselves but also by non-Koreans.
7. Bowen (1998) has also pointed out this type of Korean negotiating strategy.
8. Bowen (1998) found Koreans reluctant to exchange information.
9. According to the survey by Bowen (1998), selection of negotiators is determined by position in the company, relationship with superiors, relationship with the counterpart, and experience and expertise on the issue under negotiation. He has also found that Korean negotiators are highly experienced, technically aware and skilled negotiators.
10. Bowen (1998) has found that the majority of foreigners believe Korean negotiators lack creativity.
11. Kwon's (2006) study, based on a survey of a large number of foreign companies in Korea, found that business people from outside Korea regard the importance of personal relationships as the most arduous challenge in doing business in Korea. Lee and Park (2004) argue that Korean negotiators emphasize personal relationships more than substantive negotiation issues.
12. As pointed out by Tung (1991), Koreans are more emotional than the Japanese and Chinese during the course of negotiations. They can also become abusive, with shouting and desk-pounding in the course of arguments as well as negotiation.
13. Tung (1991) argues that Korean negotiators are more illogical than Japanese and Chinese negotiators.
14. A survey cited in Bowen (1998) found that 57 per cent of non-Koreans have experienced Koreans' requests for more concessions after closing a deal.

15.   Bowen (1998) has found a similar result.
16.   Bowen's (1998) results appear to be quite consistent with those of Lee and Park (2004).

REFERENCES

Bowen, S. (1998), 'Projections and perceptions', *AMCHAM Journal*, September–October, 1–13.

Graham, J.L. (1981), 'A hidden cause of America's trade deficit with Japan', *Columbia Journal of World Business*, Fall, 5–15.

Hahm, Hanhee (2003), 'Korean culture seen through Westerners' eyes', *Korea Journal*, 43 (1), 106–28.

Han, Kyung-Koo (2003), 'The anthropology of the discourse on the Koreanness of Koreans', *Korea Journal*, 43 (1), 5–31.

Hodgson, J.D., Y. Sano and J.L. Graham (2000), *Doing Business with the New Japan*, New York: Rowman & Littlefield Publishing.

Hofstede, G. and M.H. Bond (1988), 'The Confucius connection', *Organizational Dynamics*, 16 (4), 5–12.

Jones, Leroy P. and Il Sakong (1980), *Government, Business and Entrepreneurship in Economic Development: The Korean Case*, Cambridge: Harvard University Press.

Kweon, Sug-In (2003), 'Popular discourses on Korean culture: from the late 1980s to the present', *Korea Journal*, 43 (1), 32–57.

Kwon, O.Y. (2006), 'Recent changes in Korea's business environment: views of foreign business people in Korea', *Asia Pacific Business Review*, 12 (1), 77–94.

Lee, Jong-Keon and Hun-Joon Park (2004), 'An exploratory study of negotiation tactics in Korea' (in Korean), *International Journal of Negotiation*, 20 (1), 37–68.

Lewicki, Roy J. and Robert R. Robinson (1998), 'Ethical and unethical bargaining tactics: an empirical study', *Journal of Business Ethics*, 17 (6), 665–82.

Lewicki, R.J., D.M. Saunders, B. Barry and J.W. Minton (2004), *Essentials of Negotiation*, 3rd edn, Boston, MA: McGraw Hill Irwin, pp. 179–200.

Paik, Yongsun and R.L. Tung (1999), 'Negotiating with East Asians: how to attain "win–win" outcomes', *Management International Review*, 39 (2), 103–19.

Park, Hun-Joon and Jegoo Lee (2003), 'Korean managers' ethical/unethical bargaining tactics: a study on knowledge structure and cognitive dissonance' (in Korean), *International Journal of Negotiation*, 9 (2), 135–54.

Song, Y.J., C.L. Hale and N. Rao (2004), 'Success and failure of business negotiations for South Koreans', *Journal of International and Area Studies*, 11 (2), 45–65.

Tung, R. (1990), 'Business negotiation with the Koreans: a cross-cultural perspective', http://www.chinabiz.org/Asian_Business_Folder/Korean_Business_Negotiations.htm, accessed 7 October 2005.

Tung, R. (1991), 'Handshakes across the sea: cross-cultural negotiating for business success', *Organizational Dynamics*, 19, 30–40.

Weiss, S.E. (2004), 'International business negotiations research', in B.J. Punnett and O. Shenkar (eds), *Handbook for International Management Research*, 2nd edn, Ann Arbor, MI: University of Michigan Press, pp. 415–74.

Weiss, S.E. with W.G. Stripp (1985), 'Negotiating with foreign businesspersons: an introduction for Americans with propositions on six cultures', in S. Niemeier, C.P. Campbell and R. Dirven (eds), *The Cultural Context in Business Communication*, Amsterdam: John Benjamins, pp. 51–118.

Yi, Jeong Duk (2003), 'What is Korean culture anyway?' *Korea Journal*, 43 (1), 58–82.

7. Business ethics in Korea

7.1 INTRODUCTION

The flow of corruption that has come to light in Korea's political economy particularly since the 1997 financial crisis signals that ethics have marked Korea's corporate sector by their relative absence. A number of Korea's chaebols, including the nation's second-largest corporation, Daewoo, were forced into bankruptcy soon after the crisis. Their downfall was in conjunction with the crisis, fuelled by what is now regarded as institutionalized unethical conduct. Despite the gravity of corruption and its consequences for Korea's corporate sector, the government's far-reaching post-crisis reform program has had difficulty embedding business ethics in a corporate culture where national economic strength and quest for corporate profit still reign supreme. Ethics have been of minimal concern for many Korean businesses struggling to gain or maintain a competitive edge in domestic and international markets.

Recently, the corporate debacles that brought the massive US corporations Enron and WorldCom to bankruptcy in the early 2000s triggered greater interest in business ethics inside and outside the corporate sphere worldwide. In 2006, a corruption scandal embroiled the owner of Korea's largest automaker, Hyundai, accused of using a multi-million dollar slush fund to bribe government officials and to transfer corporate control to his son. The Hyundai case follows similar investigations into other industrial conglomerates such as Samsung and Doosan over the last few years. These large corporate scandals began to draw attention to the need for a more ethical business culture across the world.

Widespread media coverage has brought to public attention how these huge Korean corporations have ignored both ethical principles and the law. In response, the government has attempted to tighten laws and regulations to force corporate compliance with ethical standards. Beyond the force of law, the force of the market is also beginning to compel corporations to recognize the significance of ethical behavior, since alert consumers can exert market pressure on non-compliant companies. However, both forces have had a limited impact on corporate behavior. Korean people and their government have not favored severe punishment of Korean corporations for corrupt practices through the courts or through the markets, believing that this will impact negatively on the national economy, which they hold as a top national priority. Thus, without a driving popular and political will and the institutionalized imperative of severe legal punishment to compel compliance with ethical standards, transformation to a more ethical business environment in Korea has been slow, as the chain of corruption cases suggests.

Recognizing the rising importance of business ethics and their relative absence for the nation's economy as well as for international business in Korea, this chapter examines business ethics in Korea and the greater attention given to them since the disturbing string of corporate collapses after the 1997 financial crisis. This is done based on the extant literature in both English and Korean. To this end, conceptual issues of business ethics will first be reviewed as a contextual discussion. Then, the increasing importance of business ethics and the underlying international business environments which help foster and enforce ethical corporate conduct will be investigated. Under the conceptual and international backgrounds of business ethics, the recent status of business ethics in Korea, particularly in the wake of the financial crisis, will be examined. To understand what gave rise to the weak ethical foundation of Korean business when the financial crisis unfolded, the principal causes of the relatively poor development of business ethics in Korea through the decades of post-war economic development will be examined. Finally, the anti-corruption measures introduced by the Korean government to fortify the economy by producing a more ethical business culture will be assessed. Added to this is an assessment of measures that some companies have undertaken independently of legal requirements, recognizing the need to meet the demands for more ethically motivated consumers and contribute to social and environmental wellbeing as increasingly important dimensions of profit maximization.

7.2   CONCEPTUAL ISSUES IN BUSINESS ETHICS

Ethics are usually understood as a system of moral principles and rules of responsible conduct. Business ethics involve the normative application of particular ethical standards to the conduct of business as the basis for judgment about what is right or wrong in corporate life, and what a corporation ought to do and not do if it is to be a responsible actor in society. Ethical standards for corporate behavior therefore vary across cultures, nations and time, in accordance with the dominant values and beliefs of society.

Arguments for compliance with business ethics have been put forward from both a normative and a positive sense. Those who foremost support the interests of corporations have argued that a company's primary purpose is to maximize profits to maximize the financial returns to its shareholders to whom it is exclusively responsible. Implicit in this rationale is the understanding that it is beyond a company's responsibility – and thus may be unethical – for a company to consider the interests, rights and concerns of anyone else. However, some corporate supporters have come to acknowledge that companies need to comply with basic ethical standards and fulfill certain responsibilities to society beyond those specified under law. Business transactions in the free market system are based on trust and reliability between buyers and sellers to a significant extent. Thus, the free market system may not survive if economic units, whether companies or individuals, do not respect moral duties to a certain extent.

In this normative sense, Carroll (1991) has identified social as well as economic and legal responsibilities of businesses. As businesses increase their societal role and impact, they become responsible not only to their shareholders, but also to other stakeholders such as employees, customers, suppliers and the general public within which they operate. Carroll (1991) argues that these stakeholders have certain rights with regard to the conduct of business, and businesses have social responsibilities to these stakeholders. Business ethics therefore require that while maximizing profits for shareholders, businesses treat other stakeholders fairly in all aspects of business operations including finance, accounting and taxation, human resources management, production, sales and marketing, intellectual property and treatment of the physical environment. Carroll (1991) has also identified a fourth responsibility of business: to make a contribution to the society in which it operates. This is the morally grounded expectation that businesses will give some of their gains back to society, not just for further self-promotion but as acknowledgment of support received. This responsibility gains ground while governments in many countries reduce their role in society and corporate altruism is expected to contribute more.

From a positive sense, it is recognized that observance of basic moral obligations, whether these are legally codified or not, can be beneficial for business and sometimes even essential for its survival. Business performance in the market depends not only on its cost-efficiency and productivity, but also on its image toward society and employees, its reliability toward customers, and its brand as perceived by society. The dominant perceptions of a business within society, including popular concerns about the ethicality of business behavior, can impact profoundly on business image and brand, giving these public perceptions the potential to bear heavily on business performance. Today it is not just the impact of domestic ethical forces that compels corporations toward behavior that acknowledges corporate social responsibilities. Globalization of the world economy has broadened the field of ethical influence on business. Now, international standards of business ethics shape the ethical terrain of business, wherever it takes place. Companies are now constrained in their business conduct not only by domestic rules and ethics, but also by international standards of business ethics established by international and intergovernmental organizations. The responses of non-governmental organizations to business practices also steer companies toward socially responsible behavior since these organizations are generally oriented toward certain ethical causes that are of concern to society.

Ethical management means that companies run their business in consistence with business ethics together with compliance with laws and regulations. In ethical management, companies establish their ethical norms, and seek to maximize profits within the confines of laws and regulations as well as ethical norms. More specifically, ethical management refers to transparent, fair and scrupulous management in such areas as corporate governance, accounting and financing, tax payments, working conditions, environmental protection and human rights, as well as adherence to the law.

7.3   THE INCREASING IMPORTANCE OF BUSINESS ETHICS

The importance of business ethics has recently been rising because adherence to basic ethical standards is beneficial for business performance and is required for business operation by various domestic and international institutions. In a normative sense, business ethics argue that a company has moral duties that extend well beyond serving the interest of its owners or stockholders, and that these duties consist of more than simply obeying the law. Under the normative ethical principle, however, it is not incumbent on companies to adhere to moral duties. The fulfillment of moral duties will raise costs to a company and may lead to a loss of competitiveness if its competitors ignore them. Hence, companies are inclined to comply with business ethics to a minimum extent.

The importance of business ethics has recently increased in its positive context. Companies have come to appreciate that ethical conduct serves their own interests as well as those of society. Moves by international organizations to institutionalize and enforce ethical conduct in international business have helped to promote more ethically conscious business cultures. Companies recognize a positive relationship between the 'cost' of ethics – to conduct ethical management and fulfill social responsibilities; and the 'benefit' of ethics – favorable company image and reputation, which can have a profound influence on their profits and market value. Thus, companies see ethical conduct as a kind of necessary investment. Over the 1999–2002 period in Korea, the stock prices of companies that have implemented ethical management, with established codes of ethics and ethics officers, have increased significantly over those companies without ethical management (Federation of Korean Industries – FKI 2004, p. 27). The same study has found that operational profit was significantly higher for companies with ethical management than those without it over the 1998–2001 period.[1] The stock prices of the 'ten most respectable companies' selected by *Fortune Magazine* increased by 25.6 per cent over 1996 to 2001, as compared to 10.7 per cent for other standard and poors (S&Ps) 500 companies (FKI 2004, p. 28). It was also found that companies in Korea with codes of business ethics and ethics officers have attracted significantly more foreign capital than others (Yoon 2005, p. 16).

Ethics have been a more important concern for business in the era of globalization. A key reason is that ethics have been increasingly institutionalized and enforceable by international regulatory bodies seeking to establish fairness in international business transactions. The huge growth of international business through globalization of the world economy has inspired international organizations such as the UN and the OECD to establish international ethical guidelines for business conduct in areas such as employment relations, consumer protection, environmental pollution and basic human rights.[2] A clear example is the OECD's five basic principles of corporate governance (OECD 1999) that give international legal weight to: protection of shareholders' rights; equitable treatment of all shareholders; recognition of the rights of stakeholders as established by law; disclosure and transparency on all material matters including the company's financial situation, performance, ownership and governance; and responsibility of the company board to ensure strategic guidance of the company and effective monitoring of management, and the board's accountability to the company and its shareholders.

Among a raft of regulations against corruption, the OECD established in 1997 the Convention on Combating Bribery of Foreign Public Officials in International Business Transactions (Park 2005) and the UN adopted in 2003 its Convention against Corruption (Kim 2004, p. 90). The OECD Convention obliged signatory countries to make the bribery of a foreign public official a crime under their domestic laws by 1999. The provisions of the OECD Convention are binding on the participants for serious sanctions. The UN Convention against Corruption requires countries to establish criminal and other offences to cover a wide range of acts of corruption so that corruption can be prosecuted. The UN Convention also requires prevention of corruption by enhancing transparency in the financing of election campaigns and political parties, and in recruiting civil servants. Although the UN

Convention is mainly concerned with corruption at the government level, it will also have important implications for international business transactions.

International trade rules under WTO jurisdiction seek to institutionalize ethical trade behavior and corporate social responsibility. These rules result from rounds of talks on environmental issues, labor standards, intellectual property rights, fair competition and unethical business practices. The Ethics Round intends to prevent international trade of products produced by firms that conduct any unethical activities. Unethical activities include bribery, tax evasion, inappropriate financial transactions, capital flight, slush funds, false advertising, price manipulation, improper labor management, and environmental damage. As part of this round, the WTO established the Agreement on Government Procurement to enhance fair international competition through measures requiring more transparent government procurement laws.

Non-government organizations (NGOs) have also been active in this area. A pre-eminent example is Transparency International (TI), an international NGO established in 1993, that draws together civil society, business and governments in a powerful global coalition to combat corruption in government, business and banks (TI 2005a). TI focuses on systems for prevention and reform and its measurement instruments are highly regarded worldwide. These include the Corruption Perceptions Index (CPI) for comparing corruption in national contexts, and the Bribe Payers Index (BPI) for measuring the propensity of companies to bribe foreign officials to win business. TI's Six Step Implementation Process provides a practicable model for companies to steer clear of bribery. The six steps are: deciding to adopt a no-bribes policy; getting commitment from the top; setting up a cross-functional project team; deciding the extent of any public disclosure; focusing on meeting the timetable; and identifying obstacles to the implementation process.

The US, which is an important leader of global business ethics, introduced the Foreign Corrupt Practices Act in 1977 by which US firms are prohibited from paying bribes in foreign countries. In the wake of a series of corporate financial scandals including Enron, Tyco International and WorldCom, the US enacted in 2002 a law known as the Public Company Accounting Reform and Investor Protection Act. The law requires all companies listed with the US securities markets to establish an accounting oversight board under the US Securities and Exchange Commission, which in turn monitors the conduct of listed companies, auditor independence, corporate responsibility including certification of financial reports by chief executive officers (CEOs) and chief financial officers (CFOs), and enhanced financial disclosure. This law is expected to apply to all listed companies in the US including both domestic and foreign firms.

In sum, institutional pressure has dovetailed with the quest for ethical profit-making to elevate the importance of business ethics in domestic and international contexts. In recognition of the importance and value of ethical business conducts and their social responsibilities, more companies have earnestly undertaken ethical management. They have codified their ethical standards in charters or in-house guidelines for business conduct. These codes and charters are generally meant to identify the company's expectations of workers, and to offer guidance on handling some of the more common ethical problems that arise in the course of doing business. Having such an internal corporate ethical policy leads to a greater ethical awareness, consistency in application and the avoidance of ethical disasters. Some companies appoint ethics officers to make recommendations regarding ethical matters, disseminate pertinent information to employees, and uncover or prevent illegal or unethical business conduct.

7.4   BUSINESS ETHICS IN KOREA

Although Korean companies started to pay some attention to business ethics from the beginning of the 1990s, it is since the 1997 financial crisis that they have seriously taken up ethical issues. The search for causes of the crisis in Korea finally exposed the nature of Korean business practices to a critical lens and drew attention to the paucity of ethical considerations in some aspects of Korean business. Cronyism between companies and politicians, corporate governance that blocked transparency and accountability, and moral hazard, were particularly evident among chaebols and banks. The government's reform program has reached extensively across the Korean economy, seeking to address the opacity and absence of accountability among Korean businesses that had produced such unexpected failure in the national economy. Primary concerns of reform have been economic recovery and stability rather than ensuring corporate morality. Nevertheless, recognizing that business ethics are an important foundation for sustainable corporate success, reform planners have pursued a number of regulations to enforce more ethical business conduct. One particular area is corporate governance, especially increasing the accountability of principal shareholders (owners). New laws have come into effect to increase the number of outside members on company boards, expand the authority of internal auditing, protect minority shareholders and increase the transparency of financial statements.[3]

It appears, however, that ethical management has not taken root in Korea. Implementation of ethical management includes the following stages: establishing the code of ethics, developing implementation manuals, appointing ethics officers, providing ethics education for employees, and protecting whistle-blowers. Many Korean companies do not yet have a code of ethics. The 2002 survey by the FKI (2004) found that just under half of sampled companies (49.7 per cent) had a code of ethics, as compared to 90 per cent in Japan (FKI 2004, p. 126). Kim (2004, p. 112) found similar results: only 45 per cent of large companies and 21 per cent of small and medium-sized companies had a code of business ethics as of 2004. A 2005 survey by the Korean Chamber of Commerce and Industry (KCCI 2005) found 53.2 per cent of the 300 companies surveyed had a code of ethics, 64.4 per cent had ethics guidelines for employees, 30.9 per cent had an ethics officer, 48.2 per cent had whistle-blowing and monitoring systems, and 56.8 per cent offered ethics education to senior managers and employees. These survey results indicate the underdevelopment of business ethics in Korea and the necessity of institutionalizing business ethics within Korean corporate culture. Although some companies have established codes of ethics, they are mainly externally oriented, and ethics offices are either not established or not functioning properly (FKI 2004, p. 127). Kim (2004) has designated Korea at the third of the five development stages of business ethics identified by Reidenback and Robin (1991).[4]

Another indication of unethical management in Korea is the lack of transparency in business operations. One important area of the post-crisis reform program has been to address the lack of transparency in business operations, which is particularly important for attracting and securing the confidence of foreign investment and business partners. The significance of lack of business transparency was demonstrated clearly when foreign investors pulled their investment from Korea as the true picture of the Korean companies in which they had invested or partnered was suddenly brought to full public light in 1997. Yet it appears that even after the 1997 crisis, Korean companies have not come to appreciate the value of business transparency. A KCCI survey of 300 companies in 2005 found that after the 1997 crisis 68 per cent accepted the need for transparent business operations, but only 57 per cent claimed that they had increased their transparency since 1997 (KCCI 2005). As for companies' views on transparent management, the survey found that 34.5 per cent believe it enhances international competition, 27 per cent believe it improves profitability, 20 per cent believe it improves company image, and 18 per cent believe it is necessary for fulfilling corporate social responsibility (KCCI 2005). However, Korean companies acknowledge that the level of their management transparency falls quite far below that of their counterparts in developed nations, and only 20 per cent consider the transparency level of their company is equivalent to the levels most common in economically developed nations (KCCI 2004a).

The lack of transparency is regarded as an important cause of the so-called 'Korea discount' for stock prices. According to a survey of 30 foreign stock experts, conducted by the Korea Chamber of Commerce and Industry in December 2004, these foreign experts estimated that the extent of the 'Korean discount' – the percentage to which the average stock price of listed Korean companies would be higher than the actual price – was then 31 per cent. These foreign experts attributed 22 per cent of the discount to Korean companies' lack of transparency, 30 per cent to country risk such as nuclear threat, and 24 per cent to lack of policy consistency (KCCI 2004b).

Transparency and corruption are closely related. The lack of transparency begets corruption. Hence, an important indicator of the low level of business ethics in Korea is the level of corruption. With inadequate corporate governance and a lack of transparency, companies conduct socially irresponsible and unethical activities such as the controversial inheritance of company wealth and management. Kim (2004, p. 112) has considered the many types of corruption that permeate the Korean business community, such as illegal political contributions, collusion in the tendering process, bribery in business licensing and controlling, and bribery in taxation.[5] The annual Corruption Perceptions Index (CPI) developed by Transparency International provides comparative assessment of national corruption levels and is critically important in informing foreign investors and businesses in considering opportunities in Korea. CPI scores indicate the degree of corruption as seen by business people and country analysts, on a scale of 0 (highest level of corruption) to 10 (lowest level of corruption). The CPI for Korea indicates that the international business community perceives a high level of corruption in Korea. As shown in Table 7.1, Korea's score has recorded an uneven but gradual rise, although in 2005 this score was still low, with Korea ranked 40th out of 158 countries.

Table 7.1 Trends in Korea's CPI (1997–2005)

Year	1997	1998	1999	2000	2001	2002	2003	2004	2005
CPI	4.3	4.2	3.8	4	4.2	4.5	4.3	4.5	5.0
Korea's rank	34	43	50	48	42	40	50	47	40
Total number of countries surveyed	52	85	99	90	91	103	133	146	158

Sources: Transparency International (TI) (2005b). Figures for 1997–2004 are from Park (2005).

Another aspect of corruption is the propensity of companies to pay bribes to foreign officials to win business. The Bribe Payers Index constructed by

Transparency International ranks leading exporting countries in terms of the degree to which international companies headquartered in those countries are likely to pay bribes to senior public officials in emerging market economies to win business. In this index, the lower the score, the higher the perceived propensity to pay bribes, with 10 a perfect score indicating zero perceived propensity to pay bribes. For 2002 Korea's score was 3.9, ranking 18th out of 21 leading exporting countries (Table 7.2), indicating that Korean companies are highly likely to conduct business unethically and unfairly against competitors in international markets by offering bribes to win business.[6]

Table 7.2 Bribe payers' index (1999 and 2002)

Rank	Country	1999	2002	Rank	Country	1999	2002
1	Australia	8.1	8.5	12	France	5.2	5.5
2	Sweden	8.3	8.4	13	US	6.1	5.3
3	Switzerland	7.7	8.4	14	Japan	5.1	5.3
4	Austria	7.8	8.2	15	Malaysia	3.9	4.3
5	Canada	8.1	8.1	16	Hong Kong		4.3
6	Netherlands	7.4	7.8	17	Italy	3.7	4.1
7	Belgium	6.8	7.8	18	Korea	3.4	3.9
8	UK	7.2	6.9	19	Taiwan	3.5	3.8
9	Singapore	5.7	6.3	20	China	3.1	3.5
10	Germany	6.2	6.3	21	Russia		3.2
11	Spain	5.3	5.8	22			

Source: Transparency International (2002).

7.5 WHY LOW-LEVEL ETHICS AND HIGH-LEVEL CORRUPTION IN KOREA?

The data discussed above indicate that by comparison with business cultures in other nations, the Korean corporate sector is still perceived internationally as relatively high on corruption and, by extension, relatively low on ethics. Several factors help to explain this. First, Korean companies do not appreciate the value of business ethics in the emerging globalization era. Most Korean companies regard business ethics as a dispensable corporate social responsibility rather than an indispensable requirement for business success and long-term survival. Kim (2004, p. 104) shows that 71 per cent of Korean companies regarded business ethics as a social responsibility in 2004, while only 14 per cent saw ethical management as necessary for a successful business operation and survival. Korean companies fail to appreciate how business ethics are vital for legitimizing corporate image and branding, for establishing credibility with customers, and for supporting the morale of employees. They fail to recognize that ethical business behavior enables the free market to operate with minimal regulation, and that the trust on which the fiduciary relationships between market actors depend is sustained by expectations of ethical behavior in the market. Since many Korean companies do not understand the vital functions of ethical behavior for a strong market economy and for their own corporate success, business ethics have not taken firm root in Korean business culture.

Second, many Korean companies do not comprehend the raft of international rules and ethical guidelines established by international organizations for international business transactions. As Kim (2004, p. 105) explains, many Korean businesses do not understand the ethical guidelines established by international organizations for international business transactions, such as the UN Convention against Corruption, the WTO global code of ethics, the OECD Convention on Combating Bribery of Foreign Public Officials in International Business Transactions, and ethical guidelines by NGOs.

Third, inadequate corporate governance of Korean companies and particularly chaebols was regarded as the major culprit for the lack of transparency in business operations and unethical and unlawful corporate behavior particularly prior to the 1997 crisis. Before the crisis, a pyramid ownership structure resulting from cross-ownership, and a style of corporate governance that gave considerable freedom to the founders of chaebols and their families enabled these people to control and manage chaebols even though they held only a minor portion of total shares (Hwang 2002). By holding controlling interests in affiliates, which in turn held controlling interests in other affiliates, the controlling shareholder participated in the management of all affiliates. And although the board of directors had the critical role of monitoring management, because boards were comprised almost entirely of members of the families who controlled the chaebols, boards did not carry out effectively their vital duty of monitoring and disciplining management.

External monitoring and disciplining of management was also ineffective. Commercial banks as creditors had little monitoring power over chaebols because even these banks were under government control, including in their credit allocations. The hostile takeover of chaebols was banned in the name of national economic stability. Controlling shareholders therefore enjoyed almost full discretion without challenge from outside shareholders, and could ignore requirements for transparency and disclosure concerning their business operations. These circumstances generated agency problems, with controlling shareholders and managers attempting to maximize value for themselves rather than for all shareholders.[7]

Chaebols' treatment of shareholders was inequitable and inconsistent with OECD corporate governance principles. Minority shareholders had few legal protections or rights to prevent the controlling shareholders from pursuing their own interests. Shareholders with less than 5 per cent of issued shares could not remove a director, file an injunction, demand a convocation, inspect accounting books, and inspect records of company affairs and company property. By 1997, over 98 per cent of shareholders were small investors who held less than 1 per cent of shares (Joh 2001).

These circumstances that allowed the owners of chaebols to operate without transparency in their operations meant that the market lacked accurate and reliable information on chaebols' performance and management. Since chaebols relied heavily on debt financing there was no compulsion for financial transparency or reliable information to attract equity investors. Chaebols were not required to provide consolidated financial reports for the whole group of chaebols. And accounting standards in Korea were lower than international standards. The systemic features discussed here clearly indicate that without institutionalized regulations to ensure the ethical conduct of chaebols, those who owned and managed chaebols could continue operations without regard for business ethics or for the trust required of them as the domestic market's biggest players.

Inevitably, when the financial crisis in 1997 proved that these circumstances could not sustain the national economy, measures to institutionalize business ethics by improving corporate governance and management transparency were a significant concern in the government's reform program. To improve transparency, which is at the core of good corporate governance, in 1998 the government amended the Generally Accepted Accounting Principles requiring companies to prepare financial statements that conform to international standards. Chaebols are now required to prepare and publish consolidated financial statements, to disclose intra-group transactions, and detail cross-shareholdings among affiliates, intra-group guarantees and credit trading (SERI 2005). From 2004, CEOs are required to certify and sign their financial statements and ensure the veracity of signed documents (SERI 2005).

To improve the accountability of controlling owners to their shareholders, a cumulative voting system was introduced for selection of board members, and appointment of independent or outside directors for up to 50 per cent of the board was made compulsory. The independence of auditors was strengthened by establishing external auditors' committees that must include outside directors, major creditors and shareholders. Lowering the shareholding threshold to enable small shareholders to initiate or participate in certain actions strengthened the voting rights of minority shareholders, and institutional investors were given the right to vote freely by abolishing 'shadow voting'.[8] Class actions by shareholders were allowed for the first time in 2004, although these are legally limited to flagrant cases of fraudulent accounting and false disclosure (SERI 2005).

The corporate governance system has therefore been improved substantially through the laws and other measures undertaken in the reform program in the wake of the 1997 crisis. However, improvements are far from complete, and corporate governance of chaebols still falls far short on all of the OECD corporate governance principles (Kang 2004). It is still difficult for minority shareholders to check and prevent the moral hazard of managers. For individual shareholders in a large corporation it is almost impossible to mobilize those who have the threshold amount of shares to do anything against controlling shareholders or management. The post-crisis law, which enables class actions by minority shareholders, was quickly whittled away to become almost meaningless (Lee 2003, p. 56). Although institutional investors are permitted to exercise their voting rights, there is still a lack of activism (Kang 2004).The law that limits cross-shareholding up to 25 per cent of net capital has also been rendered almost impotent, with many loopholes and exceptions attached (Lee 2003, p. 56). In fact, the proportion of internally held shares in chaebols has increased after the crisis, which has strengthened the clout of controlling shareholders at the expense of minority shareholders, thereby maintaining their influence in the management of chaebols (Jang 2002).

While new laws on the selection method for company directors were to widen the scope of people chosen, even in 2000, 85 per cent of elected outside directors were recommended by controlling families, managers and related associations (Jang 2002, p. 113). The duties and responsibilities of the outside directors have not been clearly defined, and in practice give these people little or no weight on company boards (Lee 2003, p. 56; Joh, 2001, p. 127). Hence, it is still the case that neither the board nor outside investors carry out the important duties of monitoring and disciplining management. With these circumstances prevailing, both domestic and foreign investors recognize that Korean firms do not operate with transparent and accountable governance (Jang 2002, p. 116). In sum, corporate governance in Korea still falls far short of global standards. This inadequacy contributes to the low development level of business ethics.

Fourth, one important reason for the state of ethics and corruption in Korea is that the business climate tolerates and sustains it with deficiencies in the legal system and its enforcement. The nation's legal system was not crafted to enforce ethical business behavior but primarily to sustain a post-war industrial policy for rebuilding the economy quickly, particularly through the chaebols, with intensive concentration of industrial clout and extensive government support. As noted above, legal arrangements have been introduced as part of the reform program in the wake of the crisis to make business operations more transparent and to overhaul the governance of Korean companies, particularly chaebols.[9] However, corporate laws have weak teeth, have not been taken far enough, and are not enforced fully or consistently, as attested by the acquittals of Samsung and Doosan in 2005, while for a similar offence the Hyundai Motors chairman was indicted in 2006. Korean people also tolerate the deficiency of law enforcement against such malfeasance from their concern about the adverse effects of corporate laws on the economy.

Fifth, many types of difficulties internal and external to the company have been pointed out in implementing ethics management in Korea. A study was conducted in 2005 by the Federation of Korean Industry (FKI 2005) to identify internal and external obstacles to ethical management in Korean companies. The FKI carried out a questionnaire survey of 500 companies to identify in particular the views held by company CEOs. As we see in Table 7.3, on difficulties internal to the company, 17 per cent claimed lack of information and know-how in ethical management, 14 per cent claimed the shortage of human and other resources, 14 per cent the conflict with short-term operational outcomes, and 13 per cent the indifference of employees. The data in this table indicate that companies lack full awareness and understanding of business ethics, and have not paid serious attention to implementing an ethical management style. This situation highlights the need for a national ethical association representing the business sector in Korea to produce business ethics guidelines that are applicable across all businesses and require compliance by all members. Another useful remedial measure would be a requirement that the boards of all Korean companies establish an ethics committee to oversee the establishment of a code of ethics by the company and its adherence to this code.

On difficulties external to the company in implementing ethical management, as shown in Table 7.4, 25 per cent of respondents pointed to corruption in the public sector, 22 per cent to unscrupulous politicians, 22 per cent to the lack of transparency in the public sector, 19 per cent to the public sector bureaucracy, and 13 per cent to illicit political funds (FKI 2005). All of these external difficulties tie into the venality of politicians and civil servants and the structure of corporate–government links that foster it.

These findings highlight the systemic nature of the ethics problem in Korean business culture. They indicate that in order to institutionalize ethical management in the private sector, the government must simultaneously implement its own anti-corruption policy so that implementation of ethical management is comprehensive across both sectors and is mutually reinforcing. Inconsistent implementation across public and private sectors will ensure that there will always be loopholes and flexibility that enable participants from both sectors to evade or abuse the system and render it corrupt and ineffective.

Table 7.3 Internal obstacles to ethical business management

Types of internal difficulties	%
1. Lack of required information and know-how	17
2. Shortage of required human and other resources	14
3. Conflict with short-term business performance	14
4. Indifference of employees	13
5. Conflicts among employees	9
6. Compensation system against company's value	7
7. Uncertainty among employees	5
8. Damaging the image of the company	5
9. Lack of serious intention by the top manager	4
10. Others	12

Source: FKI (2005).

Table 7.4 External difficulties in ethical management

Types of external difficulties	%
1. Corruption in the public sector	25
2. Unscrupulous politicians	22
3. Lack of transparency in the public sector	22
4. Bureaucracy in the public sector	19
5. Illicit political funds	13

Source: FKI (2005).

7.6   WHAT HAS BEEN DONE IN KOREA TO IMPROVE BUSINESS ETHICS?

Particularly since the financial crisis revealed the flaws in the Korean business model and the dire consequences of these flaws for the national economy, the Korean government has pursued a raft of policy measures, particularly legislation, to address entrenched corruption. An initial step in the reform package was the establishment of the Regulatory Reform Committee in 1998 in response to recognition that some government regulations were generating corruption, and this committee has abolished 8000 (57 per cent) of 14 000 central government regulations. Also that year, the Act to Combat Bribery of Foreign Public Officials in International Business was enacted to bring Korea into compliance with OECD convention (Park 2005). Subsequent legislation was aimed more specifically at addressing corruption: the Anti-Corruption Act and the Money Laundering Prevention Act were enacted in 2001 and the Code of Conduct for Public Officials was established in 2003 (Chung 2004). The government has tried to make best use of information technology while putting its policy into practice, especially to increase transparency in public and corporate governance.

Of particular significance for institutionalizing more ethical corporate behavior, the Korean Independent Commission Against Corruption (KICAC) was established in 2002 under the 2001 Anti-Corruption Act to set the direction for anti-corruption policy at the national level and lay the foundation for government-wide implementation and public and civic cooperation. The KICAC has pursued four major anti-corruption areas in particular: policy formulation and assessment; institutional improvement; corruption-report handling; and education and promotion (Park 2005). The KICAC is responsible for handling whistle-blowing cases, providing protection for whistle-blowers from retaliation and discrimination in the workplace, and rewarding them for anti-corruption efforts.

Despite these government efforts since the crisis, the dominant international and domestic perception is that corruption still marks the landscape of Korea's political economy. The KICAC's national survey of the general public in 2002 found that 53 per cent thought civil servants (including politicians) were corrupt, and 59.5 per cent thought that corruption had not decreased over the past year (KICAC 2003). The survey identified strongest public concern for action against corruption aimed at politicians, the judicial system, the media, public administration and private corporations. The survey found that corruption was perceived to be widespread in the public sector, especially in construction, legal affairs, taxation, defense, policing, education, health care, environment and procurement. These survey results indicate the need for further anti-corruption measures across the public sector as well as the private sector, and a government that has the political will to attend to this task seriously. At the time of writing in 2006, the KICAC appears keen to crack down on corruption and to have the support of government and the legal system, as is evident in moves to indict the Hyundai Motors chairman over establishing slush funds.

7.7 CONCLUSION

This chapter on business ethics in Korea has shed light on their relatively underdeveloped status in the nation's political economy. It has been shown that the developments in business ethics in a global context still have considerable distance to travel in Korean corporate culture. This is so even though the financial crisis of 1997 forced open the window on how the post-war Korean business model sustained the capacity of business to ignore important ethical considerations and thus fostered entrenched corruption. Until the crisis, a corporate culture that easily disregarded ethics, particularly in matters of governance and transparency, had produced considerable corporate success. But because it was built on a business model blind to certain ethical considerations, such corporate 'success' was patently unsustainable over time. The ethical considerations that could be easily dismissed in this corporate culture were some of the very concerns that are vital in market operations, as the crisis proved at great expense to the corporate sector and the national economy at large.

Business environments have recently changed domestically and internationally, requiring an increasing compliance with business ethics. The ethical imperative is at work in business culture, based on the recognition that maintaining business ethics is a valuable corporate strategy that serves corporate interests. Studies have demonstrated how upholding business ethics can be critical to business success, particularly given the influence of a company's public reputation and image on its capacity to make profits. In this view, upholding business ethics is an indispensable investment in a company's continued success, rather than a dispensable cost.

In the current international context, globalization and free markets have a deeper influence on economic life, forcing ethical considerations into a more prominent position in shaping business behavior. These forces have also helped to change the nature of business ethics, which now involve social as well as legal responsibility. Business ethics now require companies to consider beyond the concerns of shareholders, and to take into account other stakeholders such as employees, customers, suppliers, and the general public who share the consequences of business operations, whether beneficial or deleterious. Ethical guidelines are also more firmly institutionalized through domestic and intergovernmental organizations such as the UN, OECD and WTO, and non-governmental organizations such as TI, that foster adherence to international rules and regulations on corporate behavior.

Nonetheless, the understanding of business ethics as an investment for corporate image, business success and long-term survival has not taken deep root in Korean business culture. The empirical evidence discussed in this chapter indicates how the understanding of ethics among Korean CEOs is poorly informed. Empirical evidence also indicates that business behavior, particularly by large Korean corporations, leaves Korea ranked poorly on international comparisons of perceived corruption (the Corruption Perceptions Index) and sustain the perception among the Korean public and the international business community that business ethics in Korea still fall well short of international standards despite widespread reform attempts since the crisis.

Indeed, we have seen in this chapter that both the corporate sector and the national government took action in the wake of the financial crisis. Many companies moved toward adopting a code of ethics and appointing ethics officers to promote ethical behavior. Yet by 2005 around half of Korean companies still did not have a code of business ethics and many of the ethics officers were not functioning properly. The national government has moved more extensively to prevent unethical behavior as part of its post-crisis corporate reform program. As well as abolishing more than half of the old government regulations and introducing a raft of new laws and regulations, the government established the Korea Independent Commission Against Corruption to set the direction for anti-corruption policy and lay the foundations for nationwide implementation.

Despite these moves to institutionalize corporate ethics in Korea, the regulatory system is still failing. Preventing unethical business behavior involves dislodging the concentration of corporate power held firmly by chaebols. The pre-crisis system of corporate governance that blocked transparency and accountability sustained a firm grip on corporate power by chaebols. They have maintained their corporate power with relative impunity since the political, legal and social institutions have been inadequate and have failed to enforce punitive action. A succession of governments since the crisis has lacked the political will to punish unethical conduct, in the face of resistance by the corporate elite and their own collusion in this system as recipients of substantial support from the corporations. These governments have embarked on extensive corporate reforms but have moved gingerly on enforcing ethical behavior in the political system, the public sector and the corporate sector. Government has allowed the passage of ineffectual laws and accepted the courts' failure to enforce them. Korean society has also accepted these outcomes in the belief that punishing the corporations will harm the economy. By 2005, Korean consumers had not used their market behavior effectively to punish corporations for unethical conduct, or used their electoral behavior to bring to power governments that would seriously attend to unlawful ethical breeches by the corporations.

Clearly there is a long way to go for business ethics in Korea to reach the level sustained by most OECD countries. As studies by Nwabuzor (2005) and Sanyal (2005) show, corruption retards economic development. Korean society must therefore realize that a firm national commitment to end corruption and enhance business ethics is critically important in developing the national economy to the level of developed countries. Globalization will continue to influence the Korean economy and encourage Korean businesses and corporations to comply further with international ethical standards. This trend is under way all over the world, and the Korean business community will benefit from corporate compliance with a higher level of business ethics. To this end, corporate governance and transparency require serious remedial action in order to conform with OECD principles. Government too must overhaul all spheres of operation to improve transparency and accountability, and anti-corruption institutions must be overhauled to conform to international standards. The business community must do its share, implementing ethical management up to the level of advanced countries.

Korea's political economy is in transition. As the nation's democracy and economy mature further, a more open and transparent political system develops, which is less susceptible to political corruption. In the process of advancing to the level of developed countries, the Korean economy will be globalized further and realize the imperative of compliance with international business standards. The trend demanding an increasing level of business ethics is rising all over the world. In appreciation of the trend, the Korean business community will further realize benefits arising from complying with a high level of business ethics. Over this transitional period of the Korean politics and economy, business ethics in Korea is likely to improve, albeit gradually, to the level commensurate to its economic power and to catch up with the level of developed countries.

NOTES

1. A similar result has been found by Yoon (2005, p. 14) over the 2001–03 period. That is, both the share prices and operating profit were higher for companies with ethical management than those without it.
2. The United Nations Universal Declaration of Human Rights in 1948 is the basic ethical guideline in dealing with human rights whereby multinational enterprises should respect the rights of all persons to life, liberty, security and privacy (Frederick 1991).
3. For detailed examination of the development of corporate governance of chaebols before and after the 1997 financial crisis, see Kwon (2005).
4. Reidenback and Robin (1991) cast the five stages in development of business ethics as:
   a. the amoral organization with a culture of winning at any cost and no code of ethics;
   b. the legalistic corporation concerned with obedience to laws and regulations but not with morality;
   c. the responsive organization upholding values beyond productivity and a sense of legality;
   d. the emergent ethical organization with a proper sense of balancing profit and ethics, a code of ethics for the core organizational values and with an ethics officer; and
   e. the ethical organization with a balanced concern for ethical and economic outcomes and an ethical profile in all phases of organizational conduct.

5.   According to Kwon (2006), which is based on a survey of a large number of foreign companies in Korea, foreign business people regard cronyism, corruption, excessive discretionary power of bureaucrats and excessive government regulations as difficult areas in doing business in Korea.
6.   Park (2005) cites other international institutes whose perceptions of Korea with regard to the corruption level and the lack of transparency are similar to those indicated by Transparency International.
7.   As one indication of the agency problem, in 1995 the total amount of donations by chaebols for the sake of their social reputation was greater than that of dividends (Jang 2002, p. 111).
8.   Shadow voting means that the votes held by institutional investors, who were not allowed to cast their votes by themselves, were distributed in proportion to the voting result at the shareholders' meeting. In effect, therefore, institutional investors were immaterial at the shareholders' meetings.
9.   For a further detailed examination of the development of corporate governance of chaebols before and after the 1997 financial crisis, see Kwon (2005).

REFERENCES

Carroll, A.B. (1991), 'The pyramid of corporate social responsibility', *Business Horizon*, 34 (4), 39–48.

Chung, Soung-jin (2004), 'Anti-corruption strategy of Korea', mimeo, presented at the 2nd Anti-Corruption Agency Forum, Malaysia.

Federation of Korean Industries (FKI) (2004), *Ethical Management: Understanding and Implementation* (in Korean), Seoul: Federation of Korean Industries.

Federation of Korean Industries (FKI) (2005), 'Implementation status and issues of ethics management viewed by CEO' (in Korean), mimeo.

Frederick, William C. (1991), 'The moral authority of transnational corporate codes', *Journal of Business Ethics*, 10, 165–77.

Hwang, Inhak (2002), 'Chaebol structure, diversification and performance', in Z. Rhee and E. Chang (eds), *Korean Business and Management: The Reality and the Vision*, Elizabeth, NJ: Hollym, pp. 171–203.

Jang, Hasung (2002), 'After the economic crisis: an analysis of the effects of corporate restructuring', in Z. Rhee and E. Chang (eds), *Korean Business and Management: The Reality and the Vision*, Elizabeth, NJ: Hollym, pp. 79–131.

Joh, Sung Wook (2001), 'The Korean corporate sector: crisis and reform', in O.Y. Kwon and W. Shepherd (eds), *Korea's Economic Prospects: From Financial Crisis to Prosperity*, Cheltenham, UK and Northampton, MA, USA: Edward Elgar Publishing, pp. 116–32.

Kang, Moon-Soo (2004), 'Corporate governance in Korea', http://coe21-policy.sfc. keio.ac.jp/ja/event/file/s1-5_Kang.pdf, accessed 27 May 2006.

KCCI (Korea Chamber of Commerce and Industry) (2004a), 'Perception and issues of transparent and ethical management' (in Korean), *KCCI Report*, 619.

KCCI (Korea Chamber of Commerce and Industry) (2004b), 'Status, causes and prospects of the "Korean discount" of stock prices' (in Korean), *KCCI Report*, 768.

KCCI (Korea Chamber of Commerce and Industry) (2005), 'Ethical management of Korean global companies: the current status and impacts on business performance' (in Korean), *KCCI Report*, 842.

Kim, Sung-Soo (2004), *Ethics Management*, Seoul: Samyoung-sa.

Korea Independent Commission Against Corruption (KICAC) (2003), 'Perception of corruption survey', http://www.kicac.go.kr/eng_content/news_02.jsp?bbsid=eng2 &seq=1602&pnum=12.

Kwon, O.Y. (2005), 'The Korean corporate sector (chaebol): development and reform', mimeo.

Kwon, O.Y. (2006), 'Recent changes in Korea's business environment: views of foreign business people in Korea', *Asia Pacific Business Review*, 12 (1), 77–94.

Lee, Jaymin (2003), 'Economic crisis and structural reform in Korea', in C.H. Sohn (ed.), *Structural Reforms and Economic Development: Experiences of the Northeast Asia*, Seoul: Korea Institute for International Economic Policy, pp. 35–64.

Nwabuzor, A. (2005), 'Corruption and development: new initiatives in economic openness and strengthened rule of law', *Journal of Business Ethics*, 59 (1–2), 121–38.

OECD (1999), *OECD Principles of Corporate Governance*, Paris: OECD.

Park, Y.S. (2005), 'International efforts to combat corruption and Korea's anti-corruption drive', *Korea Observer*, 36 (2), 323–49.

Reidenback, R.E. and D.P. Robin (1991), 'A conceptual model of corporate moral development', *Journal of Business Ethics*, 10, 273–84.

Sanyal, R. (2005), 'Determinants of bribery in international business: the cultural and economic factors', *Journal of Business Ethics*, 59 (1–2), 139–4.

SERI (Samsung Economic Research Institute) (2005), 'Korea economic trends', Seoul: SERI, 26 February.

Transparency International (TI) (2002), 'Transparency international bribe payers index 2002', www.transparency.org, accessed 7 March 2006.

Transparency International (TI) (2005a), 'TI history', www.transparency.org, accessed 7 March 2006.

Transparency International (TI) (2005b), 'TI corruption perceptions index 2005', www.transparency.org, accessed 7 March 2006.

Yoon, Dae Hyeok (2005), *Business Ethics* (in Korean), Seoul: Trade Management Company.

8. The Korean management system in transition

8.1 INTRODUCTION

Neo-classical economics regards the firm as a technical 'black box' that transforms inputs into outputs in the most efficient way to achieve maximum profit. This is premised on the existence of an efficient market that promotes efficient forms of business organizations and destroys inefficient ones. Under this presumption of market equilibrium, neither the internal working of the firm (including management), nor the social context of the firm is regarded as relevant. This argument can be extended across countries, with management systems in market economies having to converge under competitive globalization pressures.

The neo-classical economic view of the firm and its management has been challenged by a number of critics, particularly in sociology with Granovetter (1985), Whitley (1987) and Baker (1987), and by neo-institutional economists such as Williamson (1975, 1985) and North (1990). These critics argue that markets are imperfect, that firms do matter as economic actors, and that firms and markets are in fact socially or institutionally constituted. Thus, major institutions vary considerably across countries, as do the rational and efficient internal operations of firms. Although neo-institutional economics also puts forward the argument that economic efficiency is institutionally constructed and varies across different institutional contexts, it does not adequately deal with the nature of the management system.

Management is the process of planning, organizing, leading and controlling the work of organizational members to achieve stated organization goals (Stoner and Freeman 1989, p. 3; Bartol et al. 2005, p. 5). Human beings are by nature socio-cultural creatures, and our behavior is influenced by social institutions. In this way, managers are strongly influenced by social institutions throughout the management process. For this study, institutions are considered as the 'rules of the game' in a society (Yeager 1999, p. 9). They are the rules that society establishes in order to reduce the uncertainty involved in human interaction. Because of the set of institutions we have, we know how we are supposed to act in social settings. The institutional framework is comprised of three components:

1. informal rules such as customs, traditions and norms;
2. formal rules such as the legal system, policy, judiciary and bureaucracy; and
3. enforcement or the governance mechanism which aligns the enforcement structure with the game (Williamson 2000).

As these institutions are different across countries, so too are their management systems. This does not mean that management systems are completely disparate across countries. Some commonalities and similarities are bound to develop between cross-cultural management systems, as all businesses seek to survive and to be efficient under market competition.

The rapid growth of the Korean economy between 1963 and 1996 has been ascribed to many factors, including effective government economic policy, entrepreneurial talent and the hardworking nature of Koreans. In addition to these, Song (1997) and Chang (1998) add that Korea's unique management system has contributed to rapid economic growth. The Korean business sector is comprised of a large number of small- and medium-sized enterprises (SMEs) and a limited number of chaebols. Although the former group contains the overwhelming majority of enterprises, the few chaebols have played the overriding role in Korea's economic growth with concentrated economic power. Therefore, this chapter will focus on the management system employed by chaebols as the Korean management system. The management system of SMEs slightly varies from that of the chaebols, as government policy has been quite different toward these two groups of businesses over time. However, the chaebol management system is regarded as the basis of generally applied Korean management practices because of a shared cultural background and the emulation of the chaebol management system by other businesses (Rowley and Bae 2003, p. 189).

This chapter will proceed as follows. First, major characteristics of the Korean management system, particularly up to the 1997 financial crisis, will be reviewed in section 8.2. Then, section 8.3 will analyze the salient characteristics of the management system in light of underlying institutions. Recent changes in the institutions relevant to chaebol management will be examined in section 8.4. Based on these institutional changes, the prospects of the Korean management system will be assessed. Finally, findings from a sample survey of the recent changes in the Korean management system as perceived by foreign business people working in Korea will be reviewed in the final section. While the bulk of the analysis of this chapter is based on secondary material, fieldwork and a survey undertaken in 2002 contribute greatly to the analysis.

8.2   SALIENT CHARACTERISTICS OF THE KOREAN MANAGEMENT SYSTEM

Management is predicated on organizational or strategic goal. The planning phase of management involves the important process of selecting goals for the organization and identifying and selecting a course of action to achieve those goals (Bartol et al. 2005, p. 5). In contrast to Western companies, which primarily consider maximizing shareholder returns as their management goal, the strategic goals of chaebols are, in general, growth and diversification. This is in contrast to the claims made by chaebols themselves that their management goals are profitability, stability and growth (Lee 1989). In fact, in research conducted by Lee (1989), maximizing returns to shareholders was one of the least frequently stated objectives of chaebols. The total assets of the top 30 chaebols grew at an annual average rate of 20.1 per cent from 1990 to 1997 (Jang 2002). During the same period, the average net profit ratio to equity capital was minus 0.2 per cent, although the ratio was about 2 to 3 per cent in the early 1990s (Jang 2002).[1] This indicates that the strategic goal of chaebols was growth rather than profit maximization.

Another important strategic goal of chaebols has been diversification. There is little doubt that the chaebols adopted aggressive diversification strategies and, as a result, developed a large number of subsidiaries and affiliates across unrelated business areas. Chaebols increased the number of their affiliates over time and in 1997, when the financial crisis occurred, the top 30 chaebols had an average of 27.3 affiliates across, on average, 19.1 different business categories (Jang 2002). Extensive diversification across different businesses indicates that chaebols did not rely on subcontractors or intra-enterprise transactions; consequently, the growth of the SME sector was stifled.[2]

The decision-making process is also a vital component of the planning process. The Korean management system is characterized by 'top-down' decision-making, that is, upper levels of management generally make key decisions with limited consultation with subordinates. In this decision-making process, a member of the company will draw up a proposal typically based on the instructions of his or her superior. This proposal is then circulated within the managerial hierarchy and reviewed by them. Their views on the proposal are taken into account and the original proposal is revised until there is consensus (Chen 2004, p. 179). However, the proposal still must be approved by the president of the company (Chang and Chang

1994, p. 131). Although this process appears to involve group participation to reach consensus, it is little more than a formal process to rationalize and build consensus over decisions already made. Even if an operational decision is made by a lower-ranking manger, the decisions will merely be a reflection of what their superiors want. Thus, even if the decision-making process appears to be consensual and participatory, it is highly centralized (Chang and Chang 1994, p. 134). Horizontal communications across organizational units are relatively difficult in chaebols because personal loyalty is toward individual superiors rather than toward the organization in Korea.

Korean chaebols, the key positions of which are held by family or clan members (Chen 2004, p. 146), are highly centralized compared to a Western multidivisional company, reinforcing the hierarchical nature of the planning and decision-making process. With regard to planning and decision-making, the most important element in a chaebol is the planning group, commonly referred to as the chairman's secretariat office.[3] The office, regarded as a 'think tank', is staffed by elite recruits, including top managers and employees, and acts as the key advising and implementing agency for the chairman's decisions. They formulate strategic plans and put forward blueprints for future operations. Other key tasks include monitoring performance and allocating finance and managers between member firms. The chairman's secretariat office analyzes the chaebol's domestic and international environments and suggests strategies to address them.

Korean companies generally have a 'tall' structure of organization with many hierarchical levels. For instance, some large companies could have ten or more hierarchal levels in their formal organizational structure. In this type of structure, managerial control is vertically concentrated in top management. Along with this vertical and hierarchical control, areas such as finance and human resources are formalized with strong functional control held by their individual departments. Although the organizational structure is centralized and its functions formalized, individual jobs are not formally structured in Korean business firms. Thus, individual employees are not given job descriptions or job specifications, and their job tasks and responsibilities are largely determined by their supervisor. The absence of job descriptions is an attempt to develop employees as generalists instead of specialists. This system makes it easier for chaebols to move managers and engineers between member companies and to transfer expertise and develop loyalty within the chaebol groups. This movement of skilled staff enhances the overall capability of the chaebol group and, at the same time, promotes the development of a uniform group culture and reinforces centralized control.

Authority and power in Korean firms are not only concentrated in upper levels of management, but are also concentrated in a few key executive positions. Three types of groups hold these positions that are based on formal and informal power groups, indicating the crucial importance of personal relationships in Korean management (Chen 2004, p. 181). Firstly, the family members of owners constitute the strongest power group in management, as ownership and management are not separated in most Korean business firms. The second power group consists of professional executives and managers who have worked continuously for the company over a long period of time and who were initially hired through open and competitive graduate examinations (Lee 1989). The third type of power group is formed on the basis of the school and common regional ties of the owners, and it is common for owners to bring their hometown or school friends into the top management group. Kim (2004) argues that such a hierarchical structure grants rights and privileges to superiors, which often lead to corruption and deprive the subordinates of rights.

The leading phase of management, which is also referred to as the directing, motivating or actuating function, involves motivating the members of an organization to perform in ways that will help achieve established objectives. H.C. Lee (1989) points out that Korean employees as a group tend to place a relatively greater emphasis on extrinsic factors (job security and predictability, working conditions and wages, including monetary and non-monetary benefits) for motivation. This contrasts with the emphasis on intrinsic factors such as achievement, creativity and recognition by Western companies in motivation tools. For Korean businesses, intrinsic needs such as achievement and recognition tend to be fulfilled within the company's overall spirit of harmony. Korean companies use group motivational methods such as group bonuses and group spirit, while Western companies employ individual methods, with an emphasis on individual promotion and monetary compensation. Job security is most important to Korean workers and is the main source of individual motivation although, due to the traditional system of lifetime employment, this is for the most part not an immediate motivation tool (H.C. Lee 1989, p. 160). This emphasis on extrinsic motivational factors is attributable to the emphasis on harmony (*inhwa*) and stability in interpersonal relations in Korean organizational culture (H.C. Lee 1989). Identifying employees as family members (calling them 'families') and treating them like family members is greatly emphasized and practiced for motivation. Additionally, harmonious formal and informal interactions between workers and executives are stressed.

Leadership is the process of directing and influencing workers to perform the task-related activities of the organization and plays a critical role in organizational effectiveness (Bartol et al. 2005, p. 6). Managerial leadership in Korean firms is characterized as strongly paternalistic and authoritarian, with a group harmony (*inhwa*) orientation (H.C. Lee 1989, p. 160; Kim and Kim 1989, p. 213; Cho and Yoon 2002, p. 76; Park and Yu 2002, p. 379).

Chaebols were established by self-made businessmen, and many of them are still led by their founder-owners or their descendants. Generally, these founders have led their companies paternalistically and in an authoritarian style. Accordingly, chaebols emphasize strong family-like bonds among employees, considering employees as family members, and founder-managers are thus considered quasi-father figures (Cho and Yoon 2002, p. 76). The owner-managers control most decision-making, including the non-critical issues around them, and they maintain their authoritarian leadership. The leadership of these chaebols has had an enormous impact on Korean business and management, as chaebol leaders were considered as role models and their conduct was emulated by other businessmen (S.M. Lee 1989, p. 185).

Despite their strongly authoritarian style, Korean managerial leaders stress group harmony (*inhwa*), emphasizing teamwork, employee participation and consensus, and promoting corporations as family units or corporate familism (S.M. Lee 1989, p. 189; El Kahl 2001, p. 169). To this end, Korean managers tend to have frequent informal interactions with employees, as well as formal communications with them. However, since most managerial decisions in Korean firms are made at the top of the organization, there is little opportunity for employees to be involved in group decisions.

Another characteristic of Korean managerial leadership is an emphasis on moral superiority rather than technical efficacy (Whitley 1992, p. 113). Under Confucian influence, which stressed the moral virtuousness of social and ruling elites, Korean leaders were regarded as a morally superior group throughout Korea's long history. They were expected to behave benevolently by showing their interest in workers' welfare and to be knowledgeable of, and abide by, Confucian doctrines (Shin 1992, p. 658). Beyond this, Korean leaders did not need to justify their status further by performing useful functions. Thus, criticism of decisions made by ruling elites and any suggestion of alternatives were seen as personal attacks on the integrity of leaders rather than as relatively technical discussions of the advantages of different choices. As a result, a strong authoritarian and didactic leadership has developed over time. Under this type of leadership, a vertical communication process has developed, where the supervisors give directions while subordinates are expected to implement the directions obediently without voicing their opinions (Chen 2004, p. 183).

The control function of management is the process of assuring that actual activities conform to planned activities. It is a matter of controlling the internal operation of business by comparing its actual performance against planned results and then undertaking corrective action (Bartol et al. 2005, p. 6). Although Lee (2004, p. 3) argued that in terms of people management, Korean managers tend to demonstrate tight control over their subordinates, the control function in management has not been well developed in Korea. When companies continuously expand, grow and diversify, the need for internal operational control may not be vital. Under the perception of chaebols being 'too big to fail', management was not particularly concerned with control. Additionally, since Korean chaebols have maintained strong central control of operations as well as planning decisions, the autonomy of working groups has been weak (Whitley 1992, p. 65), retarding the development of the control function of management. Finally, the control function requires that corrective action be taken to address poor performance. However, when personnel management is based not on performance but on a seniority system and lifetime employment as is the case in Korea, taking corrective action against individual employees or reprimanding them would be difficult, rendering the control function inefficient.

Notwithstanding the difficulties indicated above, the Korean management system contains a control function of sorts. In the past, consistent with corporate strategic goals of growth and diversification, control was based on the short-term external achievements of expansion, growth and diversification (Shin 1992, pp. 331–60). Thus, the key performance standard was the growth of the firm or the establishment of new businesses, rather than being concerned with the internal operation of each business. Another important performance standard used for controlling purposes was the level of exports. As part of its export drive, the government provided companies with credits and awarded export prizes according to their export amounts. As a result, companies have strived to expand exports even at a loss.

There is ample evidence, however, that points to the inefficiency of the control function in Korean management. Excessive expansion and diversification of chaebols is an indication of their poor control. Just before the 1997 financial crisis, the average debt–equity ratio of the top 30 chaebols was 519 per cent (Joh 2001), clearly indicating inefficient controlling practices. Heavy reliance on foreign technologies that are licensed or emulated by Korean companies, instead of developing their own technologies, is also indicative of the inadequate control role of management.

8.3   INSTITUTIONAL INFLUENCE ON KOREAN MANAGEMENT

As mentioned earlier, the managerial practices of Korean managers are strongly influenced by various types of institutions, including culture, formal institutions and governance systems. Korea's unique institutional framework is indeed reflected in the salient characteristics of the Korean management system that have been examined above. For the planning and decision-making processes, for instance, the strategic goal of chaebols was expansion, growth and diversification in line with the government's drive for maximum economic growth over the three decades from the 1960s. Chaebols were provided with a variety of privileges such as credit allocation, cross-debt guaranteeing, cross-ownership, cross-subsidization, intra-group trading and capital flows among their affiliates. This institutional framework favoring chaebols generated the perception of them as being 'too big to fail'. A corollary of this perception is that chaebols expanded and diversified in order to survive. The ineffective corporate governance system specifically contributed to chaebols adopting the strategic goal of expansion, because the owners were allowed to wield concentrated control over their expanding enterprises.

The 'top-down' decision-making process is a reflection of Korean traditional culture. As examined in Chapter 3, the salient traits of Korean culture, which are molded under a strong Confucian influence, include hierarchical collectivism, patriarchal familism, authoritarianism and status-consciousness. In line with its culture, Korean society is vertically structured and hierarchical in nature. Since the owner-managers are regarded as quasi-fathers, they have decision-making authority. Additionally, employees are expected to be obedient and loyal to their superiors as well as the top decision-makers in line with Korean culture. Influenced by cultural traits of patriarchal familism and authoritarianism, a bureaucracy has developed in decision-making and management (Kim and Yi 1998/9).

The Korean decision-making process is highly concentrated in a group of family members and their associates established through personal relationships, which are in turn important elements underlying overall managerial practices in Korea. Collectivism developed under Confucianism implies the existence of exclusionism. Exclusionism is reinforced by a strong sense of commonality or 'groupness' among people, based on family, hometown or school attended. The level of trust among insiders of a group is higher than that of their trust toward outsiders. When this traditional exclusionism is applied to modern enterprises, a closed group has formed with the owner at the centre using concentrated decision-making power.

Due to the underdeveloped nature of institutional frameworks, loyalty has developed in Korea toward individual superiors rather than toward organizations. This cultural facet minimizes horizontal communications across organizational units, leading to the decision-making power being concentrated in a small group of managers. Over the Yi Dynasty period, no institutional framework was developed for public administration or business operations (Whitley 1992, p. 187). As explained in Chapter 2, political power was highly concentrated in the King and a limited number of aristocrats, with little tolerance for local power groups or the concentration of economic power in private hands. The aristocracy competed for state office and engaged in bitter personal and factional battles over these positions. The resulting insecurity and instability of official power made families the major source of stability and encouraged opportunistic changes of allegiance. In the absence of a proper institutional framework and political and official security and stability, the transaction costs of business were bound to be high. Hence, business people sought to align themselves with dominant factions and families and to protect themselves through their personal ties with them (Whitley 1992, p. 187). Through these socio-economic and political circumstances, personal loyalty has developed toward individual superiors rather than toward organizations. Even after the Korean War, the underdeveloped institutional framework and continuous social and political instability have directed Koreans' personal loyalty toward individuals.

The highly centralized and formal structure of Korean companies is also a reflection of Korean culture. The tall organizational structure with many hierarchical levels and with managerial power concentrated on top management reflects the stratified and hierarchical nature of Korean society. The lack of job description and specialization may reflect the holistic approach to problem-solving under oriental as well as Korean culture, compared to the analytic approach of the Western world. In addition, high transferability of staff members across different divisions and affiliates has facilitated expansion of chaebols, which has in turn resulted from formal and governance institutions.

Korean motivational tools are based on extrinsic factors such as job security and predictability, and can be traced back to cultural roots. As identified by Hofstede (1991), Koreans are quite risk averse. Hence job security, such as lifetime employment, is highly valued. Confucianism in Korea traditionally promoted social stratification and, subsequently, Koreans are keenly conscious of their status within society or in an organization. Hence, job predictability and maintenance of relative status within a firm are highly regarded, and the seniority system is an important motivation tool.

The paternalistic and authoritarian characteristics of managerial leadership in Korea are direct reflections of the key characteristics in traditional Korean families. Leadership in the traditional Korean family contains two-dimensional characteristics: despotic authority and a strong desire for harmony (Kim and Kim 1989, p. 211). The father, as the family head, controls his family members with firm authority, while the family members are required to be obedient and respectful to the family head. The father's role also includes maintaining harmony among family members and ensuring that utmost care and concern is given to them. Likewise, the head of a company wields authoritarian power and concurrently stresses group harmony.

In line with the strategic goal of growth and diversification, the managerial control function of a Korean firm is mainly concerned with short-term external achievements such as expansion, growth and diversification rather than internal operational control. As indicated above, institutional settings in Korea have encouraged firms to adopt such strategic goals. Internal control is a challenging issue for Korean companies due to the concentrated control of planning decisions and operations and the minimum amount of autonomy delegated to junior managers. Furthermore, control is also difficult under a Korean human resource management philosophy that embraces the seniority system and lifetime employment practice, both of which are culturally embedded.

In summary, institutions, including the traditional value system, formal rules such as government–business relations, and the corporate governance system, have undoubtedly influenced the Korean management system. Managerial practices are, however, not static; they change as institutions change. Thus, institutional changes and their possible impacts on Korean management will be examined in the following section.

8.4 INSTITUTIONAL CHANGES IN THE RECENT PAST

Although traditional Korean society and culture had been modified gradually over time, it was industrialization of the Korean economy after the 1960s that transformed the traditional Korean society into an industrial society, which entailed rapid urbanization and rural depopulation. In Korea's modern urban society, economic opportunities do not correspond with traditional social status, and thus social stratification has been eroded, developing a sense of greater equality. The size and composition of Korean families have changed and the traditional emphasis placed on family has also changed. The large, traditional family has become a 'nuclear family'. Furthermore, family moral values, such as respect for parents and ancestors, have declined remarkably and traditional patriarchal familism has been eclipsed. Even the legal system that supported Korean patriarchal familism has been revised, enhancing the status of women. Industrialization has also shifted emphasis in the value system from morality and humaneness to materialism and quality of life. The quality-of-life concept, which is espoused by the younger generation today, emphasizes such values as: freedom of speech; active involvement in the workplace, community and politics; and development toward a humane society.

As examined in Chapter 3, an epoch-making transformation of Korean culture occurred in conjunction with the 1997 financial crisis. The crisis made the general public appreciate the inevitability of globalization and provided an opportunity for them to review their value system. Confucian tradition, which strongly emphasizes the family and hierarchical group society, has subsequently been modified. The loyalty of workers toward their leaders and companies has declined significantly. Koreans have come to value foreign business and culture, and the prevailing strong patriotism has faded significantly. At the same time, Korean society has been gradually transforming from a group society to an individualistic one similar to Western society. Korean society has opened up to the international community, along with the internationalization of the economy.

In the wake of the 1997 financial crisis the government undertook dramatic reforms of institutions related to business operations, particularly chaebols. These reforms were aimed at improving corporate governance and financial structure and other business-related institutions. In the area of corporate governance, the power of controlling shareholders has been curtailed, and other stakeholders have had their rights expanded. Management transparency and accountability, which are at the core of good governance, have also been enhanced. Chaebols are now required to provide consolidated financial statements. Additionally, up to 25 per cent of chaebol board members are required to be independent directors. Chaebols are required to phase out existing cross-guarantees among groups' affiliates. They are also required to reduce their debt–equity ratios to 200 per cent. To streamline the exit procedure of non-viable firms, M&A, including hostile ones, are permitted, and bankruptcy and corporate reorganization laws have been revised.

As a result of corporate reform, most of the institutionalized privileges bestowed on chaebols have been eliminated. In addition, by letting some of the chaebols go bankrupt, the 'too big to fail' perception has been reduced significantly. The painful experience of the financial crisis has forced a shift in the Korean economic policy paradigm from a government-led economy to a market economy. The government has abandoned its policy of protecting domestic industries and has liberalized the economy to a considerable extent. The Korean market is now open to international competition through trade, FDI and M&As. The banking sector has also been reformed to a remarkable extent and has been exposed to greater foreign competition, thereby reinforcing its monitoring role over chaebols. Foreign investors who participate in equity capital of domestic financial institutions are able to strengthen their monitoring of debtor companies. Accordingly, companies that are not transparent or accountable and have low profitability and high debt–equity ratios will have difficulty raising money from banks. In the absence of the privileges favoring chaebols, financial institutions will lend to these companies only if they have evidence of sound business operations. This will force chaebols to concentrate on their core areas of competence and to divest themselves of marginal interests. An intriguing question then arises as to how these institutional changes – including Korean society and culture, rules and regulations related to business operations and corporate governance – will affect the management system. This will be addressed in the following section.

8.5 KOREAN MANAGEMENT IN TRANSITION

It is expected that institutional (including cultural) changes in Korea after the 1997 financial crisis will change management practices substantially (El Kahl 2001, p. 166). With the opening of the domestic market to international competition, and the removal of chaebols' privileges and potential to collude with the government, Korean companies are no longer able to enjoy monopolistic operations within a shielded domestic market. They will have to compete against foreign counterparts that are well equipped with capital and technology. Korean companies will increasingly be monitored and become the target of intervention by their foreign investors and creditor banks with foreign investment. The myth that big companies never fail has already disappeared. In order to survive, therefore, Korean companies will need to operate as efficiently as their foreign counterparts. In order to do so, Korean companies will be unable to retain the traditional Korean management system, although parts that are deeply ingrained in Korean culture are unlikely to disappear easily.

Under the emerging new business environment, Korean companies will change their strategic management, incorporating various aspects of Western management techniques into their system (Rowley and Bae 2003). They will have to yield their strategic goals of expansion and diversification as they are incompatible with the new Korean business environment. To compete in this new business environment and the global market place, they will need to strengthen competitiveness. To this end, their strategic direction should be focused on their core competent businesses and international collaborations, and their strategic goals will have to be focused on maximizing profit or shareholder returns.

The top-down decision-making process may also have to be modified. For the sake of their survival, Korean companies will need to replace management by owners and their family members with management by efficient professionals. Since the chairman's secretariat office has been eliminated by law after the financial crisis, having centralized control over the planning and decision-making processes will become increasingly difficult. Additionally, as the emphasis on hierarchical relationships in Korean society declines and the loyalty of employees toward companies and leaders abates, the practicability of top-down decision-making will be undermined. In this regard, Lee (2004) argues that a more risk-oriented and individualistic approach to decision-making has been accepted in Korean management.

Compared to the flat organizational structure of Western companies, the tall and hierarchical organizational structure of Korean companies is too inefficient to compete effectively in the globalizing world market (Lee 2004). In addition, the traditional approach of training employees as generalists instead of specialists may be disadvantageous under increasing competitive forces of globalization, even though it may have been beneficial in the past when chaebols were continuously expanding with minimum competition in domestic and international markets. Under the new institutional setting, Korean companies need highly trained and experienced specialists to sustain their international competitiveness. This will allow firms to concentrate on their core capabilities. Besides, ambitious and competent employees are likely to want to improve their mobility by being specialists instead of generalists.

It is questionable whether Korean management, with an emphasis on personal relationships, can be competitive against the efficiency-focused Western management style of emphasizing arm's-length business transactions. As foreign companies and Korean companies with foreign capital participation play an increasingly important role in the Korean economy, greater transparency and accountability will be required in business operations, the importance of personal relationships will diminish, and the existing business networks will necessarily change. Under the scrutiny of foreigners, personal relationships may not influence business operations as they did so powerfully in the past.[4]

The Korean emphasis on job security and the predictability in motivating employees by practicing lifetime employment and the seniority system is disadvantageous when compared to the motivational forces of achievement, creativity and recognition employed by Western companies. The recent introduction of lay-offs, part-time employment and flexible working hours will break the costly and inefficient convention of guaranteeing lifetime employment for workers. The seniority system with its hierarchical structure will also decay in the long term. In replacing lifetime employment and the seniority system, an individual-oriented approach to motivation should be introduced. In such an approach, individual employees are rewarded for their creativity, innovation and performance rather than their seniority or rank.

The paternalistic and authoritarian style of managerial leadership in Korean firms may not remain consistent with the emerging Korean culture and society. Junior and competent employees consider 'environment for voluntary participation' as the most effective work incentive (H.C. Lee

1989). The traditional authoritarian leadership may discourage the contribution of these modern creative workers. Declining job security in domestic companies and the increasing willingness of young workers to seek better jobs, including those in foreign companies, are emerging trends. This will make it difficult for Korean companies to retain efficient workers through a traditional leadership approach. Rather, Korean companies will have to increase the participation of employees and enhance their feeling of partnership with managers to retain them.

Finally, the control function of management has to improve in Korea. The past control criteria of expansion, growth and diversification are no longer valid. Korean companies will need to provide more autonomy to working groups and make them responsible and accountable for their operations. In conjunction with the decline in practices of lifetime employment and the seniority system, Korean companies will have to develop appropriate performance criteria whereby actual performance can be compared, and to introduce performance-oriented control practices.

Korean companies will likely encounter cultural inertia that will make it difficult to adopt an innovative management system as envisaged above. Even though formal institutions related to management have been substantially reformed after the 1997 crisis, changing corporate culture will be a difficult and long-term process, as traditional values are deeply ingrained among employees. Korean companies appear to have difficulty in implementing a decision-making process that includes the participation of subordinate officers because of lingering authoritarianism and hierarchical rigidity in Korean society. In addition, many Korean companies retain a tall and hierarchical organizational structure. Kwun and Cho (2002) illustrate difficulties involved in undertaking organizational changes due to a variety of inertia, including cultural inertia.

It will be difficult to lessen the importance of personal relationships in business management and operations as this is deeply ingrained in the collectivist nature of Korean society. Although lifetime employment practices have disappeared to a discernible extent, the seniority system remains more or less a common practice, particularly in large organizations. It appears therefore that objective performance measurements have not taken root in management practices in Korean companies. Even if performance was to be properly measured, taking corrective actions against particular persons runs counter to the Korean culture of emphasizing 'face'. Thus performance measurements will not easily be adopted in Korean companies.

Assessing the extent to which companies in Korea have transformed their management system is an extremely difficult task. As a way of assessing the management reform undertaken in Korea, a sample survey was undertaken between May and July 2002 of foreign workers who were employed by foreign companies in Korea. The findings of the survey shed light on the extent and success of management reform in Korea and will be discussed in the following section.

8.6   FOREIGN PERCEPTIONS OF KOREAN MANAGEMENT IN TRANSITION

It has been argued by Korea observers that the Korean management system has changed considerably since the financial crisis in 1997 to reflect more Western practices. To assess perceptions of change in the Korean management system held by foreign business people, the survey asked 12 questions related to various aspects of the management system: the objectives of firms, decision-making process, organization, leadership, human resource management, overall management efficiency and overall change (Kwon 2006).

Respondents had an overall negative view toward the changes in the Korean management system. This was indicated by an overall average score of 2.686 out of the scale from 1 to 5 for the 12 types of possible changes in Korean management included in the questionnaire (Table 8.1). Foreign business people surveyed had a positive view of a change in the strategic goal of Korean companies toward 'more profit-oriented management', with an average rating of 3.349, the highest score out of the 12 possible changes. This finding suggests that Korean firms are moving from their traditional business objective of maximum growth or maximum market share toward profit maximization, as is generally the case for Western firms. Foreign respondents also agreed that the lifetime employment practices were disappearing and that lay-offs of workers were increasing (Kwon 2006).

Other than the changes in the strategic goal, lifetime employment practices and job security, foreign business people generally viewed the Korean management system as having changed little, as reflected in the average scores of less than the neutral value of 3 in the survey for various aspects of management. These include the hierarchical organizational structure, authoritarian decision-making, paternalistic leadership, and human resources management. In particular, foreign respondents disagreed that significant changes were being made to the overall efficiency of Korean management and that the Korean management system was becoming similar to their own system (Kwon 2006). These survey findings suggest that from the perspective of foreign expatriates in Korea, the Korean management system remains more or less unchanged, except for it becoming more profit-oriented and discarding lifetime employment.[5]

Table 8.1 Respondents' view of changes in the Korean management system

Types of change	N	Average rating	Standard deviation
Becoming more profit-oriented management	63	3.349	1.003
Decreasing layers in the hierarchical organizational structure	66	2.591	1.007
Fading of the top-down, authoritarian decision-making system	65	2.262	1.065
Fading paternalistic leadership	64	2.594	1.050
Disappearing lifetime employment practices	64	3.156	1.130
Increases in the lay-off of workers	63	3.032	0.999
Merit-based promotion and compensation	65	2.615	0.963
Willingness to hire foreign workers	64	2.719	1.046
Recruitment by merit, rather than by personal connections or university background	65	2.462	1.047
Disappearing seniority system	66	2.394	1.080
Rising overall management efficiency	64	2.734	0.840
Korean management becoming more like yours	61	2.328	0.944
Average	64	2.686	1.015

Source: Kwon (2006).

8.7 CONCLUSION

The Korean management system has developed under the influences of its institutions such as culture, formal institutions and governance systems. With a heavy Confucian influence, Korean society exhibits characteristics such as collectivism, family orientation, paternalism, authoritarianism and a hierarchical structure. Since the early 1960s, the formal institutional framework provided a variety of privileges to chaebols in Korea including credit allocation, cross-debt guaranteeing, cross-ownership, cross-subsidization, intra-group trading and capital flow among affiliates. The corporate governance system was skewed in favor of the principal shareholder and, along with institutional privileges, this generated a perception of the infallibility of chaebols.

With this institutional background, Korean management developed in a unique way. Korean management focused primarily on the strategic goals of growth, expansion and diversification. The decision-making process has been a 'top-down' process, with decision-making power concentrated in the upper levels of management. With a tall organizational structure and many hierarchical levels, authority and power was concentrated in a few key executives, particularly owners, their clan and personally related associates, indicating the importance of personal relationships in management. Managerial leadership in Korean firms has been characterized as paternalistic and authoritarian. Korean companies have relied on job security and stability in motivation practices and have focused on lifetime employment and seniority. Finally, the control function of management, based on external achievements in growth, expansion and diversification, has been ineffectual in controlling the internal operations of business.

The institutional framework related to business management has undertaken a metamorphosis since the 1997 financial crisis. In order to survive in the new milieu, Korean companies have been required to operate as efficiently as their foreign counterparts. To this end, they have had to overhaul each component of their management system. Their strategic direction needs to focus on their core competent areas and their goals should be profit maximization. Professional management needs to take over management by owners, and consultative decision-making processes should replace the traditional top-down decision-making process. The organization of Korean companies should also be comparable to that of Western companies, resembling a more flat and efficient structure. Practices of lifetime employment and the seniority system should be replaced by a system rewarding creativity, innovation and performance. Managerial leadership should also eliminate the paternalistic and authoritarian style in leadership and encourage the participation of employees and their sense of partnership with management. The control function of management has to improve in Korea. To this end, Korean companies should develop appropriate performance criteria and introduce performance-oriented control practices.

While the transition of the Korean management system, as envisaged above, is a commendable aim, it will be a long-term process because of cultural inertia. The difficulties in transforming the Korean management system are indicated by the results of a survey of foreign business people in Korea. The overall perceptions of many of these people are that the Korean management system has not transformed significantly, although there are some movements toward the Western system.

To succeed in the new business environment and in the competitive global market place, Korean companies must ramp up their reform efforts in management, including planning and decision-making, organization, motivation, leadership and control. To succeed in transforming their management systems to embrace worldwide best practices, it appears that the cooperation of employees is critically important. To ensure that employees adopt the new management vision, values and strategies, Korean companies must maintain appropriate communication channels with employees and provide adequate education and training.

NOTES

1. Even during the 1970s and 1980s, profitability in the key manufacturing sector was about 3 per cent (Whitley 1992, p. 46).
2. Whitley (1992, p. 43) points out that the diversification of Korean chaebols is much more extensive than that of their Japanese counterparts.
3. As explained later, the chairman's secretariat office, as such, is no longer allowed as a result of the corporate reform in the wake of the 1997 financial crisis.
4. Kim (2004) argues that a focus on personal relationships leads to cronyism.
5. For a detailed explanation and discussion of the survey results, see Kwon (2006).

REFERENCES

Baker, W.E. (1987), 'What is money? A social structural interpretation', in M.S. Mizruchi and M. Schwartz (eds), *Intercorporate Relations: The Structural Analysis of Business*, Cambridgeshire, NY: Cambridge University Press, pp. 109–44.
Bartol, K., M. Tein, G. Matthews and D. Martin (2005), *Management: A Pacific Rim Focus*, North Ryde: McGraw-Hill Australia.
Chang, C.S. (1998), 'The Confucian capitalism: impact of culture and the management system on economic growth in South Korea', *Journal of Third World Studies*, 15 (2), 53–66.
Chang, Chan Sup and N.J. Chang (1994), *The Korean Management System*, Westport, CT: Quorum Books.
Chen, M. (2004), *Asian Management Systems*, 2nd edn, London: Thomson Learning.
Cho, Yung-Ho and J.K. Yoon (2002), 'The origin and function of dynamic collectivism: an analysis of Korean corporate culture', in Chris Rowley, T.W. Sohn and J.S. Bae (eds), *Managing Korean Business: Organization, Culture, Human Resources and Change*, London: Frank Cass, pp. 70–88.
El Kahl, S. (2001), *Business in Asia Pacific: Text and Cases*, Oxford: Oxford University Press.
Granovetter, M. (1985), 'Economic action, social structure and embeddedness', *American Journal of Sociology*, 91, 481–510.
Hofstede, G. (1991), *Cultures and Organizations: Software of the Mind*, London: McGraw-Hill.
Jang, Hasung (2002), 'After the economic crisis: an analysis of the effects of corporate restructuring', in Z. Rhee and E. Chang (eds), *Korean Business and Management: The Reality and the Vision*, Elizabeth, NJ: Hollym, pp. 79–131.

Joh, Sung Wook (2001), 'The Korean corporate sector: crisis and reform', in O.Y. Kwon and W. Shepherd (eds), *Korea's Economic Prospects: From Financial Crisis to Prosperity*, Cheltenham, UK and Northampton, MA, USA: Edward Elgar Publishing, pp. 116–32.

Kim, A.E. (2004), 'The social perils of the Korean financial crisis', *Journal of Contemporary Asia*, 34 (2), 221–37.

Kim, Dong Ki and C.W. Kim (1989), 'Korean value systems and managerial practices', in K. Chung and H. Lee (eds), *Korean Managerial Dynamics*, New York: Praeger, pp. 206–16.

Kim, L. and G. Yi (1998/9), 'Reinventing Korea's national management system', *International Studies of Management and Organisation*, 28 (4), 73–83.

Kwon, O. Yul (2006), 'Recent changes in Korea's business equipment: views of foreign business people in Korea', *Asia Pacific Business Review*, 12 (1), 77–94, http://www.informaworld.com.

Kwun, Seog K. and N.S. Cho (2002), 'Organizational change and inertia: Korea Telecom', in C. Rowley, T.W. Soh and J.S. Bae (eds), *Managing Korean Business: Organisation, Culture, and Human Resources and Change*, London: Frank Cass, pp. 111–36.

Lee, H.C. (1989), 'Managerial characteristics of Korean firms', in K. Chung and H. Lee (eds), *Korean Managerial Dynamics*, New York: Praeger, pp. 147–62.

Lee, Sang M. (1989), 'Management styles of Korean chaebols', in K. Chung and H. Lee (eds), *Korean Managerial Dynamics*, New York: Praeger, pp. 181–92.

Lee, Y. (2004), 'South Korean companies in transition: an evolving strategic management style', *Strategic Change*, 13 (1), 29–35.

North, D. (1990), *Institutions, Institutional Change and Economic Performance*, Cambridge: Cambridge University Press.

Park, Woo-Sung and Gyu-Chang Yu (2002), 'HRM in Korea: transformation and new patterns', in Z. Rhee and E. Chang (eds), *Korean Business and Management: The Reality and the Vision*, Elizabeth, NJ: Hollym, pp. 367–93.

Rowley, C. and J. Bae (2003), 'Culture and management in South Korea', in M. Warner (ed.), *Culture and Management in Asia*, London: RoutledgeCurzon, pp. 187–209.

Shin, Yoo-Keun (1992), *Korean Management* (in Korean), Seoul: Parkyung-Sa.

Song, B.N (1997), *The Rise of the Korean Economy*, Hong Kong: Oxford University Press.

Stoner, J.A.F. and R.E. Freeman (1989), *Management*, 4th edn, New York: Prentice Hall.

Whitley, R.D. (1987), 'Taking firms seriously as economic actors: towards a sociology of firm behaviour', *Organization Studies*, 8 (2), 125–47.

Whitley, R.D. (1992), *Business Systems in East Asia: Firms, Markets and Society*, London: Sage Publications.

Williamson, O.E. (1975), *Markets and Hierarchies: Analysis and Antitrust Implications*, New York: Free Press.

Williamson, O.E. (1985), *The Economic Institutions of Capitalism*, New York: Free Press.

Williamson, Oliver E. (2000), 'The new institutional economics: taking stock, looking ahead', *Journal of Economic Literature*, 38 (3), 595–613.

Yeager, Timothy J. (1999), *Institutions, Transition Economies, and Economic Development: The Political Economy of Global Interdependence*, Boulder, CO and Oxford: Westview Press.

9. Korea's labor market and human resource management in transition

9.1 INTRODUCTION

Human resource management refers to the activities that an organization conducts to utilize its human resources effectively. These activities include recruitment, placement, performance evaluation, compensation and promotion, training and development, and labor relations (Hill 2003). As human resource management (HRM) is part and parcel of the overall strategy and management of a company, each component of HRM should function in line with the company's strategic direction.

International human resource management of MNEs is more complex as each HRM function must be performed in an international context. Compared to the human resource management of a domestic company, international human resource management of MNEs contains two further aspects: one is related to the management of expatriates and the other is related to the management of local human resources in the host countries. It appears that the second aspect of international human resource management draws little attention in the literature, yet it is as important as the management of expatriates because overseas subsidiaries of MNEs are staffed largely by the local human resources of host countries.[1]

This chapter examines Korea's human resource management from the perspective of foreign MNEs using Korea as a host country. Although the labor market may not be regarded as a field of HRM as such, the characteristics and trends of the Korean labor market are examined, as such knowledge will be particularly useful for existing foreign MNEs in Korea or those contemplating entering Korea. In addition, foreign MNEs should acquire an understanding of the rules and practices of industrial relations and labor standards in Korea. This chapter will thus proceed as follows. Section 9.2 deals with the Korean labor market and related institutions, and is followed by an examination of rules and regulations regarding industrial relations and labor standards in section 9.3. Section 9.4 examines the salient characteristics of Korea's human resource management including changes in relevant institutions. Almost all aspects of Korea's business and economy, including macro aspects of the labor market as well as human resource management, have undertaken a metamorphosis in conjunction with the 1997 financial crisis. Hence, particular attention will be paid to changes in industrial relations, labor standards and human resource management in the wake of the crisis. In light of relevant institutional changes, the prospects for Korean human resource management will be assessed. Finally, findings from a sample survey of the recent changes in Korean human resource management as perceived by foreign business people in Korea will be examined in the final section. Although the bulk of the chapter's analysis is based on secondary material, fieldwork and a survey undertaken by the author in 2002 contributes to the analysis.

9.2 THE KOREAN LABOR MARKET

9.2.1 Supply of Human Resources

It has often been argued that one of the most important factors for the high level of Korean economic growth during the three decades from the 1960s has been the abundance of diligent and well-educated human capital and the government's ability to utilize it (Kim and Lee 1997). Demand for labor increased rapidly during the 1960s as a result of the labor-intensive industrialization strategy. Through this strategy Korea changed its labor surplus in the early 1960s into a labor shortage by the mid-1970s (Kim 2001). How then has Korea supplied the human resources required for the sustained high economic growth since the mid-1970s? What are the prospects for the supply of human resources in Korea? This section will discuss these questions.

Since the 1960s, the supply of human resources increased rapidly as a result of an increasing population, the mobilization of underemployed farm labor, rising labor force participation, and rising education. As shown in Table 9.1, the population grew from 27.3 million in 1963 to 48.3 million in 2005, an average 1.8 per cent annual growth over the period. However, a declining trend in population growth has clearly been set. The population grew at a rate of 2.56 per cent annually during the 1960s, gradually declined to 1.75 per cent in the 1970s, and declined even further to less than 1 per cent during the 1990s (Tables 9.1 and 9.2). The population growth rate has further declined to 0.44 per cent in 2005 (Table 9.1). The fertility rate started to decline from the early 1960s, reached a level below that of replacement in the late 1980s, and further decreased to 1.47 in 2000 (T.H. Kwon 2003). The fertility rate is expected to decline further to 1.36 by 2010. Taking into account the declining fertility rate, it is estimated that the population will grow to around 51 million by around 2020 (T.H. Kwon 2003).

Table 9.1 Major indicators of the Korean labor market (1963–2005)

	1963	1970	1980	1990	1997	1998	1999	2000	2001	2002	2003	2004	2005
Population (millions)	27.3	32.2	38.1	42.9	46.0	46.3	46.6	47.0	47.3	47.6	47.8	48.1	48.3
Pop growth	2.82	2.21	1.57	0.99	0.94	0.72	0.71	0.84	0.71	0.63	0.49	0.49	0.44
Population over 65 (%)	3.1[b]	3.1	3.8	5.1	6.4	6.6	6.9	8.2	8.6	9.1	9.5	10.0	10.5
Economically active pop (millions)	8.2	10.0	14.4	18.5	21.8	21.4	21.7	21.1	22.4	22.9	22.9	23.4	23.7
Participation rate: all (%)	56.6	57.6	59.0	60.0	62.5	60.6	60.6	61.0	61.3	61.9	61.5	62.1	62.0
Participation rate: female (%)	n.a.	n.a.	42.3[a]	47.0	49.8	47.1	47.6	48.6	49.2	49.7	49.0	49.9	50.1
Employed (millions)	7.7	9.6	13.7	18.1	21.2	19.9	20.3	21.2	21.6	22.2	22.1	22.5	22.8
Unemployment rate (%)	8.2	4.4	5.2	2.4	2.6	7.0	6.3	4.1	3.8	3.1	3.6	3.7	3.7
Share of employment (%)													
Agriculture	63.1	50.4	34.0	17.9	11.3	12.4	11.3	10.9	10.3	9.3	8.8	8.2	7.9
Manufacturing	8.7	14.3	22.5	27.6	21.4	19.5	19.9	20.1	19.7	19.1	19.1	19.1	18.6
Services	28.3	35.3	43.5	54.5	67.3	68.1	68.7	69.0	70.0	71.6	72.1	72.8	73.5
Working hours per week	n.a.	51.6	51.6	48.2	46.7	45.9	47.9	47.5	47.0	46.2	45.9	45.7	45.0
Nominal wage change (%)	n.a.	n.a.	23.4	18.8	7.0	−2.5	12.1	8.0	5.6	11.6	9.4	6.5	6.4
Real wage change (%)	n.a.	n.a.	−4.2	9.4	2.5	−9.8	11.1	5.6	1.5	8.7	5.7	2.8	3.6
Labor productivity/hr	n.a	n.a	n.a	6.6	4.3	4.3	5.1	3.1	1.9	4.8	4.6	3.1	3.6
Trade unions (000s)	n.a	3.5	2.6	7.7	5.7	5.6	5.6	5.7	6.2	6.5	6.3	6.1	n.a.
Union members (000s)	n.a.	473	948	1887	1484	1402	1481	1527	1569	1605	1549	1537	n.a.
Union organization rate (%)[c]	n.a.	12.6	14.7	17.2	11.1	11.4	11.7	11.4	11.5	10.8	10.8	10.3	n.a.
Industrial disputes (000s)	n.a.	n.a.	206	322	78	128	198	250	234	321	320	462	287

Notes:
[a] Figure for 1981.
[b] Figure for 1965.
[c] The union organization rate equals the number of union members divided by total employees.

Sources: Korea National Statistical Office (KNSO) (2002b); Korea Labor Institute (KLI) (2003); Korea National Statistical Office (2006); Korea National Statistical Office (2003); Korea National Statistical Office (2004); and Korea Labor Institute (2006b).

As indicated in Chapter 4, the Korean population is rapidly ageing, with the proportion of citizens older than 65 being 3.1 per cent in 1970, 5.1 per cent in 1990, and reaching 10.5 per cent in 2005 (Table 9.1). It is estimated that the proportion of the population aged over 65 will reach 15.1 per cent in 2020 and up to 34.4 per cent in 2050 (T.H. Kwon 2003).[2] These demographic trends in Korea will result in profound changes in the size and structure of the Korean labor force. Unlike the last four decades, the labor force proportion of the population will increase slowly, and the absolute size of the labor force population is estimated to shrink after 2015 (T.H. Kwon 2003), raising the prospect of a shortage in the labor supply.

Although the labor force participation rate grew slowly from 56.6 per cent in 1963 to 62 per cent in 2005, about a 0.2 per cent annual growth rate over the period (Table 9.1), it is still some 3 per cent below the OECD average (Martin et al. 2004, pp. 89–90). The participation rate remained more or less unchanged during the 1970s and 1980s, at the levels of the 1960s.[3] Combining the growth of the population and the labor force participation rate, the labor force (economically active population) grew at a rate of 4.5 per cent per annum over the period 1963–2005 (Table 9.1). It should be noted, however, that the number of average working hours per week declined substantially from 51.6 hours in 1980 to 45 hours in 2005.[4]

This slow growth of the labor force could be eased to a large extent by increasing women's participation and extending the age for leaving the workforce. Despite having increased faster than the overall participation rate, women's labor force participation remained low at 50.1 per cent in 2005, compared to 62 per cent for all workers. Increasing the number of elderly workers could also boost labor force growth. Yet, the government contrarily lowered the age of retirement for teachers and public sector employees in 2002.

The concept of labor as an economic resource has not only a quantitative dimension, analyzed above, but also a qualitative dimension. The qualitative aspects of labor's contribution to economic development largely depend on education, culture and work ethic. Because of the influence of Confucianism, Korean workers are generally regarded as hardworking, industrious, disciplined, well educated, easy to train, highly motivated, dedicated and loyal to their companies.[5] Historically, education has always been highly emphasized under Confucianism, and education of the Korean labor force has increased remarkably over the last three decades. The Confucian influence has led to the development of a subtle social status identified by an individual's level of education, with scholars maintaining the highest social status throughout Korean history. Koreans continue to perceive education as being directly linked not only to improved social status but also to material success, thereby establishing a special place for education in Korean life. Because of Korea's close-knit family-oriented society, concerns and wishes for economic success and improved social status are regarded in terms of the family unit rather than at an individual level. Thus, parents willingly devote large portions of their finances to the education of their children, and even siblings financially support each other's education.

The educational zeal of Koreans was suppressed during the Japanese colonial rule, resulting in an illiteracy rate of 78 per cent among Koreans in 1945. However, after the Korean War, the illiteracy rate started to decrease dramatically, and by the mid-1970s it had decreased to such an insignificant level that it was no longer published by the Korean National Statistical Office. As the economy has developed, education has further expanded toward tertiary education, as university education enhances social status and employment prospects. The number of students enrolled at tertiary educational institutions increased from 101 000 in 1960 to 3 million in 2005, a 7.8 per cent annual growth over this period (KNSO 2006). The proportion of high school graduates pursuing post-secondary education was 74 per cent in 2003. This is compared to the rates of 63 per cent and 45 per cent, respectively, in the US and Japan (*Chosun Ilbo* 2004). Despite a heavy social demand for higher education, the government has long enforced a strict enrolment quota system. Given the limited opportunities for university education under the quota system, the zeal for education has led to the inevitable development of fierce competition for university entrance. Primary and high school students, all geared toward university entrance examinations, work extremely hard. This competition for university entrance is another factor contributing to the Korean work ethic, described above.

The zeal for education, resulting from Korean cultural influences, has been accompanied by heavy spending on education. The private sector accounts for the lion's share of increased education expenses. The government's education expenditure accounted for 13.2 per cent of the total budget in 1974, increasing to 18.7 per cent in 2004 (KNSO 2006). Although increasing, government expenditure on education accounts for only one-third of the total national spending on education, with the remainder being made by private individuals (L. Kim and S-M. Seong 1997, p. 394). In addition, it has been argued that the government has not provided adequate resources for education, as compared to national income. The ratio of government educational expenditure to GDP remained unchanged over the period 1990–2002, although the ratio increased from 1.8 per cent in 1970 to 3.1 per cent in 1990.

There is no doubt that rapid economic growth in Korea owes a great deal to increases in the general level of education. However, the Korean education system and education policy have faced a number of serious challenges. In particular, the quality of tertiary education has become an issue of public concern. The development of science and technology, business and vocational courses are not sufficient to cope with the demands of a rapidly industrializing society (L. Kim 1995). Because of the paramount importance of examinations for university entrance and employment recruitment, the education system tends to encourage rote learning of factual information, rather than the development of the skills of scientific inquiry and critical thinking which are necessary to meet the demands of the latest industrialization policy.

9.2.2   Employment of Human Resources

Along with industrialization and the rapid growth of the economy, the number of employed has increased at an average annual rate of 4.7 per cent between 1963 and 2005 (Table 9.1). Demand for labor expanded faster than labor supply, particularly evident during the initial stages of Korea's industrialization during the 1960s and the early 1970s. As a result, since the 1970s the unemployment rate has remained quite low, except for the period 1998–99 in the wake of the 1997 financial crisis (Table 9.1).

The share of employment by industry has changed remarkably over the last four decades, reflecting Korea's industrialization. The share of employment in the agricultural sector declined steadily from 63.1 per cent in 1963 to 7.9 per cent in 2005, while the share in the manufacturing sector increased from 8.7 per cent in 1963 to its maximum of 28 per cent in 1991, then gradually declined to 18.6 per cent in 2005. The service sector steadily increased its employment share from 28.3 per cent in 1963 to 73.5 per cent in 2005.

The Korean labor market has been unique in that the mobility and adaptability of labor has been relatively free of social limitations such as social class structure, regional and religious differences. As a result, the labor turnover rate was relatively high during the 1970s and 1980s at about 4 to 5 per cent (K.S. Kim and J.K. Kim 1995), indicating a competitive labor market. However, the turnover rate gradually declined to below 3 per cent during the 1990s, and reached 2.41 per cent in 2002 (KLI 2006a, p. 36). Although the real wage rate for the economy as a whole increased substantially, it was less than the increase in labor productivity. As shown in Table 9.2, over the period 1980–2002, the former increased at 5.6 per cent per annum, while the latter increased by 9.7 per cent.[6]

Table 9.2 Trends of major indicators of the labor market (annual average over the period)

	1963–69	1970–79	1980–89	1990–99	1963–96	1963–2002	1998–2002	2002–2005
GDP growth (%)	9.8	9.7	8.3	6.2	8.7	8.2	4.6	4.7
Pop growth (%)	2.56	1.75	1.24	0.94	1.64	1.51	0.72	0.47
Real wage increments (%)	n.a.	n.a.	5.8	5.6	n.a.	5.6d	3.5	5.7e
Productivity growth (%)a	n.a	8.9b	9.6	11.2	9.8c	9.7d	8.6	8.4e

Notes:
a Labor productivity is measured as the index of constant GDP divided by the index of labor man-hour input.
b Indicates value for 1971–79.
c Indicates value for 1971–96.
d Indicates value for 1980–2002.
e Indicates value for 2003.

Sources: Korea National Statistical Office (KNSO) (2002b); Korea National Statistical Office (2003); Korea National Statistical Office (2004); Korea National Statistical Office (2006); Korea Labor Institute (2003).

9.3 INDUSTRIAL RELATIONS AND LABOR STANDARDS

9.3.1 Industrial Relations in Transition

The labor market is the area in which the Korean government has intervened most extensively. Up until the late 1980s, the generation of employment in line with the policy of maximum growth was the focus of government labor policy. Because strong authoritarian regimes had all emphasized maximum growth policies, anti-competitive institutional arrangements such as minimum wage laws, labor protection laws and union monopolies that could have raised real wages and labor costs either did not exist or were not implemented until the late 1980s. In addition, the government also frequently imposed wage guidelines. As part of this labor policy, the government promoted the rights of management at the expense of the rights of labor, suppressing union activities and intervening in labor disputes. Management, taking advantage of government policy and intervention, has applied an authoritarian method of labor management. Whenever labor disputes occurred, management often relied on the government to resolve the disputes instead of learning and practicing appropriate methods of dispute resolution. Therefore although, as Kim and Lee (1997) argue, the Korean labor market appeared competitive and efficient, it was under strict government control and had not progressed toward the sort of labor market seen in advanced countries.

The Korean labor market has changed markedly since the late 1980s. In conjunction with political democratization in 1987, labor market democratization also occurred, and government power and influence on labor management fell dramatically. This, together with the shortage of labor experienced in the late 1980s, led to numerous labor disputes during the 1987–89 period. It thus became apparent that past practices of labor relations management would no longer work in Korea. From the early 1990s, globalization forces also exerted substantial influence over industrial relations and government labor policy. Faced with growing global competition, the government and employers sought to control wage increases and maintain flexibility in the labor market. Trade unions on the other hand demanded that labor rights be strengthened to be aligned with international standards. After several confrontations across the nation, Korean labor laws were amended in early 1997, lifting most of the restrictions on union activities (Lee and Lee 2003, p. 178).

The outbreak of the 1997 financial crisis had a profound impact on industrial relations in Korea. The Tripartite Commission was established in January 1998 to promote cooperation among the three key parties –

government, labor unions and employers – in overcoming the economic crisis. The Commission concluded a historic social pact covering an extensive agenda and, accordingly, the Labour Standards Act was amended in February 1998 (Lee and Lee 2003, p. 179). One of the key contents of the amended Act was to enhance labor market flexibility by allowing the dismissal of workers for 'managerial reasons' and introducing a 'dispatched worker system'.[7]

9.3.2 Current Industrial Relations and Labor Standards

Trade unions in Korea are predominantly enterprise-based, although industrial unions have appeared in the recent past (Lee and Lee 2003, p. 180), and the union density rate is not high.[8] The numbers of both unions and union members increased to their maximum values in 1989, and declined more or less steadily until 2001 when both of them increased somewhat above the values of the preceding year (Table 9.1). As of 2004, there were 6107 unions and 1.5 million union members. The union density rate increased to its highest rate of 18.6 per cent in 1989, and declined steadily to 10.3 per cent in 2004 (Table 9.1). The number of industrial disputes has varied from year to year. It was 206 in 1980 and peaked to 3749 in 1987 with political democratization. Since 1990, the number of labor disputes has ranged from about 100 to 300 annually (Table 9.1; KLI 2006a).

The major actors involved in current industrial relations in Korea are unions, employers and the government. There are two national federations of unions: the Federation of Korean Trade Unions (FKTU) and the Korean Confederation of Trade Unions (KCTU). The FKTU had 3754 unions with 872 000 union members, and the KCTU had 1362 unions and 615 000 union members at the end of 2000 (Lee and Lee 2003, p. 181). The KCTU, which gained legal recognition in 1999, leans toward militant activism. The FKTU shows a more cooperative stance toward the government and employers. The two national-level organizations representing employers are the Korea Employers Federation (KEF) and the Federation of Korean Industries (FKI). The FKI consists mainly of chaebols and deals with economic policy issues, while the KEF, which represents about 4000 members of small firms as well as chaebols, focuses on industrial relations issues. The KEF represents the official voice of Korean employers for national-level negotiations and consultations. The Ministry of Labour is the government body that administers labor policies.

As trade unions are enterprise-based unions, collective bargaining at most unionized firms is conducted primarily at the firm level. Nevertheless, the influence of national federations of unions on company-level bargaining has been rising in the recent past. At the beginning of every year, the

FKTU and KCTU make nationwide bargaining demands for wages and other contractual changes, which serve as an influential guideline to enterprise-level collective bargaining. In response to these proposals by national union houses, the KEF offers its own negotiation guidelines to member companies.

To facilitate communication and cooperation between employees and employers, labor–management councils are formed by law at all companies with more than 30 workers (Lee and Lee 2003, p. 182). The council is composed of the same number of representatives from employees and management, and holds regular meetings every quarter. The official mediator of labor disputes in Korea is the Labour Relations Commission (LRC), which consists of representatives of trade unions, management and the public interest.

The Labour Standards Act (LSA) outlines the basic framework for labor standards in Korea. The Act, as amended in 1998, provides workers' rights and labor standards up to levels close to international standards. The Act prohibits discriminatory treatment, including gender discrimination and exploitation of workers. The Act sets forth the minimum level of working conditions required to guarantee workers' dignity, safety and occupational health. It also stipulates the minimum wage as a guarantee for workers' basic needs, although workers earning less than the minimum wage amounted to only 2.1 per cent of workers in 2001 (Lee and Lee 2003, p. 187). In 2003, the Act was amended after serious contestations between employers and employees to make Saturday a non-work day, thereby reducing the number of working hours from 44 to 40 per week. Despite this, Korean labor standards fall short of international standards in a number of areas such as the prohibition on unemployed workers remaining members of unions, the prohibition of more than one union at enterprise level, the prohibition on employers' payment of union officials, and the very broad definition of an essential public service on which strike action is prohibited (Martin et al. 2004, pp. 79–80).

There remain a number of thorny issues within Korea's labor relations. First, even though collective dismissal of workers for managerial reasons has been legislated, it is extremely difficult to dismiss workers because employers must meet a number of requirements, including giving 60 days advance notification of the dismissal plan to trade unions (Lee and Lee 2003, p. 185). In practice, therefore, employers rely more on 'honorable retirements', early retirement or attrition rather than dismissal for employment adjustment when restructuring their businesses (Park et al. 2001). Employers claim that honorable retirements are an expensive mode of employment adjustment due to severance payments, and that the labor market still lacks flexibility.[9]

It appears that employment adjustment through dismissals will not become the dominant mode of adjustment because of the strong collectivism that prevails in Korean society, the poor social safety net and the difficulty of middle managers in finding new jobs once they are dismissed. Another contentious issue is a rapid increase in temporary workers, the highest among OECD member countries in 2002.[10] The share of temporary workers increased from 45.9 per cent in 1997 to 52.4 per cent in 2000, yet their labor rights have not been well protected. Within this group, the even less secure category of daily workers made up 18.3 per cent of total employment in 2000 (Rowley and Bae 2004, p. 71). Reflecting this increase in temporary workers, average job tenure in Korea is low by international comparison. In enterprises with five or more employees, tenure was less than six years under the same employer in 2000. This contrasts with average employment tenures of ten years in the EU, and 12 years in Japan (Martin et al. 2004, pp. 95–6).[11] Finally, even though the union density rate is quite low, industrial disputes have been high profile, large scale and confrontational, thereby disrupting economic and social order and tarnishing the national image in the eyes of foreigners.

9.4 HUMAN RESOURCE MANAGEMENT

9.4.1 Traditional HRM

As management, HRM is influenced by social institutions, including tradition and culture, formal rules and regulations, and enforcement mechanisms. Korea's HRM system has evolved over a long history and reflects its unique institutional background. Institutions do not remain static but evolve over time. Similarly, social institutions in Korea have also transformed over time. In particular, as examined in Chapter 3, Korean society witnessed drastic changes in various aspects of social institutions in conjunction with the 1997 financial crisis and ensuing economic and business reforms. Consequently, the Korean economy has been engulfed by the globalization of the world economy, and companies seek to adopt the best practices of HRM to survive the fierce competition in the global economy. In addition, foreign investors have penetrated the Korean business sector as equity participants, business partners under strategic alliances, or domestic competitors with their direct investments. The ratio of FDI stock to GDP increased from 2.1 per cent in 1995 to 7.9 per cent in 1999. Further to this, the number of Korean companies with a foreign-owned equity stake of more than 10 per cent increased from 4419 in 1997, to 11 515 in 2001 (Kwon 2003, p. 40). The rising presence of foreign capital, business firms and ideas will force Korean companies to adopt more competitive HRM practices.

Whither then Korea's HRM system? Various facets of Korean social institutions have been transforming toward Western institutions (see Chapter 3). In addition, Western systems of management and HRM have been regarded more favorably than Korean systems, particularly since the 1997 crisis. Hence, it is expected that Korean companies would change their HRM toward a Western system. However, in spite of institutional reforms since 1997, serious doubt has been cast on the extent of the transformation of Korea's HRM in view of institutional inertia and path dependency. Even with their pursuit of competitiveness and efficiency, Korean companies will not quickly and lightly discard key cultural norms. Rather, they will seek to maintain the strengths of their traditional HRM, such as group harmony and employees' loyalty and commitment, while adopting other Western practices. Many employees would prefer job security and certainty protected by traditional HRM. Guillen (2001) has pointed out that most empirical studies in social sciences do not find convergence in political, social or organizational patterns of behavior as a result of globalization, and that national cultures and values change over time, although in 'path-dependent' rather convergent ways, with no common global culture emerging on the horizon. How then would Korean companies weigh the two countervailing forces and come up with their optimal model of HRM?

The objective of this section is to examine Korea's traditional HRM and assess the new approach to HRM that has been transpiring in the recent past. This will be done by analyzing the HRM of chaebols, as their HRM practices are clearly illustrated and also chaebols are in the vanguard of the transformation of management and HRM systems in Korea. It is anticipated that other Korean companies will quickly emulate new systems adopted by chaebols in pursuit of the efficiency and competitiveness required for their own survival.

As mentioned earlier, HRM is predicated on management strategy. In the past, as examined in Chapter 8, the Korean management system was geared toward growth-oriented strategies and paternalistic and authoritarian-style management under Confucian influences. Under such a management system, the guiding philosophy of Korean HRM was anchored on the maintenance of employees' loyalty and commitment and group harmony by providing job security and certainty through the seniority and lifetime employment systems (see Table 9.3 for summary). Under these principles, Korean HRM traditionally emphasized teamwork and promoted the corporation as a family unit (S.M. Lee 1989, p. 189). In accordance with the perception of the firm being a type of family unit, and the prevailing Confucian responsibility to care for family members as best as possible, traditional Korean HRM practices were group- or family-oriented, yet autocratic.

Table 9.3   Korean human resource management: traditional and new approaches

Functions	Traditional HRM approach	New HRM approach
Corporate strategy	Growth-oriented strategy	Profit-oriented strategy (efficiency and international competitiveness)
	Paternalistic management	Participative management
Philosophy of HRM	Long-term loyalty	Competence and merit
	Harmony (familism)	Cooperative
	Autocratic	Democratic
	Seniority	Seniority influence reduced
	Job security (life-time employment)	Life-time employment influence reduced
	People-based	Job-based
Recruitment	Generalists	Specialists
	Internal	Internal and external
Selection	Family members, university- and regional-based preference	Merit-based
	Fresh graduates: (twice/year)	Experienced: when needed with aptitude and personality testing
Promotion	Seniority	Performance
	Internal promotion	Internal and external promotion

215

Table 9.3 (continued)

Functions	Traditional HRM approach	New HRM approach
Compensation	Seniority-based	Performance-based
	Group-based incentives	Differential incentives
	Numerous fringe benefits	Limited fringe benefits
	No profit sharing	Profit sharing (limited)
	Monthly pay system by *hobong*	Annual pay by individual ability
Labor relations	Lifetime employment	No guarantee of lifetime employment
	No part-time workers	Part-time workers (contract-based)
	No lay-off	Lay-offs if necessary
Training and Development	Extensive	Less extensive

Bearing in mind changes in these underlying basic principles, each of the traditional HRM functions (recruitment, training and development, promotion and compensation) will be examined first, and an examination of changes in these functions will follow.

Recruitment
Recruitment in most Korean companies has traditionally not been based on ability or skills, but on personal connections such as family, educational and regional ties (Chang and Chang 1994, p. 65; S.M. Lee 1989, p. 188). Korean society is the most family-centered society among Asian countries and it was considered a basic responsibility of family to provide for its members. Thus, family owner-managers were expected to recruit clan members into management. However, as chaebols became far too large to be staffed solely by family members, educational and regional ties were also considered as important sources of recruitment.

Traditionally, chaebols recruited new graduates twice a year through open examinations with strong preference given to those graduates from a few prestigious universities in Korea. They were hired as generalists, in that job descriptions were not provided to them, and academic disciplines were not considered seriously during recruitment. Regional ties were also an important consideration. Koreans believed that people from the same region would share a similar culture, trust each other better, and work harmoniously together. Internal promotion was taken for granted, and ties by family, school and region were all considered important aspects of promotion. This indicates a very limited reliance on external recruitment.

Korean companies also engaged in other kinds of discriminatory HRM practices. They treated blue-collar workers unfavorably, compared to white-collar workers. They also discriminated heavily against female workers. Due to a commonly held perception that once women had children they would leave the corporations and not return, women were less likely to be employed in the first place, even though they were equally qualified with the same educational background. Furthermore, women were discriminated against when recruiting for upper management positions, as it was not considered appropriate for women to hold such leadership roles in Confucian society. Even though labor laws were in place prohibiting gender discrimination, women in upper management positions were rare in Korean companies.

Training and development
Under the strong perception that workers, once hired, would stay with the same company for their career with lifetime employment practices, chaebols put strong emphasis on training their employees. A number of chaebols also

established their own well-resourced and supported training centers. Leading Korean companies provided their new employees with a long orientation period to promote corporate values, group harmony and loyalty through group training. To develop generalists, all-purpose general skills, team spirit and adaptability were emphasized in training, and job rotations were regularly practiced. As companies relied on the internal promotion system, they provided extensive training to all levels of senior managers at their centers.

Promotion and compensation

Traditionally, under seniority payments and lifetime employment practices, the system of performance evaluation was not important as it did not affect promotion or compensation significantly. As Korean culture places great value on 'face-saving', a fair and objective evaluation was difficult. Any harsh criticism of an employee by a manager was deemed to be detrimental to *inhwa* – group harmony – thus managers were particularly reluctant to identify poor performers. For this reason staff were not informed of their manager's evaluation and no feedback was given.

Promotion has been a particularly important component of Korean HRM. In a highly Confucian society such as Korea, the success of a person is judged by his status or rank, and promotion brings great prestige to himself and his family. In most cases, promotions were sourced in-house and were based on seniority, with external promotion being a rare exception. Normally the process for promotion would involve an assessment of an employee's seniority, performance, personality, educational credentials, sincere efforts (or diligence) and results of tests conducted by companies for promotion purposes.[12] Of all these criteria, seniority was generally the most important. The assessment of an employee based on these criteria was then compared to management's expectations and desires. The employee that was evaluated as most suited to management's expectations was then promoted (Pucik and Lim 2002, p. 148).

Traditionally, compensation was based on seniority and educational qualifications. Korean wage structures have been complicated, consisting of a contracted basic wage, various allowances, bonuses and fringe benefits. Basic wages and numerous allowances were paid monthly, and bonus payments proportionate to basic wages were normally given three to five times a year to every staff member. Approximately half of Korean corporations decided these wages and salaries through collective bargaining and informal labor management negotiations in 1987 (Chang and Chang 1994, p. 96). Under the corporate familism and also under the perception of lifetime employment, fringe benefits were another important component of the Korean compensation system and were related to the financial needs of employees.

Many companies assisted their workers financially by providing housing loans and tuition fees for their employees' children. Additionally, many companies supported their employees' pursuit of higher education, from masters to doctoral programs.

9.4.2 Emergence of a New Approach to HRM[13]

Since the 1997 crisis with the ensuing new institutional framework, the corporate strategy of Korean companies has changed from a growth-oriented strategy to a profitability-driven strategy (Park and Yu 2002, p. 127). This reorientation in management strategy has led Korean firms to seek international competitiveness, and in pursuing this they have begun reforming various components of the traditional HRM system. In addition, soon after the crisis, labor laws changed to allow management to retrench workers. Under these new laws, corporate restructuring has caused many companies to downsize and lay off a large number of workers.[14] Cho and Keum (2004, p. 375) argue that most of these dismissals did not comply with the required procedures, particularly in small to medium-sized businesses (SMEs) where unions have traditionally had very little bargaining power. This was a watershed in the cultural basis underlying the traditional HRM system and transformed the guiding philosophy for HRM from both managers' and employees' perspectives. Managers can no longer guarantee job security to employees, and employees' commitment and loyalty to the company have started to ebb.[15] Under these circumstances, the guiding principles of HRM in many companies have begun to shift from seniority and lifetime employment practices to performance-based and job-based management and remuneration (Rowley and Bae 2004). In addition, autocratic HRM and corporate familism have declined, and participative HRM has been increasingly adopted (Table 9.3).

Another development in the Korean economy that has accelerated the transition of HRM has been the explosion of venture businesses based on information technology (Park et al. 2001). Venture firms do not adhere to the traditional HRM practices; they do not guarantee job security and prefer recruiting the workforce from the external labor market, offering attractive compensation such as stock options. The increasing success of venture companies has contributed to fresh graduates and young and innovative workers considering venture companies as being a more attractive employment opportunity than the cumbersome and ageing chaebols. The increasing attractiveness of these venture companies and their HRM practices has had a significant impact on the HRM of chaebols. Some chaebols have already started trying to compete with the more attractive HRM systems of venture businesses, introducing new incentive systems and attempting to create work environments that encourage creativity and give a degree of autonomy to the new generation of employees, as venture firms do (Park et al. 2001; Rowley and Bae 2004).

Korean companies have, therefore, faced a daunting challenge for their HRM. The new HRM system has to accommodate both the employees who are used to and comfortable with traditional HRM practices with job security, and the younger generations who crave challenges and high merit-based compensations with little commitment and loyalty to the company. The new HRM practices have to focus on attracting the younger generations as well as retaining and motivating them. At the same time, they should improve management efficiency for employees who are accustomed to the traditional system.

Recruitment
An important trend in staffing has been the emergence of a new emphasis on recruitment of specialists rather than generalists. Even though leading Korean companies still recruit new graduates twice a year, they now seek specialized professionals, rather than generalists. For professional staffing, the important selection criteria are creativity and challenge, integrity, cooperation and technical competence, rather than the prestige and status of universities from which candidates graduate (Park et al. 2001). Thus, the selection process places emphasis on aptitude tests to assess the potential competency of applicants, and an increasingly higher emphasis is placed on interviews to assess applicants' personality characteristics, their values and creativity. Many companies, including Samsung, do not require the names of schools of applicants. This eliminates any prejudice based on school names (Pucik and Lim 2002).[16]

Leading Korean companies now rely not only on internal human resources but also on the external labor market for recruitment. Given the significant change in the preference of many graduates toward venture businesses, Korean chaebols are now scanning the external labor market more actively (Pucik and Lim 202). Park et al. (2001) point out that 79 per cent of the companies sampled by the Korea Labor Institute in 2000 have had experience of recruitment from outside sources. This is a remarkable transition in recruitment practices given that internal recruitment or internal promotion was the cornerstone of traditional HRM in Korea.

Training and development
The focus of training and development has changed significantly. Prior to the crisis, management expended significant resources on promoting corporate values, group harmony and loyalty. However, such HRM practices do not appeal to the new breed of young and educated employees with individual

talents and aspirations (Pucik and Lim 2002, p. 138). For these young employees, training has to be focused on the development of specialized professionals rather than the development of generalists. Samsung Electronics, for instance, focuses its staff training on cultivating experts in technology, marketing and customer services, and on career development programs for selected staff members with noteworthy capacity and talent (Samsung 2007). As Park and Yu (2002) point out, the intensity of training for management development purposes could have declined because of declining practices of long-term employment and the emerging importance of the external labor market for recruitment. Nonetheless, Korean companies seek to maintain the strengths of the traditional HRM, such as group harmony and employees' loyalty and commitment. To this end, companies look for a balance between these competing demands and continue to operate traditional training programs focusing on enhancing corporate culture.

Compensation and promotion
As mentioned above, evaluation was not important under the traditional HRM system because of the seniority system for compensation and promotion, and concerns about the potential negative impact on employees' morale and group harmony. However, as companies increasingly implement performance-based compensation and promotion and differential incentives, evaluation has become an important part of some chaebols' HRM. Under the new HRM, evaluation emphasizes performance in tasks, duties and responsibilities, and competence in skills and knowledge, compared to the traditional emphasis on seniority, educational credentials, family background and diligence (Pucik and Lim 2002, p. 148). Park et al. (2001) have found that while companies undertook evaluation mainly for promotional purposes in the past, some of them now utilize evaluation as a tool for career development as well.

The cornerstone of Korean traditional HRM practices was promotion based on seniority and from internal human resources. That is, vacant positions within a company were previously given to existing employees in the form of a seniority-based promotion. However, as explained above, workers that have been recruited externally are increasingly staffing these positions (Park et al. 2001). In addition, promotion is increasingly being based on performance and ability. For example, Samsung introduced a merit-based promotion system, although it was intended to supplement, not to replace, seniority-based promotion (Pucik and Lim 2001).

Traditionally, compensation was primarily based on seniority and rank (Kim and Briscoe 1997). As Korean firms encountered rapidly rising wages from the late 1980s, however, they started to fine-tune their compensation schemes to take into account other considerations (H.C. Lee 1989). In particular, many companies introduced performance-based pay systems, limited though they were. For instance, based on a survey of 4303 business units in January 1999, 15.1 per cent of the firms surveyed had already adopted an annual pay system based on performance and ability. Further to this, 11.2 per cent had made a decision to adopt the system and were preparing for its implementation, with a further 25 per cent in the planning stages of adopting such a system (Rowley 2002, p. 186). As of 2003, approximately one-third of companies with 100 or more workers were using performance-based remuneration systems, and in the case of companies with 1000 or more workers, the proportion was 61 per cent (Economist Intelligence Unit 2003, p. 60).[17]

One of the key characteristics of the Korean compensation system is that the compensation package consists of basic salary, allowances and bonuses, with bonuses making up about one-third of the total. Bonus systems are increasingly focused on what has been achieved relevant to individual performance, while still being influenced substantially by the group. Koreans generally regard the importance of incentive payments relatively highly compared to other developed countries, yet they rate the desirability of performance-based incentive payments quite low (Lowe et al. 2002). Thus, bonuses are still largely group-based rather than individual performance-based.

Another innovation in compensation that has been introduced by venture companies and chaebols is a profit-sharing program. Since regulations related to share options have been amended to make it easier for companies to adopt share option incentives, many venture companies have adopted the Employee Stock Ownership Plans (ESOPs). A number of chaebols have introduced ESOPs, although only to a limited extent, mainly providing them only to R&D employees.

As the annual salary system based on performance is increasingly introduced and the concept of corporate familism declines, fringe benefits (voluntary) should decrease as companies try to reduce excessive spending as part of their drive to be internationally competitive. However, it appears that fringe benefits are still used quite extensively. Many companies provide fringe benefits of various types such as subsidies for housing and lunch, child education support and support for leisure and sport activities. It should be noted that these fringe benefits are based on financial need or the individual circumstances of staff members – not on performance.

9.5   FOREIGN PERCEPTIONS OF KOREAN HRM

It is useful in setting up a business strategy to understand foreign perceptions of Korean HRM. To assess perceptions held by foreign business people of change in the Korean HRM system, a sample survey of foreign workers who were employed by foreign companies in Korea was undertaken between May and July 2002. The findings of the survey shed light on the extent of the transformation of Korean HRM perceived by foreign business people (Kwon 2006).

The survey asked six questions related to important functions of HRM, as shown in Table 9.4. Respondents generally viewed HRM in Korea as having changed little, as indicated by an average score of 2.73 for the six types of possible changes in HRM (Table 9.4). Of those six possible types of changes, two types were rated higher than 3, while four were rated less than 3. Foreigners generally agreed with the view that 'lifetime employment practices are disappearing', with a score of 3.156, and marginally agreed with the view that 'lay-off of workers is increasing', with a score of 3.032 (Kwon 2006). This indicates a perception that, although lifetime employment practices are disappearing, other conventional human resource management practices are changing little. These include the practices of promotion and compensation, recruitment and the seniority system. Foreigners also disagreed, although marginally, that change was evident in Korean companies' willingness to hire foreign workers.[18]

Table 9.4 Respondents' view of changes in the Korean HRM system

Types of change	No.	Average rating	Standard deviation
Disappearing life time employment practices	64	3.156	1.130
Increases in the lay-off of workers	63	3.032	0.999
Merit-based promotion and compensation	65	2.615	0.963
Willingness to hire foreign workers	64	2.719	1.046
Recruitment by merit – rather than by personal connections or university background	65	2.462	1.047
Disappearing seniority system	66	2.394	1.080
Average	64	2.730	1.015

Source: From Table 6 in Kwon (2006).

9.6 CONCLUSION

Since the 1997 financial crisis, the Korean economy has been transformed in a variety of ways. The corporate and financial sectors and the labor market have been reformed, and the economy has been liberalized and internationalized. Hence, the Korean business environment has changed remarkably. Businesses are now faced with unprecedented competition both domestically and internationally. They have had to respond to this new situation in terms of their strategy and management, and have had to enhance their operational efficiency and international competitiveness for their own survival.

Korean HRM, therefore, faces a daunting challenge. Korean companies have had to eliminate inefficiency in HRM under the traditional system yet, at the same time, endeavor to maintain its strengths in such areas as workers' commitment and loyalty, which the empirical evidence suggests are in decline. They have also had to accommodate HRM to demographic changes and new labor laws, while appreciating the concepts of path dependency and institutional inertia, particularly the resilient customs and cultural values related to HRM.

The HRM system of Korean companies has had to transform in line with this new strategic direction and to accommodate the emerging social institutions. Companies have shifted their strategic goals from maximum growth to profitability. Additionally, a clear trend is set in Korea's demographics with population growth slowing significantly and the population ageing quickly. This type of demographic change has serious implications for HRM. Formal institutions related to the labor market have also needed to change. Though difficult, retrenchment of workers has been allowed for 'managerial reasons'. Although unions are still enterprise-based, industry-based unions are rising. Two federations of trade unions coexist, multiple unions at the enterprise level have been allowed from 2002, and union tactics are considered quite confrontational (Rowley et al. 2004). The Labour Standard Act, as amended in 1998, provides for labor rights more or less up to international standards. Finally, five working days a week with 40 hours of work has been introduced by law.

Korean companies, with chaebols as vanguards, have already begun transforming various functions of HRM in the recent past. They have been implementing HRM systems that are performance-based, moving away from the traditional, authoritarian and paternalistic HRM system with seniority and lifetime employment practices. Regarding recruitment, traditional in-house staffing policies have been modified to include the external labor market. Selection criteria have also changed, with less emphasis being placed on traditional criteria such as personal, school and regional ties, and more emphasis on competencies and individual traits. Staff evaluation is moving away from a reliance on seniority and family background toward an emphasis on performance in tasks, duties and responsibilities, and knowledge.

Part of the cornerstone of Korean traditional HRM practices was promotion based on seniority. However, increasingly, workers that have been recruited externally are staffing vacant positions, and promotion is based on performance and ability. While traditionally based on seniority and rank, compensation systems are including new and innovative incentives increasingly based on performance. Finally, management has increasingly attempted to approach labor relations in a more democratic way, emphasizing harmonious communication through regular labor–management consultations.

Based on the above examination of the HRM practices after 1997, an intriguing question arises as to the real extent of the HRM transformation. There is no doubt that significant transformations in Korea's HRM have been undertaken, particularly by many leading chaebols driven by the pressures of internationalization and globalization together with the new institutional framework. However, they do not amount to a complete conversion to Western systems. Rather, it appears that the traditional system still remains strong. According to a survey of 107 HRM specialists (both academics and HRM practitioners) conducted in 1999 by Park et al. (2001), the majority of respondents claimed that the HRM paradigm has shifted in four aspects:

1. from seniority-based to performance-based;
2. paternalistic to contract;
3. autocratic to democratic;
4. generalist to specialist HRM.

However, the respondents were unsure of a shift from people-based to job-based HRM. People-related HRM includes those practices of seniority-based compensation and generalist staffing (Park et al. 2002). This is contradictory to the claims of shifts in (1) and (4) above, indicating that compensation and promotion, a key HRM function closely related to culture, has not transformed to any easily discernible extent.

Based on the information and the results of empirical studies examined above, it appears that the transformations in Korean HRM have not been extensive, although these changes will certainly continue into the future. Although many companies have introduced some combination of seniority and performance-related pay systems, the pay system is still largely based on seniority. Rowley et al. (2004) suggest that the transformation in compensation from a seniority to a performance-based system is still in its infancy. New and innovative bonus systems have been introduced, yet they are implemented largely on a group basis.[19] Even most of the fringe benefits that remain an important component of Korean compensation systems are still based on individual circumstances rather than on performance. In addition, although selection criteria have changed significantly, with more emphasis on competencies and individual traits, recruitment is still largely internal.[20]

As perceived by foreign business people in Korea, HRM in Korea has changed little. Although there is a view that the practice of lifetime employment is declining and lay-offs of workers are rising, other components of Korean HRM remain unchanged. In particular, foreign business people take the view that the recruitment process of Korean companies has not opened up to foreigners.

Culturally, Koreans have a high preference for the traditional HRM system. As pointed out by Hofstede (1991), Koreans are highly risk averse and have high power distance. They are also the most family-oriented people in Asia. Koreans therefore have a high preference for job security and certainty, and are tolerant to authoritarian and paternalistic management due to Confucian culture. An overriding concern for job security is particularly prevalent among those with lower educational attainment and income levels (Park and Kim 2005). Therefore, it is likely that the seniority and lifetime employment systems will remain important elements of the Korean HRM system for the foreseeable future. Hence, the challenge of Korean HRM is to enhance its efficiency, embracing and taking advantage of its unique institutional framework. Foreign MNEs should not overlook Korea's unique cultural features and its traditional HRM system when implementing HRM 'best approach', as suggested by Von Glinow et al. (2002, p. 127).

In conclusion, various functions of the Korean HRM system have been transforming toward the new approach in leading chaebols, as summarized in Table 9.3. However, because of institutional inertia and path dependency, the transformation is unlikely to be completed in the near future. In fact, the Korean system may never converge fully toward Western systems. It is highly likely that managerial attempts to maintain the strengths of employees' loyalty and commitment to companies will continue. Thus management will not readily be able to discard the traditional HRM system.

NOTES

1. Textbooks of international business and management typically deal only with human resource management of expatriates (Hill 2003, pp. 606–29; Cullen 2002, pp. 428–56). There are studies in the literature to identify the tendency of convergence or divergence of HRM practices and to identify the 'best practices' of HRM across countries. Although there is a converging tendency, HRM practices still remain quite divergent across countries according to their cultural and institutional backgrounds (Von Glinow et al. 2002; Rowley et al. 2004).

2. One of the most important features of population ageing in Korea is that its pace is unprecedented. It took 175 years in France for the proportion of population aged 65 and

above to reach 12 per cent, 65 years in the United States and 40 years in Japan. This change is estimated to take less than 25 years in Korea (T.H. Kwon 2003).

3. This may be attributable to changes in the composition of the labor force. As the economy has developed, participation by the younger age group (aged 15–19) declined as a rising proportion of younger people remained at school, while the participation rate of the oldest age group increased as more job opportunities become available.

4. Korea National Statistical Office (2006), *Statistical Database*, http://kosis.nso.go.kr/, accessed 21 August 2006. Weekly working hours are estimated from working hours per month at firms with ten or more employees in all non-farm industries, multiplying them by 12 and dividing them by 52.143. For monthly working hours, see KLI (2003, p. 92).

5. According to a survey of foreign business people in Korea in 2002, Kwon (2003a) found that foreign business people viewed Korean workers as having such characteristics.

6. Nam and Kim (1997) argue that real wage rates in the manufacturing sector increased substantially faster than increases in labor productivity over the 1964–94 period.

7. The dispatched worker system refers to hiring arrangements whereby an employer can employ workers through temporary work agencies instead of hiring them directly. The managerial reasons include an absolutely unavoidable case and cases arising as a consequence of mergers and acquisitions.

8. The union density rate refers to the number of union members as a percentage of the total number of employed workers.

9. Park and Yu (2002) argue that the new Labour Law has helped troubled companies reduce their workforce, particularly soon after the 1997 crisis.

10. In 2002, temporary workers comprised 51.6 per cent of the Korean labor force compared with 32 per cent in Spain, 27 per cent in Australia, 13 per cent in Germany and 12 per cent in Japan (Park and Kim 2005, pp. 38–9).

11. Cho and Keum (2004, pp. 376–7) also point out that length of job tenure among wage earners declined by 20.4 per cent between 1994 and 1999.

12. To show their efforts, employees usually do not leave their office, even after official working hours, until their superior officers leave.

13. As mentioned earlier, this section is an analysis of new HRM practices in chaebols, companies that have traditionally been the vanguard in the transformation in HRM, in the expectation that other Korean companies will emulate chaebols.

14. After the crisis, 66 per cent of listed companies were reported to lay off their workers (Park and Yu 2002, p. 128).

15. In a survey of workers in 33 countries in 2002, only 36 per cent of Korean respondents expressed dedication to their work, by comparison with a global average of 57 per cent; 35 per cent of Korean workers expressed commitment to their company; and only 25 per cent were found to be committed to both work and company, as compared with a global average of 43 per cent (Park and Kim 2005, pp. 43–4).

16. According to the *Chosun Ilbo* (2002), over the six-year period 1997–2002 Samsung Electronics hired only 5 per cent of its total newly recruited employees from the five outstanding universities in Korea, followed by 21 per cent from the first-tier universities, 59 per cent from the second-tier universities and 14 per cent from the remaining universities. This indicates quite clearly that applicants' universities and regions are no longer important criteria for recruitment in Korea.

17. There are some variations in the types of annual pay systems used. For example, Samsung and Hyosung reduce the salary of poor performers while increasing the salary of high performers. On the other hand, S.K. Doosan and Daesang increase the salary of high performers, without reducing the salary of poor performers (Rowley 2002, p. 187).

18. For a detailed explanation and discussion of the survey results, see Kwon (2006).

19. From casual conversations with workers, it was understood that if one member of staff is given a bonus, he or she spends it all in entertaining his or her colleagues in the same section or division.

20. This observation is somewhat different from that of Rowley et al. (2004) who argue that recruitment has transformed substantially.

REFERENCES

Chang, C. and N. Chang (1994), *The Korean Management System: Cultural, Political, Economic Foundations*, Westport, Connecticut: Quorum Books.
Cho, J. and J. Keum (2004), 'Job instability in the Korean labour market: estimating the effects of the 1997 financial crisis', *International Labour Review*, 143 (4), 373–92.
Chosun Ilbo (2002), 'Status of universities: not important for recruitment' (in Korean), 24 February.
Chosun Ilbo (2004), editorial, 22 April.
Cullen, John B. (2002*)*, *Multinational Management: A Strategic Approach*, Cincinnati, OH: South-Western, Thomson Learning.
Economist Intelligence Unit (2003), *Country Commerce: South Korea*, New York: Economist Intelligence Unit.
Guillen, Mauro F. (2001), 'Is globalization civilizing, destructive or feeble? A critique of five key debates in the social science literature', *Annual Review of Sociology*, 27, 235–61.
Hill, Charles L. (2003), *International Business*, 4th edition, Boston, MA: McGraw-Hill Irwin.
Hofstede, G. (1991), *Cultures and Organizations: Software of the Mind*, London: McGraw-Hill.
Kim, K.S. and J.K. Kim (1995), 'Korean economic development: an overview' (in Korean), in D.S. Cha and K.S. Kim (eds), *The Korean Economy 1945–1995: Performance and Vision for the 21st Century* (in Korean), Seoul: Korea Development Institute, pp. 25–117.
Kim, Linsu (1995), 'Absorption capacity and industrial growth: a conceptual framework and Korea's experience', in B.H. Koo and D.H. Perkins (eds), *Social Capacity and Long-Term Economic Growth*, New York: St Martin's Press, pp. 266–87.
Kim, Linsu and S.M. Seong (1997), 'Science and technology: public policy and private strategy', in D.S. Cha, Kwong Suk Kim and Dwight H. Perkins (eds), *The Korean Economy 1945–1995: Performance and Vision for the 21st Century*, Seoul: Korea Development Institute, pp. 383–425.
Kim, Seongsu and D.R. Briscoe (1997), 'Globalisation and a new human resource policy in Korea transformation to a performance-based HRM', *Employee Relations*, 19 (4), 298–308.
Kim, Sookon (2001), 'Korea's industrial relations in transition', in O. Yul Kwon and W. Shepherd (eds), *Korea's Economic Prospects: From Financial Crisis to Prosperity*, Cheltenham, UK and Northampton, MA, USA: Edward Elgar Publishing, pp. 207–224.
Kim, Sookon and Ju-Ho Lee (1997), 'Industrial relations and human resource development', in D.S. Cha, Kwong Suk Kim and Dwight H. Perkins (eds), *The Korean Economy 1945–1995: Performance and Vision for the 21st Century*, Seoul: Korea Development Institute, pp. 586–622.
Korea Labor Institute (KLI) (2003), *KLI Labor Statistics 2003*, Seoul: Korea Labor Institute.
Korea Labor Institute (KLI) (2006a), *KLI Labor Statistics 2006*, Seoul: Korea Labor Institute.

Korea Labor Institute (KLI) (2006b), 'Labor Statistics for June 2006', http://www.kli.re.kr// Accessed 21 August 2006.

Korea National Statistical Office (KNSO) (2002a), *Korea Statistical Yearbook 2002*, Seoul: National Statistical Office.

Korea National Statistical Office (KNSO) (2002b), *Major Statistics of Korean Economy*, Seoul: National Statistical Office.

Korean National Statistical Office (KNSO) (2003), *Korea Statistical Yearbook 2002*, Seoul: National Statistical Office.

Korean National Statistical Office (KNSO) (2004), *Korea Statistical Yearbook 2003*, Seoul: National Statistical Office.

Korean National Statistical Office (KNSO) (2005), *Korea Statistical Yearbook 2004*, Seoul: National Statistical Office.

Korean National Statistical Office (KNSO) (2006), 'Statistical database', http://www.nso.go.kr/eng/index.html, accessed 21 August 2006.

Korea Productivity Centre, www.kpc.or.kr.

Kwon, O.Y. (2003), *Foreign Direct Investment in Korea: A Foreign Perspective*, Seoul: Korea Economic Research Institute.

Kwon, O.Y. (2006), 'Recent changes in Korea's business environment: views of foreign business people in Korea', *Asia Pacific Business Review*, 12 (1), 77–94, http://www.informaworld.com.

Kwon, Tai-Hwan (2003), 'Demographic trends and their social implications', *Social Indicators Research*, 62 (1), 19–27.

Lee, H.C. (1989), 'Managerial characteristics of Korean firms', in K. Chung and H. Lee (eds), *Korean Managerial Dynamics*, New York: Praeger, pp. 147–62.

Lee, S.M. (1989), 'Management styles of Korean chaebols', in K. Chung and H. Lee (eds), *Korean Managerial Dynamics*, New York: Praeger, pp. 181–92.

Lee, Won-Duck and B.H. Lee (2003), 'Industrial relations and labor standards in Korea', in O.Y. Kwon, S.H. Jwa and K.T. Lee (eds), *Korea's New Economic Strategy in the Globalisation Era*, Cheltenham, UK and Northampton, MA, USA: Edward Elgar Publishing, pp. 173–91.

Lowe, K.B., J. Milliman, H. De Cieri and P.J. Dowling (2002), 'International compensation practices: a ten-country comparative analysis', *Human Resource Management*, 41 (1), pp. 45–66.

Martin, J.P., P. Tergeist and R. Torres (2004), 'Reforming the Korean labour market and social safety net: key pending issues' in C. Harvie, H.H. Lee and J. Oh (eds), *The Korean Economy: Post-Crisis Policies, Issues and Prospects*, Cheltenham, UK and Northampton, MA, USA: Edward Elgar Publishing, pp. 78–119.

Nam, S.W. and J.I. Kim (1997), 'Macroeconomic policies and evolution', in D.S. Cha, K.S. Kim and D.H. Perkins (eds), *The Korean Economy 1945–1995: Performance and Vision for the 21st Century*, Seoul: Korea Development Institute, pp. 143–85.

Park, D.J., J.H. Park and G.C. Yu (2001), 'Assessment of labor market response to the labor law changes introduced in 1998', in F.K Park, Y.B. Park, G. Betcheman and A. Dar (eds), *Labor Market Reforms in Korea: Policy Options for the Future*, Seoul: Korea Labor Institute, pp. 125–50.

Park, G.S. and A.E. Kim (2005), 'Changes in attitude toward work and workers' identity in Korea', *Korea Journal*, 45 (3), 36–57.

Park, W.S. and G.C. Yu (2002), 'HRM in Korea: transformation and new patterns', in Zasun Rhee and E. Chang (eds), *Korean Business and Management*, Elizabeth, NJ: Hollym, pp. 367–91.

Pucik, V. and J. Lim (2002), 'Transforming human resource management in a Korean chaebol: a case study of Samsung', in C. Rowley, T.W. Sohn and J.S. Bae (eds), *Managing Korean Business: Organization, Culture, Human Resources and Change*, London: Frank Cass, pp. 137–60.

Rowley, C. (2002), 'South Korean management in transition', in M. Warner and P. Joynt (eds), *Managing Across Cultures: Issues and Perspectives*, London: Thomson Learning, pp. 178–92.

Rowley, C. and J. Bae (2004), 'Human resource management in South Korea after the Asian financial crisis', *International Studies of Management and Organization*, 34 (1), 52–82.

Rowley, C., J. Benson and M. Warner (2004), 'Towards an Asian model of human resource management? A comparative analysis of China, Japan and South Korea', *International Journal of Human Resource Management*, 15 (4), 917–33.

Samsung Electronics (2007), 'About Samsung-Samsung Group', Samsung website, www.samsung.com/about/SAMSUNG/index.htm, accessed 30 April 2007.

Von Glinow, M.A., E.A. Drost and M.B. Teagarden (2002), 'Converging on IHRM best practices: lessons learned from a globally distributed consortium on theory and practice', *Human Resource Management*, 41 (1), 123–40.

10. International joint ventures in Korea: salient characteristics and management

10.1 INTRODUCTION

An international strategic alliance is an agreement between two or more firms from different countries to cooperate in any activity in the value chain, which includes R&D, design, production, marketing, distribution and service. According to Shenkar and Luo (2004, p. 281), international strategic alliances are the most common entry mode for MNEs. As globalization intensifies international competition for access to markets, products and technology, the importance of strategic alliances has increased.

One of the most common strategic alliances is an equity international joint venture (IJV), which entails establishing a new entity that is jointly owned and managed by two or more parent firms from different countries. A non-equity-based international strategic alliance is a contractual agreement by two or more firms from different countries to cooperate in any activity in the value chain without setting up a separate company. An MNE may take an equity IJV for one value-creating activity and a contractual cooperative alliance for another activity. Although these two types of strategic alliances are different in terms of equity, the purposes and issues they involve are quite similar and the two names are used interchangeably in practice. The analysis in this chapter focuses on equity IJVs in Korea but is also applicable to the other type of strategic alliances.

In response to the rapid rise of globalization and new technologies, Korean companies have been aggressively pursuing global strategic partnerships with leading foreign companies. A large number of IJVs have been undertaken between Korean and foreign companies in Korea and in other countries. Korea has received a large number of foreign direct investment (FDI) projects particularly since 1997. The number of approved FDI projects was about 1000 in 1997, and increased to more than 3000 in 2004 (MOCIE 2006). More than half of these have been undertaken in the form of strategic alliances (Lee and Lee 2004). Samsung Electronics alone undertook 49 strategic alliances over the period from February 2000 to March 2004

(Samsung 2004). LG Electronics undertook 25 strategic alliances over the 2000–05 period (LG 2005).

Yet IJVs in Korea have not drawn the analytical attention they deserve, particularly in the English language literature. The literature in English examines joint ventures across the Asia-Pacific broadly, but very few studies examine IJVs in Korea, and focus almost exclusively on management issues. Other available sources include media articles from newspapers and business magazines. These sources report on particular cases of joint ventures, and lack context and theoretical underpinnings of joint ventures in Korea. There are, however, a number of empirical studies in the Korean language. This chapter draws on both literatures in examining the salient characteristics, motivation and management issues of IJVs in Korea. First, attention will turn to the conceptual issues, the motivation to establish IJVs and their reasons for success as the context for this discussion of the Korean examples. Then, specific issues associated with IJVs in Korea will be examined based on the conceptual discussion.

10.2 INTERNATIONAL JOINT VENTURES: MOTIVATION AND SUCCESS FACTORS

10.2.1 Motivation to Establish IJVs

Companies create IJVs to share costs and risks and obtain the synergistic benefits that these ventures can produce. Economic benefits can result not only from reduction of costs and risks, but also from acquisition of complementary resources, improvement of economic efficiency, mitigation of competition, and expedient market entry. To create a joint venture, partners contribute complementary resources or capabilities including some form of financing, facilities, equipment, materials, technology, managerial expertise, labor, land-use rights and intellectual property rights. The home-country partner may typically obtain advanced technology, capital, marketing know-how and management expertise from the foreign partner. Foreign partners benefit from local firms' knowledge of the host country's market and social conditions, and cultural, political and legal systems. Language can also be vitally important. By combining complementary resources or capabilities, firms can pursue business activities that might be too risky and costly to pursue on their own.

Improvement of economic efficiency arises from joint ventures as partners achieve greater economies of scale and scope in various activities such as the supply of raw materials and components, research and development, and marketing and distribution. This applies in particular for small firms that improve economies of scale by combining financial and other complementary resources. Since partners share knowledge and expertise including complementary technologies, R&D results and managerial know-how, as Shenkar and Luo (2004, p. 316) argue, IJVs enable partners to acquire knowledge at significantly reduced costs. This is particularly so for the information and telecommunications areas, where technological collaboration is highly demanded to save both time and money because the life cycles of technologies become shorter over time and the R&D costs rise rapidly. Joint ventures may also improve a company's local image, enabling products produced by joint ventures to be accepted better by foreign consumers as part of domestic products.

IJVs help mitigate competition by joining firms that are potential or existing competitors, and can also help to align industry standards better. Joint ventures can help partners overcome the restrictions imposed on competition from foreigners. In emerging technology areas, competitors may align and adopt industrial standards more effectively by developing technologies jointly, instead of developing different standards, some of which may quickly become obsolete.

Joint ventures with local partners can expedite the investment and business process and may reduce political risks of the host country such as political interference or nationalization. Particularly in the developing countries, IJVs may be the only available entry mode for foreign businesses, since domestic laws may require them to set up a joint venture with a local firm as an entry condition. In developing countries, joint ventures with local partners are regarded as an effective tool in national economic development. Lasserré (1999) argues that a local presence in the form of joint ventures with local partners is necessary to conduct business in the Asia-Pacific region.

Because of these advantages as examined above, MNEs are increasingly using joint ventures as an entry mode when conducting FDI, as opposed to establishing a wholly owned subsidiary (Choi and Beamish 2004). Joint ventures appear to be the most effective mode of entry for foreign firms, given present conditions shaped by the ever-changing global environment for direct investment, increasing competition in the market, rapid changes in technologies and their rising costs. In this regard, Park (1991) points out that a majority of MNEs express preference for equity joint ventures in Korea as the most effective form of strategic alliance to cope with the ever-changing environment for direct investment.

10.2.2 Success Factors

Despite these advantages, IJVs face many types of challenges and many IJVs fail.[1] Various reasons explain these failures. First, a firm that enters into a joint venture risks loss of control over its technology and management to its partners. Particularly in developing countries where intellectual property rights are not well protected, protection of critical technologies is difficult. Thus, unless alliance activities are under firm control, local partners may disseminate the foreign partner's critical knowledge to other parties. In some cases, local partners may even become global competitors after developing skills and technology through joint ventures.

Second, management of an IJV is bound to be much more complex than that of a single enterprise. As an IJV is a new entity set up by the parent firms from different countries, it involves a set of inter- and intra-organizational relationships. These include relations between the parent companies, between the manager of the joint venture and the foreign parent, between the manager and the local parent, and among the joint venture staff with different nationalities. Conflicts can arise in each of these relationships from various sources such as cross-cultural differences, diverging strategic goals, leadership style and managerial practices. These conflicts hamper operation and management of the joint venture. It is more difficult for each partner of a joint venture to adjust its strategy in response to changes in market conditions and other business environments, as compared to doing business alone. Park et al. (2002) estimate that more than 50 per cent of IJVs fail largely because of management problems, rather than financial or technical issues.

For the success of an IJV, the selection of partners is therefore recognized as the most critical and difficult factor (Shenkar and Luo 2004, p. 319; Lasserré and Schutte 1995, p. 176). The success of an IJV depends on complementarity of resources and capabilities of the partners, their willingness to cooperate and the climate of trust between them. The managerial processes and procedures of the venture also have important bearings on IJV success.

The literature proposes a number of criteria for partner selection to maximize the possibility for success of IJVs. This chapter uses the framework of Lasserré and Schutte (1995, p. 180) that identifies suitability in four key areas of compatibility: strategic fit, resources fit, cultural fit and organizational fit.[2] A strategic fit refers to congruence between the partners' long-term strategic objectives. Partners may enter a joint venture for a variety of strategic reasons including long-term growth, expanding their market share, maximum dividends, obtaining key resources, and acquiring technology and managerial know-how, or simply for opportunistic purposes. If partners' strategic reasons differ, interpartner conflicts in the operation of the venture are inevitable over time, and partners' interests in continuing the collaboration will wane. Assessment of strategic fit can be difficult since it involves an assessment of the compatibility of partners' implicit and explicit motives for engaging in a joint venture, and the nature of benefits they expect to gain from it prior to establishing the partnership. Lasserré and Schutte (1995) argue that in assessing strategic fit the degree of partners' commitment to the joint venture is particularly important.

Resources fit exists when each partner is willing and able to contribute to the venture the critical and complementary resources (people, financing, raw materials and so forth), assets (tangible and intangible), and capability (competence, experience and expertise) that will generate synergistic effects and ultimately competitive success. In assessing resources fit, evaluating the contributions by each partner is often a thorny issue, as some of the resources, assets and capability may not have identified market prices. The extent of partners' contributions of resources is a major determinant of the venture's ownership structure, including the percentage of equity held by each partner, which is critical in organizing an equity joint venture. In the case of two partners, the ownership can be split equally between them or unequally with a majority and minority owner. A 50:50 ownership allows both partners to be involved equally in operations and to share the fruits of the enterprise equally. Since technology development is the principal reason for partnerships in the rapidly expanding field of high technology, equal ownership accounts for more than half of joint ventures in this field so that partners can share the developed technology (Shenkar and Luo 2004, p. 324).

Cultural fit concerns the compatibility of the cultures of partners. Empirical studies show the problems and conflicts that incompatible cultural differences can produce among partners (Lasserré and Schutte 1995). There may be many differences in national and business cultures between IJV partners, including understanding the role of business in society, the time horizon for business, management systems, human resource management (HRM), human relationships, risk aversion, and social stratification. Given these differences, organizational skills and the ability to overcome cultural barriers are critically important for the success of an IJV.

Organizational fit refers to the compatibility of corporate management systems, including the decision-making, operational and controlling mechanisms employed by partners in the operation of a joint venture. If these mechanisms are significantly different between partners and cannot be modified and coordinated for the joint venture, good communication and effective monitoring may not be possible, and the venture will fail.

10.3 INTERNATIONAL JOINT VENTURES IN KOREA

10.3.1 Salient Characteristics

IJVs in Korea began to boom from the late 1990s as a result of increases in foreign direct investment. The Korea government restricted and controlled

FDI, particularly up to the 1997 financial crisis, largely because of its historical obsession with protecting domestic industries and management control. A number of industrial sectors were closed to FDI by law until the mid-1990s and even in those areas where FDI was permitted, the administrative regulations and processes for FDI were complex and opaque. Neither the structure of the Korean economy nor the socio-cultural climate was conducive to inward FDI. The Korean economy was concentrated heavily in a handful of large chaebols that enjoyed various types of institutionalized advantages over foreign firms. The Korean labor market was not flexible and unions were renowned for their militant tactics. Foreigners encountered various difficulties in on-site management of their businesses resulting from the lack of transparency and accountability in the corporate governance of Korean companies, and the cronyism prevalent in business–government relations. Poor living conditions also presented problems for foreign expatriates. The low level of FDI in Korea until 1997 reflects these impediments to inward FDI (Kwon 2003).

In the wake of the 1997 financial crisis, the Korean government shifted FDI policy dramatically from 'restriction and control' to 'promotion and assistance'. A series of policy measures and all-out efforts to improve the business environment and attract FDI have seen investment procedures streamlined and up to 99.8 per cent of all business sectors opened to FDI by 2002 (Kwon 2003, p. 45). Korea now uses a negative list system, which means that a business is open to FDI unless it is specifically restricted. Restricted sectors include domestic periodical publications, telecommunications and power generation, where foreign equity ownership is limited. The capital market has been liberalized, as have M&As (including hostile M&As). The business environment has also improved remarkably since 1997. Reform of chaebols has raised the standard of corporate governance and management transparency and accountability of all Korean firms. New laws have increased substantially the flexibility of the Korean labor market. Korean society and culture have also become more conducive to the FDI environment.[3] As a result, inward FDI in Korea surged over the three-year period 1998–2000, and after some setbacks over 2001–02, increased gradually to US$7.7 billion in 2004 (UNCTAD 2005).

These changes in the conditions of FDI in Korea have shifted the pattern of FDI in Korea over time. Before the 1997 financial crisis, Korea needed FDI to stimulate economic development and to attract high technology, and foreign investors sought to gain access to Korea's relatively inexpensive labor. Thus, a typical pattern of inward FDI was to set up new companies, or greenfield investments, on their own or as new joint venture companies with Korean partners. After the financial crisis with government policy pursuing across-the-board liberalization and internationalization, including permission for M&As, a new investment pattern emerged. Foreign investors were attracted to Korean companies troubled by the crisis, and bought either all shares in acquisition or controlling block of shares to entitle them to meaningful participation as partners (Lee 1999).

Most FDI projects in Korea are undertaken in the form of joint ventures. Over the 1998–2000 period, about 55 per cent of FDI in Korea was undertaken in the form of joint ventures (Kwon 2003, p. 25), as Lee and Lee (2004) confirm. In terms of the number of FDI projects, more than 2000 were undertaken each year over the 1998–2004 period, indicating a large number of annual establishments of IJVs (MOCIE 2006). Most IJVs in Korea were established with partners from the US and Japan. Over the period 1990–99, 50 per cent of total IJVs in Korea were established with the US and 22 per cent with Japan, attributable to Korea's heavy reliance on these two countries for technology and markets (Jun and Yo 2002). Over this period, 46.8 per cent of IJVs were established in the area of technology development and sales (Jun and Yo 2002).

Some features of the Korean environment make IJVs an attractive mode of entry for foreign companies. Although the Korean market is penetrable by foreign companies, the Korean business environment is still complex and uncertain. A combination of Korea's cultural complexities, Koreans' underlying mistrust of foreigners and general preference for domestically produced products, and the high costs involved in setting up businesses, make establishing a wholly owned subsidiary not the most suitable entry option for most foreign companies (Kwon 2006). Entering a joint venture with a Korean partner offers many advantages, including access to local market knowledge, local contacts, government incentives, and overcoming negative effects from the mistrust of foreigners within the Korean community. Koreans have a general mistrust of foreigners, a disposition influenced by collective memory of the hardships that most Koreans had to endure under the Japanese occupation that finished with the end of the Second World War in 1945. Nationalism is still a powerful force in Korea to the point where it influences many aspects of consumption, down to the purchase of daily goods. Partnership with a Korean company therefore alleviates the negative commercial consequences of nationalism and xenophobic tendencies. Perhaps one of the most compelling reasons for an IJV over other entry modes is the extensive knowledge of the Korean regulatory, business and political environment and the extensive personal networking capacity that a Korean partner is likely to have. Personal relationships are of the utmost importance when conducting business in Korea (Kwon 2006).

When both the costs and risks associated with establishing and operating in a foreign market are high, a company may want to share these risks and costs with a domestic joint venture partner in that foreign market. This is especially true in costly advanced technology industries and for high-risk R&D operations. It would thus be most appropriate for companies wanting to operate in these fields in Korea to enter into a joint venture with a Korean company. By doing so, foreign companies (especially smaller companies) can gain direct access to resources that they would otherwise find too costly. This is particularly true in Korea in relation to human resources and specialist knowledge. In the recent past, in particular, many chaebols in electronics and telecommunications have entered into joint ventures with foreign counterparts for speedy development of advanced technologies.

Kwon (2003) found that most foreign firms had chosen to undertake FDI in Korea to capitalize on the emerging business opportunities in Korea by means of their firm-specific advantages including technologies and managerial and marketing know-how. They did not in general regard Korea as a target country for supply-seeking investment, or as a stepping stone to gain market access to other Asian countries. There are a number of cases of IJVs established in Korea between foreign and Korean partners to capitalize on business opportunities in Korea. An Australian banking establishment, Macquarie Bank, has also entered into joint ventures with Korean partners. With the Kookmin Bank, Macquarie developed the Kookmin Macquarie Business Cooperation, which pioneered Treasury derivatives in Korea and is now one of the leaders of the Korean market. With the Shinhan Bank, Macquarie established the Shinhan Macquarie Financial Advisory, which has a primary focus on providing investment-banking services.[4] In 1999, Samsung Corporation and Tesco PLC (UK) entered into a joint venture (Samsung-Tesco) to penetrate the Korean retail sector, for which Tesco provided capital, management skills and IT technology for retail industries, and Samsung provided a strong local background to create synergistic effects.[5]

In order to take advantage of complementary resources, Kia entered into a joint venture with Ford Motor Company in 1988. Ford was interested in Kia's distribution and after-service network, while Kia sought a premium model to complement its product line at a time when technology transfer for producing such a vehicle was too expensive (Kim et al. 2004). In 2002, Korea Petrochemical (KPIC) and Odfjell (Norway) entered into a joint venture (Odfjell Terminals Korea Co. Ltd) for complementary resources. KPIC, a producing company, needed a stable selling network, and Odfjell, a transporting company, needed to increase demand for its transport services and wanted to build a North Asia Hub in Korea.[6] In the electronics and telecommunications sector, Japan-based Nippon Electric Glass Co. entered into a joint venture with LG Philips in early 2005 to 'secure a stable supply of LCD parts as well as to improve productivity' (WWP Inc. 2005). Another Japanese company, Sony Corp., entered into a 50:50 joint venture with Samsung Electronics Co. Ltd. under the name of S-LCG Corp., to produce seventh generation TFT LCD products at a new facility at Tangjeong (WWP Inc. 2004). Relatively few IJVs have been established to use Korea as a platform for subsequent expansion into Asia more broadly. As one example, the US-based Curtiss-Wright Corporation that deals with flight and engineering products set up a joint venture with a Korean partner to expand sales of its products in the region (PR Newswire 2002).

There are also a number of IJVs established to develop new technologies and reduce risks and costs associated with their developments. Valeo (France), DuPont Electronic Technologies and US-based VAXGN are a few cases focusing on new technology developments jointly with Korean partners.[7] In addition, Perstorp (Sweden), Nortel (Canada) and SingTel (Singapore) have recently established joint ventures in Korea.[8] Jun and Yo (2002) found that of joint ventures reported in Korean news media over 1990–2000, 52.5 per cent were established in three areas – electrical and electronic, telecommunications, and computer and semiconductor – and 60.5 per cent were established to develop new technologies and reduce associated costs and risk.

10.3.2 Laws and Regulations Related to Joint Ventures in Korea

The Foreign Investment Promotion Act, enacted in 1998, has greatly reduced previous restrictions and barriers on foreign investment activities in Korea.[9] In conjunction with the negative system introduced by the Act, the approval system was replaced by a simple reporting system in so far as joint venture enterprises fall into the opened business sectors. As part of the incorporation process, a certain amount of minimum paid-in capital is required. In cases where additional funds are needed over and above the initially approved amount, there are still numerous restrictions on raising funds from Korean sources.

The Korean Commercial Code identifies four types of business organizations: the unlimited commercial partnership company, the limited commercial partnership company, the limited liability company and the stock company (Lee 1999). The stock company is by far the most commonly used form of business organization in Korea like an incorporated company in the Western world. The limited liability company is basically the same as the stock company except that it requires the number of equity holders to be no less than two and no more than 50 persons, and it requires the consent of equity holders to agree for share transfers. An IJV established as a stock company or a limited liability company will have a chief executive officer and a board of directors. IJVs, like domestic companies, are subject to the Monopoly Regulations and the Fair Trade Act and Korea's labor laws.

After formal establishment, a joint venture company needs to obtain governmental approval to operate the business in which it will engage. It must also register with the local district court in the jurisdiction where the company's head office is located, and with the local tax office. A joint venture company is subject to corporate income tax and capital gains tax. These taxes are subject to the provisions of double-taxation treaties that may be applicable to foreign partners in an IJV. Korea has tax treaties with more than 50 countries. In order to encourage FDI in selected areas, the Korean government provides tax incentives for investments involving advanced technology and investments carried out in foreign investment zones (FIZs). Companies contributing to technological innovations are exempt from company, income and dividend taxes for the first seven years of operation, and a 50 per cent reduction in these taxes is allowed for a subsequent three years. The foreign-owned share of an IJV is exempt from local taxes for eight to 15 years and is also exempt from customs duties, consumption tax and value added tax on goods imported for industrial activities. In an attempt to attract large-scale FDI projects, FIZs were introduced, primarily targeting manufacturing. Special tax reductions and exemptions apply to foreign-invested enterprises within these FIZs.

To settle any disputes arising under an IJV or related agreement, the parties are free to resort to any court within or outside Korea. There is no legal restriction in Korea against the use of arbitration as a method of dispute resolution. Most IJV agreements between foreign and Korean parties contain an arbitration clause in their attempts to settle disputes should they arise. Typically, the forum for arbitration is not the home country of any of the joint venture partners. Korea is a signatory to the UN Convention on the Recognition and Enforcement of Foreign Arbitral Awards of 1958, and enforcement of foreign arbitral awards has been recognized between the member nations pursuant to the Convention.

10.3.3 Ownership Structure of IJVs

The percentage of equity share or ownership is one of the most sensitive and contentious issues in establishing an IJV. A majority shareholder will in general control the management of the venture. Most Korean companies, and particularly chaebols, are family-owned and managed enterprises, and they desire a majority equity position to maintain control over their enterprises (Tung 1991). Heavy reliance on debt capital by chaebols indicates their predilection for controlling their enterprises. Koreans' preference for majority ownership is reflected in Korea's overseas investment. The overseas investment projects by Korean firms with more than 50 per cent equity increased over time to 83 per cent by 1999 (Kwon and Oh 2001, p. 24). A similar tendency was found by Kim et al. (2000). Western companies also desire majority ownership in order to have control in managing their IJVs and to protect their intellectual property.

The division of the equity position depends on the bargaining power, strategic goals and global control requirement of each partner, in addition to their negotiation skills.[10] For IJVs inside Korea soon after the 1997 financial crisis, Korean firms were desperately in need of foreign capital for their survival, and many capitulated to the foreign partners' demand for majority ownership. Y.C. Kwon (2001) has found from his survey of 94 IJVs in Korea that 40.4 per cent of sampled foreign firms had more than 51 per cent of ownership and 33 per cent had 50 per cent ownership.

A cursory survey of the English-language business press since 2001 suggests that equity joint ventures are the most common form of IJVs established in Korea in recent times.[11] The percentage of equity invested by a foreign partner is most often a 51 per cent controlling share. This perhaps reflects typical foreign partners' concerns regarding control of IJV enterprises in Korea, or the advantage that foreign firms could exercise through their stronger bargaining power in technology and financing capacity soon after the 1997 crisis.[12] Recently a number of IJV partnerships have been established in Korea with a 50:50 equity ratio.[13] There are also IJVs with other equity configurations such as 80:20, 90:10 and so on.[14] For expeditious development of new technology, companies in the same field typically establish contractual alliances, referred to as collaborative agreements, rather than equity joint ventures.[15]

The ownership of IJVs does not remain static; in most cases it changes over time as the ventures operate. Both financial performance of the joint venture and the initial ownership structure have important bearings on future ownership. Nestlé is well known for its joint venture strategy in which it enters a foreign country including Korea in the form of joint venture with a local partner to gain access to local expertise in regulations, and buys up the local partners in a few years time. Samsung-Tesco also bought up most of the shares owned by its partner, Samsung Corporation (Kollewe 2004).[16] From their studies of IJVs in China between Korean firms and Chinese counterparts, Rhee et al. (2001) have found that the possibility of changing the ownership structure tends to increase when the financial performance of an IJV is either better or worse than an industrial average. They have also found that those with an unequal initial ownership structure are more likely to change their ownership structure than with equal initial ownership. As noted above, consistent with the study of Rhee et al. (2001), Kwon and Oh (2001) and Kim et al. (2000) have found that Korean overseas joint ventures with majority ownerships tend to increase their shares further over time.

10.4 MANAGEMENT OF IJVS IN KOREA

As mentioned earlier, IJVs have a high failure rate despite their popularity as a form of market entry for foreign businesses. In the Korean context, Lasserré (1999) found a relatively low degree of satisfaction among Western managers of IJVs. Failed IJVs are not usually reported, and only a limited number of joint venture failures in Korea have been reported since 2001. Village Roadshow, an Australian-based cinema and entertainment company, sold its 50 per cent equity share in Korean cinema group CGV to Asia Cinema Holdings, a Dutch company, because of what the Australian company perceived to be a lack of controllability (ABC News 2002). In late 2005, Europe's largest consumer electronics company, Philips, wrote off its remaining book value in LG Philips Displays, a joint venture with LG Electronics, due to deteriorating demand for TVs built on old-style technology (Bickerton 2005). The high failure rate of IJVs is generally attributed to management problems, rather than to financial or technical issues (Park et al. 2002). In the Korean context management problems usually derive from the incompatibility of partners, which becomes the principal cause for the joint venture failures.

10.4.1 Strategic Fit

One of the most important reasons for the success of IJVs is the congruence of the partners' long-term strategic goals. It is well known that Korean firms have a strong proclivity toward long-term growth and market share over short-term profit (Tung 1991). This reflects both the long-term orientation that tends to be dominant in Korean culture and the concentration of ownership of Korean firms by founders and their families. This proclivity also reflects forceful government promotion of growth and expansion strategies for roughly four decades after the Korean War. However, as Hitt et al. (1997) and other observers note, this strategic orientation by Korean firms is in direct opposition to the common preference of Western companies for increasing shareholder value through short-term profit maximization. Therefore, unless this difference is acknowledged and addressed, it is highly likely that fundamental tension will develop in IJVs between Korean and Western partners around the goal of the foreign partner to make short-term profit and quickly remit dividends outside Korea, and the local partner's goal of not only realizing company growth, but also making an overall contribution to the well-being of the Korean economy and society at large.

Y.C. Kwon (2001) found that strategic fit (and organizational fit) generates mutual trust and commitment by the partners, which in turn contributes to the partners' mutual satisfaction with their venture relationship and the achievement of the overall purpose and success of IJVs in Korea. Kwon's findings appear to be consistent with Lasserré and Schutte's (1995) argument for the critical importance of partners' commitment to the joint venture. A number of IJVs in Korea have failed largely because of differences in strategic goals. One infamous case is a 50:50 joint venture established by General Motors of the US and Daewoo Motors of Korea in 1984, which dissolved in 1992. Much of the day-to-day management of the alliance was in the hands of Daewoo, with managerial and technical advice provided by GM. Conflicts were many, around issues such as wage hikes, quality control, marketing and the impact of cultural difference in human relationships. Yet the main reason for the break-up of the joint venture lay in Daewoo's incessant expansion proposals and GM's refusal of those proposals (Hill 2001).

If partners have opportunistic motives, their commitment to the joint venture will be low, usually providing unsatisfactory performance and instability in the venture. Lee and Lee (2004) found from their empirical study of IJVs in Korea that if the parent company of a foreign partner perceives the Korean partner as having highly opportunistic motives, the parent company delegates its HRM to the joint venture to monitor closely the venture operations. If, however, the Korean partner is trusted by a foreign partner, HRM of the venture tends to be controlled remotely by the parent company.

10.4.2 Resource Fit

Before the 1997 financial crisis, in setting up IJVs with foreign companies, Korean firms had gained the reputation in the Western business community of being essentially motivated by the opportunity to extract technology from the venture partners (Tung 1991; Lasserré and Schutte 1995). Since the crisis, however, Korean firms enter IJVs not only for advanced technologies but also for foreign capital, and Korean firms will usually provide human resources and mass production facilities. When the resource fit is met and each partner gains access to the other partner's resources, the partners' needs to continue the collaboration will wane. Unless their complementarity of resources and needs is continuously identified and each partner is willing and able to contribute the resources needed to ensure competitive success in the venture, conflicts may arise between the partners and the venture may be dissolved, probably through absorption by one partner (Tung 1991).[17]

10.4.3 Cultural Fit

Empirical studies show that cultural congruence is critically important for the success of IJVs in Korea. Y.C. Kwon (2001) found that the compatibility of corporate cultures is a significant factor for maintaining a satisfactory relationship between IJV partners and achieving the goals of their venture. As explained in Chapter 3, Koreans have their own culture, heavily influenced by Confucianism, which upholds hierarchical collectivism, patriarchal familism, authoritarianism, status-consciousness, secularism and strong nationalism.[18] Therefore, as a number of studies show, unless IJV partners appreciate the distinctive cultural traits among them and seek to accommodate and adapt to each other, intercultural misunderstandings and conflicts are bound to arise in the operations of IJVs.[19]

One important source of cultural conflict in IJVs in Korea is related to the emphasis on personal relationships in Korea. Even after the 1997 crisis and in the emerging globalization era, interpersonal relationships are still especially important in Korea for every aspect of business, largely because of the tightly knit nature of Korean society compromising multilayered groups. Koreans tend to do business with those they trust. According to an extensive survey of foreign business people in Korea in 2002 this author found that foreigners regard the importance of personal relationships in business as a significant difficulty in on-site management in Korea (Kwon 2006). Koreans maintain and cherish personal relationships based on family ties, high school and college ties, regional ties and military ties throughout their lives, both personally and professionally. While Korean business people have become somewhat more objective than at earlier times in evaluating potential business relationships, having connections still gives advantage in business. Favors and opportunities are often given and contracts are signed in the Korean business community on the basis of personal relationships.[20] Another important aspect of personal relationships required in undertaking joint ventures in Korea is to build and maintain good contacts with the relevant government ministries, as the Korean government still exerts a strong influence over all aspects of the country's economy and business operations. As Koreans attach considerable importance to the duration of these personal connections, it takes time to establish and build a relationship of trust in Korea.

Given the strong emphasis on personal relationships, Koreans view the concept of contractual obligations in a way fundamentally different from Westerners. They consider contracts more as personal agreements than as binding legal arrangements, and expect contracts to change as business environments change, as a way of maintaining business relationships. Where a business contract is in place, Koreans typically prefer to resolve conflicts through informal channels without resorting to the contract documents or the legal system.

Koreans, like many East Asians, have a cultural reputation for being relatively guarded with strangers, and particularly with foreigners. In particular, there is a strong perception in Korea that a joint venture with a foreign company will have a relatively short life expectancy (Park 1991). This perception stigmatizes employment in foreign companies or IJVs as Korean people tend to be risk averse and prefer secure long-term employment where possible. Joint ventures therefore have serious difficulty in attracting top-quality local management. Added to this is that many Koreans are reluctant to take on the extra language and cultural problems associated with working with foreigners.

Park (1991) found that the level of operational cohesiveness perceived by joint venture local managers toward the companies they manage is far lower than the level perceived by Korean managers of purely local firms. This may indicate that loyalty or attachment of Korean workers toward IJVs is less than that toward purely Korean firms. Park's survey found that a sense of inequity in rewards was the most significant variable reducing the sense of operational cohesiveness of joint venture local managers. Following this was the 'negative group image' that Koreans attach to foreign companies. The status of the company for which Koreans work and their employment status within the company both serve to influence the individual's social status outside the company. Because of the 'sense of temporality' resulting from the perceived short-term orientation of foreign enterprises, and the relatively limited number of ranks within flatly organized foreign companies, foreign firms or IJVs are regarded by Koreans as less prestigious than Korean firms. Thus, foreign companies are relatively disadvantaged in the status-conscious society. All these negative images lead to the disruption of joint venture management cohesiveness.

As for IJVs in any national contexts, cultural congruence is an indispensable factor for a successful joint venture in Korea. Since Korean culture places a relatively strong emphasis on personal relationships, as Y.C. Kwon (2001) points out, successful joint ventures depend on open, mutual and respectful communication about the values of the different approaches that each partner is inclined to take to the operation of the joint venture. They also require time to evolve, since it takes time to develop personal relationships. Speed or efficiency is ineffective in understanding foreign cultures and to the development of cultural congruence.

10.4.4 Organizational Fit

Salient Korean cultural traits are embedded in Korean business culture. As explained in Chapter 8, the Korean management system, including decision-making, organization, directing and controlling mechanisms, is significantly different from Western systems. Characteristics of the Korean management system include top-down decision-making, hierarchical organization with emphasis on group harmony, directing and controlling by means of seniority and lifetime employment, and authoritarian and paternalistic leadership. Underpinning all these characteristics are formal and informal personal relationships. Western business people may find Korean internal management procedures inflexible and ineffective.

Given what are usually marked differences in organizational practices between the parent companies of the Korean and foreign partners, an IJV in Korea may have to adopt its own organizational design to accommodate these differences, particularly for the protection of technology, managerial control, HRM and performance assessment considerations. As mentioned above, some Korean firms are motivated by the opportunity to extract technology from their joint venture partners, so that joint ventures must be structured to reduce the risks of partners being opportunistic, which may include stealing technology.[21] A joint venture company can be structured to have one partner's critical technologies walled off from the other partner.[22] Joint ventures may also be designed so that valuable technology can be swapped between partners, averting opportunistic behavior.

One of the more sensitive issues in organizational design is the proportion of managerial control allocated to joint venture partners. Four types of management configurations are most common: shared control management, foreign-partner dominant management, local-partner dominant management and split control management (Cullen 1999, p. 377). The type of management structure chosen for a joint venture usually depends on each partner's contribution and management preferences. In many cases, partners enter a joint venture with equal ownership and resource contributions, and adopt relatively balanced managerial systems. These balanced systems include shared and split managerial structures. The former involves both partners sharing control equally over all managerial aspects, while the latter splits aspects of managerial control and assigns specific aspects to each partner.

Where a foreign firm chooses a Korean joint venture partner with similar technologies and both parties contribute equally to the enterprise, usually a shared management structure is adopted, with each partner allocating approximately the same number of managers to strategic and operational decision-making. Where a foreign firm chooses a Korean joint venture partner with technologies different from its own and the partners contribute equally to the organization, a split management structure is usually adopted. Partners typically share control over strategic decision-making, but each partner is allocated responsibility for specific aspects of operational decision-making such as production, marketing, R&D and so forth, corresponding to their specific competencies and technologies (Cullen 1999, p. 378).

Choi and Beamish (2004) have found from their study of 71 IJVs in Korea that 'split control management' was the most successful management configuration for IJVs in Korea. They explain that the concept of split control management is based on the contribution of complementary resources and involves each partner controlling its own firm-specific advantages to maximize resource complementarity. Their empirical study found no performance differences between the remaining three management configurations, and consequently suggest strongly that foreign and local Korean partners split control and match allocation of responsibility with respective complementary resources.

Other important organizational design issues concern HRM, including recruiting, staffing and evaluating joint venture personnel. As noted above, cultural issues can further complicate the already complex issues of HRM, making the HRM practices of a joint venture quite different from those of its parent firms. When choosing the workforce for a joint venture, the parent companies must decide the proportions of staff to be hired locally and internationally, and their positions within the JV company. Assessing the desirability of using the local workforce includes such considerations as skills, labor laws, labor supply and cultural values. Korean laws provide for foreign or JV companies hiring local workers. There is a strong supply of highly educated and skilled workers in Korea, with a strong work ethic. There are likely to be differences between partners in their evaluation criteria for staff appointments. For example, Korean partners are likely to favor obedience and capacity for group work, whereas Western partners are likely to focus on initiative, independence and leadership skills. Related to this, Park (1991) argues that Western expatriate managers tend to adopt temporary, pecuniary, individual solutions to boost local employees' morale, while Korean managers employ non-monetary, honorary and group rewards.

When dealing with Koreans, foreign managers should be aware of social stratification in the Korea workforce on the basis of age and education level as well as other factors. The managers that a foreign firm sends to a joint venture should be older, highly educated and have significant workplace and management experience. This is important for the prospects of a successful venture, since Koreans associate seniority with knowledge and wisdom, and older employees expect respect from all others younger than them. Hence younger foreign managers may not be taken seriously or respected in the Korean business environment, regardless of their aptitude. Koreans also pay respect to those with higher education credentials, as reflected in a high number of PhDs held by Koreans.[23]

Empirical study by Y.C. Kwon (2001) confirms the expectation that commitment to the partnership has significantly positive influence on the performance of a joint venture. It is important for the managers of joint ventures to educate staff about the reasons for the alliance, the parent company's goals for the alliance, and its position, contribution and responsibilities in order to enhance the commitment and loyalty of staff toward the joint venture. It is generally recognized that Korean workers show loyalty to their boss first before loyalty to their company, and will feel more loyal to their Korean supervisors than to the joint venture employing them. Thus it may be most appropriate for Koreans to be supervised by Koreans. Foreign companies need to appreciate that if they send foreign-based or foreign-educated Koreans back to Korea for managerial purposes, these people, although valuable in many respects of on-site management, may feel pressured to put the interests of the Korean firms before the interests of their own company. Koreans are generally highly nationalistic and relationship-oriented, and may be easily persuaded to help out Korean friends with whom they have developed strong relationships despite their obligations to their foreign employer.

10.5 CONCLUSION

Given the recent proliferation of IJVs in Korea, this chapter has examined their salient characteristics, the motivations that inspire and sustain them, and issues concerning their management. Companies enter into joint ventures to share costs and risks and to obtain synergistic effects by combining complementary resources. In nations with emerging markets such as Korea, the typical joint venture structure is one where the foreign partner contributes firm-specific advantages such as product and process technology, brand name or trademark, and overseas marketing support. The local partner's firm-specific advantages include expertise related to local knowledge in the form of marketing and personnel practices, and management of relations with the domestic government bodies.

Despite their advantages and popularity as a form of market entry, IJVs in Korea have a high failure rate, largely attributable to the selection of incompatible and uncollaborative partners and to management problems. This chapter has considered the criteria for appropriate partner selection proposed by Lasserré and Schutte (1995), which involve fit between partners on four key fronts: strategic, resources, cultural and organizational. Poor selection of partners leads to management problems. However, if partners are congruent and compatible with each other on all four fronts, a joint venture will be usually managed effectively and successfully, leading to mutual benefit.

Foreign MNEs enter into joint ventures with Korean partners mainly to capitalize on merging business opportunities in Korea. Few joint ventures have been established in Korea as a target country for supply-seeking investment or as a platform for subsequent expansion into other Asian countries. Most strategic alliances in Korea have been with US and Japanese firms for technology development and sales. The legal framework for establishing joint ventures in Korea is comparable with that of advanced Western countries. For joint ventures established in recent years, the controlling share is held mainly by foreign partners, indicating that foreign partners have high bargaining power usually through provision of critical resources such as technology and capital. Since the post-crisis reforms, a large number of joint ventures with a 50:50 equity ratio have been established in electronics and telecommunications for expeditious development of new technology.

This chapter has considered empirical findings that point to the importance of compatibility of partners for the success of joint ventures. Incompatibilities arise from irreconcilable differences between foreign and Korean partners in their strategic orientation, business culture, managerial control, HRM, commercial privacy and confidentiality, and perceptions of contractual obligation. Korean firms' strong preference for long-term growth over the short-term profit that foreign partners usually prefer is a source of managerial problems. Partners need to maintain resource complementarity for continuous success of the joint venture, since without it the need to collaborate diminishes and one partner buys up the other's contribution.

Cultural congruence is indispensable for a successful joint venture in Korea. Korean culture places strong emphasis on personal relationships, leading foreigners to perceive considerable cultural divergence. Building cultural congruence within a joint venture is therefore an arduous challenge for all partners, requiring open, mutual, respectful communication of the value of the different approaches each partner is inclined to take to the operation of the joint venture. One of the critical issues of joint venture management is the proportion of managerial control allocated to each party. Split control management, which involves each joint venture partner controlling its own firm-specific advantages, has been the most successful configuration for IJV management in Korea, as compared with other configurations such as shared control, foreign-partner dominant and Korean-partner dominant management.

Another critical issue for joint venture management in Korea is HRM which is heavily influenced by Korean culture. Difficulties in HRM include

Korean perceptions that IJVs have short life expectancy and for employment purposes have low prestige, which creates difficulty in recruiting good, committed, loyal local staff. These difficulties lead to low levels of management cohesion and low overall commitment to joint ventures. It is thus critically important for managers of joint ventures to educate staff about the vision and long-term commitment of the alliance. In sending expatriates to the joint ventures, foreign partners should choose those who can accommodate well to local culture and, importantly, be received and respected by local colleagues.

Joint ventures are an appropriate mode of entry for foreign companies seeking to enter the Korean market that are willing to share risks and costs and generate synergistic effects with Korean partners. To achieve success, foreign partners should be first committed to establishing a long-term presence in the Korean market, and maintain complementarity and compatibility with local partners in their strategic goals, contributing resources, cultural attitudes and organizational configuration. They should be prepared to accommodate Korea's distinctive culture, management practices and local business cultures. These prerequisites for joint venture success in Korea were captured succinctly in a business analyst's assessment of the success of BAT Korea (a wholly owned subsidiary of Britain's BAT) and Samsung-Tesco (a joint venture), saying, 'Samsung Tesco and BAT Korea can be seen as two of the biggest overseas successes. They realized the importance of localization as the main key to success in the Korean market at an early stage and acted upon it, instead of insisting on operating based on business strategies that would only work elsewhere' (Park 2006).

NOTES

1. According to a survey by McKinsey & Company and Coopers & Lybrand, about 70 per cent of international strategic alliances fall short of expectation, as cited in Shenkar and Luo (2004, p. 317).
2. Shenkar and Luo (2004) and Beamish et al. (2000) have proposed a similar set of criteria, although their terminologies are somewhat different from those of Lasserré and Schutte (1995).
3. A survey conducted in 2005 found that more than 50 per cent of respondents had positive attitudes toward foreign investors and appreciated their contribution to both the Korean economy and enhancement of corporate governance (*Invest Korea Journal* 2006).
4. Macquarie Bank (2005).
5. KIEP (n.d.).
6. Invest Korea (2005) 'Success stories – Odfjell Terminals Korea Co. Ltd', http://www.investkorea.org/templet/type18/1/list.jsp, 15 May 2006.
7. See, for the three cases, respectively, PR Newswire Europe (2005), Elsevier Engineering Information (2003) and WWP Inc. (2002b).
8. See, for the three cases, respectively, Elsevier Engineering Information (2003), Invest Korea (2005) and Australian Stock Exchange Company Announcements (2002).

9. Laws and regulations related to IJVs that I discuss in this section draw on Lee (1999).
10. In the case of Korean overseas investment projects Kim et al. (2000) have found that the key determinants of bargaining power with regard to ownership are technology and financing capacity.
11. No official data on IJVs was found in government official documents including websites.
12. Recent international joint venture partnerships in Korea with a 51:49 equity ratio include Fast Retailing Co., a venture created by Uniqlo (Japan) and Korea's Lotte Shopping (*Asia Wall Street Journal* 2004), and iMax Solutions, Inc., a venture for voice-over IP-related products, established by VoIP, Inc. (US) and Korea's iCable Systems Co. (Business Wire 2004).
13. Joint ventures with a 50:50 equity ratio include auto components manufacturer Valeo Samsung Thermal Systems, a venture established by Valeo (France) and Samsung Climate Control Group (PR News Wire Europe 2005) and SD Flex Company, an electronic circuit manufacturer, between DuPont Electronic Technologies (US) and Samsung subsidiary Cheil Industries (Elsevier Engineering Information 2004).
14. A sustainable energy-based venture between Lahmeyer International of Germany and Korea's Union Industrial Co. Ltd has an 80:20 equity ratio (WWP Inc. 2002a).
15. A joint venture called CELLTRION, between US-based firm VAXGN and Korea Tobacco is a contractual joint venture (WWP Inc. 2002b).
16. It appears that few studies have studied the changes in the ownerships of IJVs in Korea.
17. A partner with financial capacity may propose expanding the joint venture, which the other partner cannot afford, and the former may absorb the latter. As noted above, Nestlé is well known for its joint venture strategy of that nature. Nestlé entered into a joint venture with Doosan in Korea and bought up Doosan's share within a few years. Through a similar process, Samsung-Tesco also bought up most of the shares owned by its partner, Samsung Corporation (Kollewe 2004).
18. Park et al. (2002) argue that Korean culture is one of the most dissimilar cultures from that of the US in interpersonal terms.
19. On conflicts arising from cultural differences in Korea, see Park et al. (2002), Park (1991) and De Mente (1994).
20. Park (1991) argues that many business decisions in Korea are based solely on personal relationships rather than strict policy or official procedures.
21. De Mente (1994) points out that the 'concept of privacy within a company is very weak in Korea', and it is difficult to keep internal information of companies confidential.
22. For instance, in its joint venture with a Japanese partner, Boeing was able to protect its competitive advantage by 'walling off' the key areas where Boeing considered it had a competitive advantage (marketing and R&D), and at the same time worked constructively with its Japanese partner for mutual benefit (Hill 2001, p. 446).
23. As of 2001, about 90 983 Koreans held PhDs, amounting to 0.02 per cent of the Korean population (Education State University n.d.).

REFERENCES

ABC News (2002), 'Village Roadshow to sell off Korean cinema venture', 20 September, factiva.com, accessed 21 February 2006.
Asia Wall Street Journal (2004), 'Retail: Japanese clothier to launch Korean venture', 13 October, factiva.com, accessed 21 February 2006.
Australian Stock Exchange Company Announcements (2002), 'Singapore Telecommunications Limited C2C forms Korean joint venture to provide deeper local reach', 7 June, http://global.factiva.com, accessed 12 June.
Beamish, P.W., A.J. Morrison, P.M. Rozenzweig and A.C. Inkpen (2000), *International Management: Text and Cases*, Boston, MA: Irwin McGraw-Hill.

Bickerton, Ian (2005), 'Phillips writes-off value of South Korean joint venture', *Financial Times*, 21 December, factiva.com, accessed 21 February 2006.

Business Wire (2004), 'VoIP, Inc. announces joint venture with Korean corporation', 25 May, factiva.com, accessed 21 February 2006.

Choi, Chang-Bum and Paul W. Beamish (2004), 'Split management control and international joint venture performance', *Journal of International Business Studies*, 35, 201–15.

Cullen, J. (1999), *Multinational Management: A Strategic Approach*, Mason, OH: South-Western College Publishing.

De Mente, Boye L. (1994), *Korean Etiquette and Ethics in Business*, 2nd edn, Chicago, IL: NTC Business Books.

Education.stateuniversity (n.d.), 'South Korea-educational system overview', http://education.stateuniversity.com/pages/1400/South-Korea-EDUCATIONAL-SYSTEM-OVERIVEW.html, accessed 3 October. 2007.

Elsevier Engineering Information (2003), 'Joint venture in Korea between Perstorp and Hansol approved', 10 June, factiva.com, accessed 21 February 2006.

Elsevier Engineering Information (2004), 'Materials for flexible circuits: Korean joint venture for DuPon', 4 October, factiva.com, accessed 21 February 2006.

Hill, Charles, L.W. (2001), *International Business*, 3rd edn, Boston, MA: Irwin McGraw-Hill.

Hitt, Michael A., T.M. Dacin, B.B. Tyler and D.W. Park (1997), 'Understanding the differences in Korean and U.S. executives' strategic orientations', *Strategic Management Journal*, 18 (2), 159–67.

Invest Korea (2005), 'Success stories – Odfjell Terminals Korea Co., Ltd', http://www.investkorea.org/templet/ type18/1/list.jsp, accessed 15 May 2006.

Invest Korea Journal (2005), 'LG–Nortel joint venture due in October', 23 (5), 6.

Invest Korea Journal (2006), 'Majority of Koreans positive toward foreign investors: survey', 24 (2), 6.

Jun, Yongwook and Kyongchol Yo (2002), 'A study on the alliance type and business performance in strategic alliances' (in Korean), *Korea Academy of International Business*, 13 (2), 259–87.

Kim, D.K., D. Kandemir and S.T Cavusgil (2004), 'The role of family conglomerates in emerging markets: what Western companies should know', *Thunderbird International Business Review*, 46 (1), 13–38.

Kim, T.K., Y.R. Park and S.C. Song (2000), 'Change in equity ownership of Korean overseas joint ventures: bargaining power perspective' (in Korean), *Korea Academy of International Business*, 11 (2), 197–219.

Kollewe, Julia (2004), 'Tesco raises stake in Korean venture', *Independent*, 23 October, p. 55, factiva.com, accessed 21 February 2006.

Korea Institute for International Economic Policy (KIEP) (n.d.), 'Case study of Samsung-Tesco, Korea', http://72.14.209.104/search?q=cache:3rwSJuTuQ9wJ: www.iie.com/publications/chapters_preview/356/mann-apecapp4b.pdf+Samsung-Tesco,+Korea&h1=en&gl=au&ct=clnk&cd=1.

Kwon, O.Y. (2003), *Foreign Direct Investment in Korea: A Foreign Perspective*, Seoul: Korea Economic Research Institute.

Kwon, O.Y. (2006), 'Recent changes in Korea's business environment: views of foreign business people in Korea', *Asia Pacific Business Review*, 12 (1), 77–94.

Kwon, O.Y. and I.S. Oh (2001), 'Korean direct investment in Australia: issues and prospects', Brisbane: Australian Centre for Korean Studies, Griffith University.

Kwon, Y.C. (2001), 'An empirical study on the determinants of partnership and performance in international joint ventures', *Korean Journal of Management* (in Korean), 2 (11), 1–24.

Lasserré, P. and H. Schutte (1995), *Strategies for Asia Pacific*, London: Macmillan Press.

Lasserré, Philippe (1999), 'Joint venture satisfaction in Asia Pacific', *Asia Pacific Journal of Management*, 16, 1–28.

Lee, Jae-You and Eung-Seok Lee (2004), 'A study on the structure of control and performance in international joint ventures in Korea: moderating effects of the levels of opportunitism and trust between partners' (in Korean), *Korean Academy of International Business Journal*, 14 (2), 1–37.

Lee, Tae Hee (1999), 'International joint ventures in Korea', Seoul: Lee & Ko, mimeo, http://www.leeko.co.kr, accessed 17 May 2006.

LG Electronics (2005), 'Strategic alliances', www.lge.com, 23 April 2006.

Macquarie Bank (2005), *Korea*, http://macquarie.com.au/au/about_macquarie/international_activities/asia_region.

MOCIE (Ministry of Commerce, Industry and Energy) (2006), 'Foreign direct investment', http://www.mocie.go.kr/index.jsp, 9 June 2006.

Park, Hoon (1991), 'Analysis of joint ventures local managers' behaviour and its impact on joint venture Cohesiveness: Korea case', *Journal of Global Marketing*, 5 (1–2), 201–24.

Park, H.K. (2006), 'Tesco, BAT represent success story in Korea', *Korea Times*, 25 May, http://times.hankooki.com/lpage/biz/200605/kt2006052517042711870.htm, 7 June.

Park, Hoon, M. Gowan and S.D. Hwang (2002), 'Impact of national origin and entry mode on trust and organizational commitment', *Multinational Business Review*, 10 (2), 52.

PR Newswire (2002), 'Curtiss-Wright forms Korean joint venture', 2 April, factiva.com, accessed 21 February 2006.

PR Newswire Europe (2005), 'Valeo creates a joint venture in Korea for engine cooling systems', 24 December, factiva.com, accessed 21 February 2006.

Rhee, D.K., M.S. Kim and Y.G. Cho (2001), 'Performance and change in ownership structure of international joint ventures' (in Korean), *Korea Academy of International Business*, 12 (2), 71–89.

Samsung Electronics (2004), 'Major strategic alliances', www.samsung.com, accessed 15 May 2004.

Shenkar, O. and Yadong Luo (2004), *International Business*, Hoboken, NJ: John Wiley & Sons.

Tung, R. (1991), 'Handshakes across the sea: cross-cultural negotiating for business success', *Organizational Dynamics*, 19, 30–40.

UNCTAD (2005), *World Investment Report 2005*, New York: United Nations.

WWP Inc. (2002a), 'South Korea: joint venture construction plans for proposed $110 000 000 wind power farm', *Report on Engineering Construction and Operations in the Developing World*, 11 (9), factiva.com, accessed 21 February 2006.

WWP Inc. (2002b), 'South Korea: joint venture construction start-up planned $150 000 000 build-operate (BO) pharmaceutical plant is tentatively scheduled to begin in June 2002', *Report on Oil, Gas and Petrochemicals in the Developing World*, 11 (3), factiva.com, accessed 21 February 2006.

WWP Inc. (2004), 'South Korea: joint venture construction plans for proposed $2 000 000 000 flat-panel liquid crystal display (LCD) plant', *Report on Engineering Construction & Operations in the Developing World*, 12 (4), 1 April, factiva.com, accessed 21 February 2006.
WWP Inc. (2005), 'South Korea: joint venture construction plans for proposed glass substrate plant', *Business Opportunities in Asia and the Pacific*, 14 (3), factiva.com, accessed 21 February 2006.

Index

Korea Traders' Association 18–19
Korean Chamber of Commerce and
Industry (KCCI) 105, 170–71
Korean Commercial Code 239–40
Korean Confederation of Trade Unions
(KCTU) 211–12
Korean Independent Commission
Against Corruption (KICAC) 178,
180
and whistle-blowing cases 178
Korean Institute for International
Economic Policy (KIEP) 38, 119,
121, 122
Korean management system *see*
management system in transition
Korean market in transition *see* import
market (and)
Korean National Statistical Office
(KNSO) 20, 76, 81, 87, 88, 90, 96,
103, 105, 207, 209, 227
Korean politics *see* politics
Korean War 1, 15, 68, 70, 74–5, 192,
207
Koryo Kingdom/era 67, 70
Kuznets, P.W. 20, 21
Kwack, S. 20
Kweon, S-I. 66, 69, 144
Kwon, O. Y. 2, 3, 19, 23, 28, 45, 49, 51,
60, 94, 114, 115, 123, 124, 126,
129, 130, 133, 135, 161, 181, 182,
198, 201, 213, 223, 236, 237, 238,
241, 244
Kwon, T.H. 95, 97, 204
Kwon, Y.C. 241, 243, 244, 245, 248
Kwun, S.K. 197

labor force participation rate, growth in
206
labor management and market 25
labor market 21, 114–15, 123, 203–30
see also human resource
management
employment of human resources for
208–10
flexibility of 127–8, 211
industrial relations and labor standards
210–13 *see also main entry*
and labor costs 128
notes and references 226–30
reform of 27, 125

supply of human resources for 204–8
Labour, Ministry of 211
Labour Relations Commission (LRC)
212
Land Reform Act 76
language 74, 152–3
and culture 74
studies in Korean 232
Lasserré, P. 233, 234–5, 242, 243, 248
leadership 79, 188–9
in family 192
Lee, B.H. 210, 211, 212
Lee, E-S. 231, 237, 243
Lee, H. 105, 106–107
Lee, H.C. 186, 188, 196–7, 221
Lee Hoi Chang 47
Lee, H.Y. 47
Lee, J. 94, 156, 175
Lee, J.W. 38, 39, 49
Lee, J-H. 21, 103, 110, 204, 201 (1997)
Lee, J-K. 147, 148, 153, 156, 157–8, 161
Lee, J-Y. 231, 237, 243
Lee, K-C. 22
Lee, K-T. 19
Lee, K.U 15
Lee, N.C. 98
Lee, S. 95
Lee, S.M. 189, 214, 217
Lee, T.H. 1999 239
Lee, W-D. 210, 211, 212
Lee, Y. 97, 100, 189, 196
Lee, Y.I. 3
Lee, Y-S. 39, 102, 110
legislation (Korean)
Act to Combat Bribery of Foreign
Public Officials in International
Business 178
Anti-Corruption Act (2001) 178
Antitrust Act 31
Civil Code 76
Code of Conduct for Public Officials
(2003) 178
and e-commerce 106
Equal Employment Act (1987) 81
Fair Trade Act 240
Family Law 77
for labor-management councils 212
Foreign Capital Inducement Act
(1966) 124
Foreign Investment Promotion Act